COLLEGE
AND
EIGHTH

COLLEGE
AND
EIGHTH

Herbert Hyde

College and Eighth
Copyright © 2010 by Herbert Hyde

Edited by Jeanine McCartan
Cover art by Marcus K. Anderson
Author photo by Robert Scully
Cover and book design by Melissa Mykal Batalin

To order additional copies of this title, contact your favorite local bookstore or visit www.tbmbooks.com

ISBN: 978-1-935534-47-1

Acknowledgments

I want to thank my loving wife Barbara for supporting and tolerating my dream. It was not easy listening to my incessant ranting as this memoir came to life. I also want to thank my daughters, Sharon and Denise and their husbands Rob and Joe, as well as my wonderful Grandchildren, Terra, Brandon, Sequoia and Shane for being the light of my life.

I also want to thank my loving sisters for helping me retrieve, clarify and focus these memories of my family for all to enjoy. Additionally, I want to thank my childhood buddies and neighbors for helping me bring these characters to life in a way that I could never have done without them. Thank you, Alan, Denny, Billy and Charlie for helping me revisit my childhood. Just reconnecting with you made the effort worthwhile.

In addition, I want to thank Marcus K. Anderson for his wonderful cover illustration and to Jim Robinson my photographer as well as Matt Graves for taking the time to review my book.

In conclusion I want to express my heartfelt special thanks to Jeanine McCartan. This book would not have been possible without her friendship, encouragement and guidance, along with her tremendous editing skills. She unselfishly dedicated untold hours to this project and I will be forever grateful for that help. You are a true friend!

Contents

Prologue

Memories of a time gone by. This story is told first through the eyes of a young boy and continues through those of a youth, at times lonely and shy, into early adulthood. It chronicles his foibles, insecurities and frustrations and introduces his family, friends and other assorted characters he meets along the way. Hopefully, this journey will bring humor and insight about a dynamic time of change for him as well as American society.

His was a diverse neighborhood, consisting of various ethnic and religious groups, mostly Irish, English and Italian, along with a few black families. Most families were either Catholic or Protestant. They were people of different economic means—working middle class families, where the fathers actually had jobs, and poor families where fathers did not have jobs. The poor ones either could not or would not find jobs. In some cases it seemed that the only jobs they were successful at was procreation. Most, though, had fallen on hard times after the depression and war. Many were struggling to scratch out a meager existence in order to feed and clothe their families. They learned to cope with what life handed them and to coexist with families that had more than they did without the rancor and jealousy that seems to permeate society today.

These diverse families, no matter what their economic status, shared a respect for the dignity of their neighbors. They weren't perfect, but they watched out for one another. We had a "Neighborhood Watch" long before the term became coined in today's society. When a kid did something wrong or was hurt, the message got back to their parents where the appropriate punishment was doled out. Getting whacked on the ass with a switch, paddle or a good old fashioned hand spanking was the usual response.

Political correctness and psychobabble had not yet found its way into our thinking at that time. I miss those good old days, even though I had a sore ass many more times than I wish to remember. Apparently, I didn't suffer brain damage, although some may question that statement as they read this embellished memoir.

Luckily, most of these families were able to lift themselves out of poverty, mine being one of them. It may have taken many years to do this, but I am grateful to have had the opportunity to survive poverty, live a productive life and support my family.

I was raised in Troy, New York, a city that was home to 50,000 people in the early 1950s, a city that was of great historic significance in bringing American society into the industrial age. It has since fallen onto hard economic times. Perhaps rebirth, I hope, is immanent. Troy is known as the "Collar City" for its production of dress shirts and collars manufactured at the former Cluett and Peabody factory(a mainstay employer for decades), as well as many other smaller shirt and collar manufacturing companies.

South Troy was also home to the H.Burden and Sons iron factory. Superintendent of the Troy Iron and Nail Factory, Henry Burden began the Troy iron industry in 1822. Burden's inventions, which automated work that was previously done by hand, made the factory extremely profitable. Henry Burden realized that Troy's strategic location as a hub of rail and water transportation made it possible to produce and ship an enormous quantity of finished goods—for example, fifty one million horseshoes per year. Burden's inventions inspired the citizens of Troy to believe that technology could make anything possible.

The Burden water wheel, built in 1852, was the most powerful water wheel in the world. It most likely inspired George Washington Ferris, an engineer who graduated from Rensselaer Polytechnic Institute in Troy, to build his famed Ferris Wheel which was exhibited at the Chicago World's Fair in 1893.

Troy is also known as the home of Uncle Sam. Samuel Wilson was a meat packer in the city during the War of 1812; he furnished beef to the military encamped locally at Greenbush. The barrels of meat he supplied were stamped "U.S." Soldiers recognized the beef as coming from Wilson's in Troy and affectionately called it "Uncle Sam's Beef." Thus the nickname Uncle Sam was born and has become synonymous with Troy.

Among the many other businesses located in Troy were breweries. They thrived for the most part until the mid 1950s. One of the better known ale houses was the Stanton Brewery, located on Fifth Avenue. It was a huge structure encompassing almost an entire city block. Another was the Fitzgerald Brothers Brewery located on River Street.

It was rumored that one of the perks for working at "Fitzie's Brewery" as it was affectionately called, was that the workers could enjoy all the free beer they wanted at lunch. A great marketing tool for the company. They could hook their own workers on their product. Needless to say, most guys who worked there probably had a drinking problem by the time they retired, if their livers survived that long. Who would have thunk it.

Fitzie's was the first beer I officially imbibed at the age of 12. There were certain bars in Troy where bartenders would turn their head the other way, in order to get their nickel or dime, the cost of a glass of beer back then. Fitzie's was served on tap in most of the city's storied watering holes—Woodchucks, Dempsy's, Tip's and the Armory Grill, class establishments all. Troy was noted for having a bar on every corner. Of course, that's an exaggeration: there was one on every other corner.

As a teenager I remember when the Stanton Brewery burnt to the ground in 1962. I remember how spectacular the fire was, billowing smoke and flames shooting a hundred feet in the air that could be seen for miles. Living just one and a half blocks north of the building, we had a ring side seat to this major disaster. That fire, along with the fire that destroyed Fitzgerald Brothers brewery in 1964, signaled the beginning of the end for the brewery industry in the city. Neither was ever rebuilt. It's sad to note that all Troy's breweries went the way of the dinosaur. They either burnt to the ground or were gobbled up by larger competitors. Like most major industries in this country today, only a few survived.

Troy remains an architectural jewel. Bruised and dusty, but beneath the grit of age and declining industry, Troy is still a gem, ready to be polished back to its former brilliance. Just take a tour of the elegant brownstones along Fifth Avenue or the many that surround Washington Park in South Troy or visit the Troy Public Library with its Tiffany stained glass windows or the Troy Music Hall, one of the ten finest acoustical structures in the world.

Troy streets were featured as backdrops in several important movies filmed in the city such as "The Bostonians," "The Age of Innocence," "Ironweed" and the remake of "The Time Machine."

Troy is also known for its fine educational institutions: Rensselaer Polytechnic Institute (the oldest engineering school in the western world), Russell Sage College and the female prep school, Emma Willard. Jane Fonda was one of its most renowned graduates.

As it turns out, Troy is now much more of a college town than the industrial giant it was in its heyday. In fact, Rensselaer Polytechnic Institute has recently "plopped" its huge state-of-the-art Experimental Media & Performing Arts Center costing hundreds of millions of dollars, right where my house was once located near the corner of College Avenue and Eighth Street. The houses are gone now, but not the warm, vibrant memories.

This retrospective of my childhood of which I'm about to embark will linger forever in my heart. Hopefully, it will also touch the hearts and funny bones of others.

Although I was raised in poverty as a child, my remembrances aren't as dark and bleak as the experiences described by others who have lived through poverty in a different era and have then written about those experiences in stark images. Our neighborhood was a microcosm of society at the time, but that neighborhood milieu would slowly change forever. These changes were like tectonic plates silently sliding beneath the earth's surface, gliding along unnoticed as society moved indomitably forward. What I find to be the most dispiriting aspect of those changes was that they weren't necessarily changes for the better. The physical transformation was slow and insidious, but even more insidious was the loss of social integrity and acceptance that existed for me as a child and which seemed to flourish in our little community.

Slowly, people and businesses moved out of the neighborhood but would not be replaced. Vacant buildings began to appear on Congress and Eighth Street. First, it was Helflick's Market, which would move to a new, more modern location out of the area. Then the adjacent row houses east of them would be shuttered, because the slumlords who owned them were being pressured to bring them up to code. However, those slumlords decided to ignore the warnings and the city eventually condemned the buildings to the dust bin of history. I have so many fond memories of playing with kids who lived in those ramshackle houses. In some cases they were dumps like mine, but nevertheless, they were my friends' homes, filled with caring and loving families raising their children as best they could.

Unfortunately, "progress," as some might call it, would inextricably march forward and take with it a time of social acceptance and caring for those in need, replacing it with a new paradigm of social disdain for those who, in many cases and through no fault of their own, find themselves in poverty today. However, today they don't have the social or economic means needed to extricate themselves from poverty like I had. Instead, many turn to drugs, prostitution and crime in an effort to find their illusive, American dream. Generational poverty now appears to be the norm, as opposed to the exception during my time.

When I entered the workforce in 1962, a person without a college education or in some cases, a high school education, could find work in one of the many industries that still thrived in our area. Those were the stalwarts of the industrial era: General Electric, with plants in Schenectady and Waterford; Ford Motor Company in Green Island; Allegheny-Ludlam and Altec Steel in Watervliet; finally, dozens of smaller companies in the parts, textiles and clothing industries.

Sadly, corporate greed and capital flight had already begun, surreptitiously slipping under the social and economic radar, and rapidly progressing to where we are today with millions of lower and middle class jobs being shipped overseas in order to exploit cheap labor, and at the expense of workers and the environment. Layoffs, firings and plant closings would soon become downsizing and consolidation, buzz words used as a ruse to disguise capital and corporate flight.

No longer can honest, poor people who want to work their way into the middle class in order to provide a decent life for their families find the path that I was able to follow out of poverty. Many remain trapped in a nether world of generational poverty, drugs and single parent families, with no visible means of escape, scapegoats of the radicalized extremes, labeled as having no redeeming social value, parasites feeding off the federal teat.

Having survived poverty myself, I find it hard to believe that those facing poverty today have no socially redeeming values. I believe that most people trapped in this baleful subsistence want to rise out of poverty like I was able to do. That desire to raise oneself up is part of the human spirit and the American heart, but only if given the tools and opportunities to do so.

We have to regain our moral compass as a society and attack this major problem head-on. But for the grace of God, any one of us could be in their shoes. No one knows when they might face a life changing experience, major illness, death of a spouse, loss of a job, pension or health insurance. Hopefully, we will regain our moral compass soon, before it's too late.

And so, my social discourse ends and my life's odyssey begins, not exactly like Homer's, but it does occur in Troy. My friends and family marvel at my early childhood recollections, although at times viewing them with skepticism until I refresh their memories, then *they* provide me with additional details I might have overlooked. Although I can recollect events going back to my childhood in detail, there are some days that I have trouble remembering what I ate for breakfast. Be that as it may, I'm sticking to my story!

I know some people reading this might think I'm a bit hyperbolic or a liar or both, and that's fine. I can live with that because I'm not a liar. My family and friends know that these episodes really happened and that I do have an odd sense of humor. So, in the spirit of full disclosure, I admit that I have taken some poetic liberties and embellished a bit in order to give the reader a feel for who I was as a child, and what my friends and family were really like. I have also changed the names of some of the characters and businesses to protect the innocent, the unsuspecting, and the humorless.

Mom and Dad, young and beautiful.

CHAPTER ONE

The Homestead and Family Tree

Financial security was always a problem. We were raised dirt poor, although as young kids we never knew we were "poor." We were, well, just ourselves, little brats, raising hell and driving our Mom nuts. My parents' life journey together seemed destined to be full and rewarding. It certainly had been full (ten kids, remember). Rewarding, well, that's a different story. One thing I know for sure: Ma loved her children dearly, and I believe that until the day she died she still loved her philandering husband. I also believe Dad loved Ma too, although time and circumstance had driven a wedge between them. While they did not live together at the end of their lives, we made sure that they were buried by each other's side and in my heart I'm sure that's the way they'd have wanted it.

Our home? We lived in a third floor flat infested with bedbugs, which meant that our flat would be the hottest and nastiest of them all. But it was also the only one Ma could afford with the meager rent allowance she received from the local welfare department, which also provided our used furniture. Keeping the bedbugs under control was an unending battle, and the memories of having to go to bed with the lights on (bedbugs are nocturnal and hate light) still lingers in my mind along with their indescribable smell. Once experienced, you'd never ever be able to forget that smell. I remember my mother cleaning mattresses and box springs with some type of insecticide, DDT or other toxic substance to try and keep them under control. It seemed like an unending battle.

Raising eight kids, mostly by herself, had taken its toll on this once stunningly beautiful woman. Years of personal neglect while raising this brood, as well as emotional and financial neglect by my father, had aged her well beyond her years, but she would bear yet two more offspring. Fertility was not a problem in our family, clearly. Dad, it seems, was incapable of keeping his pecker in his pants. But you know what! I'm really glad he didn't, at least as far as my immediate family is concerned, because I wouldn't have had this special group of brothers and sisters to grow up with, and I wouldn't have these wonderful memories to reprise. I loved all my siblings dearly, cherishing deeply the ones who have passed on before me and relishing every moment I still have with my surviving sisters today.

My dad was a handsome devil. I remember seeing pictures of him as young man; he looked like a young Spencer Tracy, sophisticated and debonair. He was not big in stature, only standing about 5' 7" tall, with a protruding beer belly and artificial leg. (He had lost his leg, as well as several fingers and toes to Burger's disease, a debilitating circulatory disease.)

Who would have thought that over his lifetime he would become an irresponsible, beer drinking scamp and everybody's good old boy, affectionately known by his beer-guzzling buddies as "Skinner." Among my father's barfly buddies, he was apparently considered a stud. Why "Skinner" I'd ask myself? Using my trusty thesaurus I found several synonyms for Skinner: "Boner, Meat packer and Meat Man." It appears my father may have been well endowed in certain other parts of his anatomy, and apparently his bar room buddies were better educated than I thought.

Sadly, I never really got to know my father when I was younger, because he was rarely home. He would be away for weeks on end either off working at odd jobs or felling trees in Vermont with Frank Languid, his closest friend and drinking buddy. I often wonder what our family life would have been like if Dad had spent less time with his drinking buddies and more time with us.

Rationalizing Dad's behavior further, I can now surmise that maybe it was his staid mother's pampering of him as a child that led to his narcissism. From what I was told, my Grandmother doted over him. Of the oldest of three children, Dad, Olive and Paul, Dad was her favorite. Ironically, it was Paul who doted on his mother, even though she seemed to look down on him as the good-hearted, servile son.

Ma always spoke kindly of Uncle Paul. A bachelor, Uncle Paul was very sick with emphysema and suffered for many years. But being the good son, Paul would be the one who would live with and care for his ill and aging Mother until she died at the age of eighty-six. Pure at heart and selfless, Paul was the antithesis of Dad. He was friendly, congenial, giving and always respectful to Ma and us kids whenever we visited. It's a shame Paul was taken for granted and under-appreciated by his Mother. I guess that happens in families. The good ones willfully suffer and toil in silence. But, I'm sure God has a special place by his side for people like Uncle Paul.

Our visits to Bennington usually took place on a Sunday afternoon in the fall at the peak of leaf peeping season. Although only twenty-eight miles from Troy, it seemed to take forever to get there. If we went with Dad, which we rarely did, he'd have all us kids crammed like sardines into the back of his dilapidated truck. Ma would be in the front seat holding on for dear life as Dad recklessly rambled along. It was actually fun for us kids, although not very safe. Feeling the cool autumn breeze hitting our faces was refreshing as we hurtled treacherously along on State Route 7.

We traversed rolling hills dotted with ubiquitous farms and pastures that were home to the many cows, sheep and horses. Counting them was part of the fun and made our ride more interesting. Once we passed by the Tomhannock Reservoir, shimmering placidly in the autumn sun, we soon reached the crest of the hill that would usher us along on our journey. It was at this spot where the unending rows of Burma Shave billboards would humorously appear. They would take over the mission of guiding us toward the Bennington Monument, a stoically beautiful, granite obelisk, splitting the sun-drenched mountains draped in their amber and gold blanket.

I never understood why Grandma Hyde was so intolerant and mean to us kids, especially since we rarely visited. Grandma and Grandpa Davenport, Ma's parents, were just the opposite. You'd think Grandma Hyde would be delighted to see her grandkids. Apparently not! When we visited her, we weren't allowed to budge from our seats or even speak unless spoken to.

One Sunday, Dad had Ma ring the door bell as we all stood behind her, waiting for Paul to come downstairs and let us in. It couldn't have been more than a minute or two before we heard the labored wheezing of poor Uncle Paul through the closed door.

"What the hell is taking him so long?" Dad complained to Ma after about thirty seconds.

"Jesum Cripes, Frank, you know he has trouble breathing. Have a little patience, will you?" Just as Dad was about to argue with Ma, a smiling Uncle Paul opened the door, coughing a welcoming greeting, desperately trying to catch his breath.

"Well, hi!" he gasped, in his twangy, Vermont accent. "It's so good to see all you kids again. My, Mabel," coughed Paul, "how these kids have grown."

"Like weeds," Ma laughed.

"Well, hello to you too, Franklyn," a gracious and dutiful Paul greeted. "It's been a long time. I know Ma will be so happy to see you."

"I bet," Dad responded, with a twinge of sarcasm.

"Well, come on upstairs now, you all." Paul replied.

Entering the clean, but dreary looking kitchen we saw our un-welcoming Grandma. She barely acknowledged our presence until Dad entered the room, at which time he quickly rushed over to give her a hug. In return, he received the only smile I remember from her all day. She and Ma exchanged cursory greetings, but you could sense the unease between them. Knowing from past experience that we couldn't say or do anything without getting in trouble, my sisters and I just sat passively on the wooden chairs that surrounded Grandma Hyde's kitchen table.

As was her custom, Grandma obliquely insulted Ma with remarks about our tattered clothes and what Grandma considered our unkempt look. Ma just bit her tongue and let the insults slide, knowing it was futile to argue with the old witch. Instead, she frantically puffed away on the Chesterfield Uncle Paul had given her. In a disingenuous attempt to be courteous and hospitable, Grandma offered us kids some flavorless, oatmeal cookies, along with a glass of some putrid milk substance, either rancid milk or buttermilk, I could never figure out which. All I remember is that it was disgusting. Yuk! "Drink your milk!" she demanded, as I pushed my glass away.

"It tastes awful," I mistakenly replied.

"Why, you ungrateful little snot," she shot back. It was then that Dad got angry and yelled at me to drink my milk or he'd punish me. Out of the corner of my eye I could see Ma getting red in the face. She must have bit her tongue trying not to take sides. Seeing the anger in Dad's eyes and the frustration in Ma's, I decided I'd better comply. So I reluctantly gulped down the rest of this vile, viscous poison. I could feel my body shudder as I desperately tried not to purge all over her table. Luckily, I was able to hold back the nausea that engulfed me. The hour we spent at her house seemed like an eternity. We couldn't wait to leave and visit our other grandparents where we could laugh and act like our normal bratty selves.

Ironically, Grandma Hyde was a retired elementary school teacher. I can just imagine the torture she must have put her students through all those years if she treated them the same way she treated us. She had the capacity to suck all the youthful exuberance out of us kids.

Our tortuous hour finally ended and we headed over to Grandma and Grandpa Davenport's house for a short visit. Dad was already back to his miserable self as Ma rang the doorbell. With all us kids huddled in back of Ma and Dad, it was a refreshing change to see a smiling Grandpa Davenport open the door, as the smell of a pungent lamb roast wafted over us.

"We can't stay long, Dad." Ma said to her father as he ushered us in.

"Nonsense, Mabel, you're all going to stay for dinner. We have plenty enough for all of you. Hey, Frank how have you been?"

"Ok," Dad grumbled as he shuffled through the door. "Been busting my ass with Frank Languid, clearing out a field near Hoosick Falls. Got to make some dough before winter sets in."

"Well, good for you Frank," Grandpa said. "At least you have some work. I know it's been very tough out there for all of you."

We were soon sitting around a huge dining room table, laughing as Grandpa reprised his bevy of stories and jokes. Even Dad started to lighten up as he stuffed himself with lamb, creamy mashed potatoes and a couple of beers. After finishing the day off with a big piece of apple pie and slice of sharp Vermont cheddar cheese, we headed home.

Luckily, Dad only had a couple of beers and wasn't plastered. He was able to recklessly meander his way back to Troy, usually on two wheels, speeding around curves he knew like the back of his hand. Of course, Ma was holding on for dear life, but afraid to say anything that would upset him. That would make him drive even faster. We kids, on the other hand, screamed with delight as his tattered, old, roller coaster clattered back to Troy.

Ma was the center of our universe. Some of my fondest remembrances of Ma came when she was in the kitchen. She always seemed most relaxed and at peace with herself when she was quietly preparing meals for us. Entering the kitchen one cool, fall day, I spotted Ma sitting at the kitchen table. She looked serene, immersed in her thoughts, as angular beams of golden sunlight lilted through her silver hair, creating a loving aura that surrounded her beautiful but weathered face. Outside the window, red and gold leaves sanguinely drifted by like chapters of her loving life. I just stood there for a few moments watching her, overwhelmed by a feeling of love and happiness, sensing she was at peace for a small sliver of her normally hectic day.

But of course, I unwittingly shattered her tranquility when I asked her what she was making. Startled, Ma emerged from her spiritual trance. "Oh, hi, Herbie, I didn't see you there. I'm making baked macaroni for supper."

"Great, I love that, Ma."

She made the best baked macaroni in the world. Not like the usual kind, where you cook the elbows and drown them in a puddle of oozy cheese, then bake them. Nope, Ma's was different. She meticulously sliced an entire bulb of garlic, razor thin, then sautéed them in Crisco or butter when she could afford it. She cooked them until they were just translucent, making sure not to burn them because that would make them bitter, instead of sweet and pungent. Next, she emptied two sixteen ounce cans of Pine Cone tomatoes into a large bowl, then squished them to a pulp with her aching, arthritic hands. Salt, pepper and a cup of dried parsley were then added along with the garlic mixture. She mixed all the ingredients together, including the cooked macaroni, with a large wooden spoon, before adding a pound of cubed American cheese and a half pound of sharp cheddar, if she was lucky enough to have some. Otherwise she'd use only American cheese. She always saved several slices to top the casserole, which would then turn into a dark brown, chewy crust when it came out of the oven. (You're probably thinking, ugh, why so much garlic? Well, it really tasted good, and we were never attacked by vampires, as far as I know.)

We rarely had roasts, except on holidays, turkey at Thanksgiving, ham at Christmas and Easter. The only kind of steak I can remember having as a young kid was cubed steak, smothered in onions and Worcestershire sauce. It was chewy but yummy. We were lucky if we had that twice a year. Our daily meals mainly consisted of casseroles: goulash, made with hamburger, tomatoes, chopped green peppers, and macaroni; baked spam with garlic gloves inserted to flavor it; chipped beef in white sauce served over mashed potatoes or toast; spaghetti and meatballs; and of course, Irish stew, another of the world's best.

Many times, however, when things were really tough, we'd have pancakes or toast for supper. If we were lucky, Ma might have some tiny, pullet eggs that Dad had bartered from local chicken farmers in exchange for firewood. Often Ma would have to feed us leftover pea soup or chicken soup she made in large batches from chicken carcasses or ham bones she saved, or from the ones her friends Winnie or Helen saved for her.

Ironically, Dad often managed to bring stuff home for himself, an occasional porterhouse steak or beef liver he finagled from Hooley's meat market. He had money for the things he wanted but rarely found any for bills, Ma, or us kids. He always seemed to have just enough money to keep his ever-expanding beer belly hanging over his belt.

On rare occasions, when he went on a fishing trip, he'd come home with a bunch of frogs legs instead of fish for Ma to cook. He'd skin them at the kitchen table, making a bloody mess, then force Ma to cook them. She hated cooking them and complained, "Damn it, Frank, you know I hate cooking these and you always make a mess."

It was a strange sight to see those scrawny legs hopping around in her sizzling frying pan. Ma would always turn her head away from the sight as Dad laughed at her heartily. "See, Mabel, they're so fresh they're trying to jump out of the pan."

"You're awful, killing those poor, innocent frogs," she complained.

When he brought home liver, he'd force Ma to cook him liver and onions, something she detested, because it always smelled so disgusting. Once, she gave me a tiny piece to try and I almost threw up. Yuk! It was awful and from that point on, I despised even looking at liver. To this day, I've never tried liver again, except First Prize liverwurst, which I love, in a sandwich slathered with mustard or mayo and thinly sliced onions.

At last, I come to my siblings! The oldest sibling was my brother Jack, who was born in 1930. He was followed by Kathleen, Frank (Sonny), Dorothy, Clifford (Cliff), Pat (Patty) and me. I was followed by Brenda, Jan and finally Bonnie. Sadly, Bonnie had a twin sister Sharon who died fifteen minutes after birth. (To this day I don't know where she is buried. I fear she is in an unmarked grave somewhere. I hope to someday locate her grave and give her proper respect.)

As a kid, I barely knew my two oldest brothers. Sadly, I didn't really get to know them well until I was much older. That is the one part of my life that I wish had been a little different, because I know that having them around more when I was a little kid would have profoundly affected my growing up. Having said that, I don't regret my childhood at all.

My closest brother was Cliff. He was considered the black sheep of the family (unjustifiably, I believe) because he always seemed to get into trouble. I think that he was just the unlucky, loyal one who was always took the rap for things that other kids instigated, never squealing on them. Because Cliff would never "Rat" on anyone if he got caught, he got labeled as a trouble maker.

I'm not sure what Cliff did that was so bad to be sent to Vanderheyden Hall so often. Maybe it was because he was a truant. Cliff hated school and was always taking off to go downtown to hang out with his other truant buddies. It seemed like every other day the truant officer was banging on our front door, looking for Cliff. Dad constantly brow beat Cliff. I remember him calling Cliff "stupid" all the time and then whack him with his strap if he tried to defend himself. Cliff was far from stupid. Misguided at times, yes. But, stupid? Never.

He'd get yelled at for relatively innocuous things or things he may have done a week or two earlier. I think he got yelled at most because he often disturbed Dad at his hangout, Stickley's Grill on Rock Alley. When they had nothing better to do, Cliff and his buddies peered through the window at Stickley's and watched my old man and his friends carousing, playing cards or darts, shooting pool or messing with some of the old tarts who might stagger in. Dad may have been afraid Cliff would turn him in to Ma. But Cliff never did. Given those circumstances, one would wonder why Cliff's life so closely mirrored Dad's. However, unlike my Dad, Cliff would become one of the most beloved men in the family, especially by his own children, nephews, nieces and most of his siblings. He was unpretentious, irreverent and true to himself. Cliff was Cliff.

Like most of the older kids with younger siblings, he didn't want to hang around with me. He'd usually brush me off when I'd try to hang around, yelling at me, "Go home, you little pain in the ass, I'm not your damn baby-sitter."

Even though he'd yell at me, I knew deep down that he really loved me. However, he couldn't show that in front of his buddies, because he had to project the rebel-without-a-cause image he'd been saddled with. Deep down, I knew he didn't want me to get into the same kind of trouble he got into. He was really my protector.

My brother Jack, on the other hand, was so much older than me that I wouldn't have known any of the "bad things" he might have done as a kid. Jack always seemed older than his age. He was forced to grow up quicker than me and my other younger siblings.

Although he never finished sixth grade, Jack was very smart. By then he was working part-time at the A&P store in Bennington. He taught himself bookkeeping, and through hard work and perseverance he eventually became a store manager for over thirty years.

He and my sister Kathleen were shipped away to work to my Aunt Olive and Uncle Wilber's home in Granville because Ma couldn't afford to keep and feed them. I remember my sister Kathleen relat-

ing the story of how close they became because they had been ex-
cised from the family several times during the Great Depression.

While attending grade school, Jack also had to clean out chick-
en coops after school and on weekends at a local chicken farm near
their Granville, New York home. I'm not sure how long Kathleen
stayed with Jack or if she spent time working at the farm. However,
I know Jack was there for at least four years, returning home briefly
when he was eleven. Jack and Kathleen were very close right up to
the time each married.

My brother Frank (Sonny to us kids) was considered a saint by
Ma. He couldn't do anything wrong in her eyes. He was the golden
boy, tall, athletic, smart and very handsome. He reminded me of
Ronald Reagan, the actor with those good looks. I don't really believe he was a saint though, because when I was older I'd hear stories about a few crazy things he did as a kid too. I also heard that he
was really, really tough and few kids messed with him. (I would see
that toughness play out in a different way later in life as he battled
lung cancer.)

My older brothers and sisters faced more daunting challenges
than me and my younger sisters. It's ironic that each set of brothers
and sisters had unique relationships. For instance, my brother Jack
and sister Kathleen were close and went through trying times together, distinct but similar to what Dorothy and Sonny went through.
However, Sonny's struggles were not as severe as Dorothy's. Because
they were all born during the Great Depression, out of financial ne-
cessity they were shipped off to live with various relatives.

Cliff and Patty were not shipped away like the others and had
an ambivalent relationship growing up. Cliff always seemed to get
into trouble while Patty turned out to be the most outspoken one
in the family.

Brenda and I were also very close, both in age and tempera-
ment. We were dance partners, hula hoop partners and just good
friends over the years. My younger sisters would also become very

close to my sister Patty, especially Jan who was very athletic but not quite as outspoken as Patty. Bonnie will always be the baby of the family and more on the quiet side, except at sporting events where all of us were on the lunatic fringe, giving outspoken support of our high school teams and unrelenting disdain for the refs.

Kathleen seemed to be the most tolerant of Dad's shortcomings among my sisters. It might have been because he favored her a little bit, being the first girl in the family. In any event, she didn't seem to hold as much animosity towards him as an adult, accepting him for who he was, even with all his shortcomings.

Neither Jack nor Kathleen received much formal education. Kathleen may have finished grade school, but Jack only went to the sixth grade. After quitting school, he moved to Vermont, living with my mother's parents, Harold and Mabel Davenport. Jack became very close to Grandpa Davenport and Uncle Clifford (Kip), who lived nearby. In fact, Kip, who was a butcher, got Jack a job stocking shelves at the local A&P down the street from their house. It was at the Bennington, Vermont store where he would meet and marry his first wife, Claire. She worked there as a clerk.

My mother had three brothers, Clifford (Kip), Harold and Herb, whom I was named after. Tragically, Herb was killed in a motorcycle accident at age twenty-six while Ma was pregnant with me. To this day I refuse to ride motorcycles.

Jack would get his first major promotion several years and several kids later. He was assigned to the A&P store in Ticonderoga as an assistant manager. Moving so far away meant that we would rarely see him or my nephews and nieces, Barbara, Mike, Debbie and Christopher. Occasionally, we would make the long trek up to the Adirondacks to visit him. But because he worked so many hours at the store, he rarely had the time to visit with us.

Jack always seemed older to me. He felt more like an uncle than an older brother. However, we became very close as adults. He did let me visit him and his family for a week one summer when I was a teenager. It was there that I learned he was a pretty good athlete, especially at bowling and softball. He was the team's best pitcher, leading them to several Vermont State championships.

Sadly, Jack and Claire's marriage would end in divorce, although under amicable terms. They remained close friends even though both remarried. Jack was later transferred to Saranac Lake then to Troy, where he would eventually marry a young woman, Linda, who worked in his store. Like Claire, she was also very pretty and down to earth. They soon had a son, Matthew.

I think Sonny would also have been a good role model for me if he were around more when I was young. Both he and Jack seemed so mature for their years. Jack was an adult before he was out of his teens, while Sonny was not far behind. In fact, when Sonny was a teenager, he'd hang out and play poker with most of the older men on Ed Barrow's front porch: Ed, Luke and Walt Howard, Don Delechance, and even Frank Brighton. I've heard stories that Ed thought of Sonny as one of his own sons.

Dorothy and Sonny, like Kathleen and Jack, were very close. I'm not sure if Sonny was ever shipped away for any length of time. However, Dorothy was forced to live with Grandma Hyde for three years and hated every minute of it. I guess Dad had insisted that she move there over Ma's objections. Dorothy said Grandma Hyde treated her like Cinderella. However, she never got to meet a prince or ride in a carriage or try on those glass slippers. She was basically a servant to Grandma.

I think Sonny may have stayed with Aunt Olive for a while, but I'm not totally sure about that. The one thing I do remember about Sonny: he had an uncanny ability to walk on his hands. He could be seen walking down to Harry's store without ever stopping or losing his balance. The most amazing part was that he started his jaunt from our third floor apartment.

Dorothy told me she was very upset when she finally returned from Grandma Hyde's. It seems Ma said she didn't know what to do with her. You see, times had not gotten any better while she was away and now Ma had another mouth to feed with no additional help from Dad. It was during those early, formative years that I began sensing how we functioned as a family.

Uncle Herb (my namesake) and family.

CHAPTER TWO

Twinkle, Twinkle

My earliest memories date back to about age two, you know, that delightful period of time for most parents when their former infants begin to exercise their independence, as they enter toddler-hood, or as some fondly refer to it, *the terrible two's*. However, for Ma, the terrible two's had a different connotation as they related to me. Instead of lasting just a couple years like most kids, she probably felt mine lasted about two decades. I think that might be a slight exaggeration, but nonetheless, the beginning of my terrible two's certainly was an eye opener for her that lasted for many years.

Early one steamy morning I took it upon myself to seek a little adventure. I was awake but no one was paying any attention to my infantile babbling. Since the lock on our apartment door was broken, it was easy for me to open and I was able to slip out without making a sound. My sopping wet diaper and I wiggled our way all the way down two flights of stairs to the bottom landing.

After struggling a bit to pry open the unlocked bottom door, I was able to make my dash, or should I say waddle, to freedom, down the fronts step and onward to Moore's corner store. I found a bottle cap, which I immediately put in my diaper, and a cigarette butt, which I promptly put in my mouth.

That was when I was inexorably snatched up by Winnie Koch, Ma's best friend. Luckily for me and Ma, Winnie had been unable to sleep that morning. Sitting on her front porch in her house coat, she was startled to see me waddling down the street in a droopy diaper with a butt hanging out of my mouth. Although she could hardly restrain a chuckle from this incongruous sight, she also sensed the danger. She raced down her porch steps to grab me before I slipped over the embankment and into the road. Winnie would later relate to Ma that I looked like my old man in miniature, with my little pot belly and cigarette butt hanging out of my mouth. Well, that may be true, but I don't ever remember my old man in a diaper and, although he had an artificial leg, I didn't.

Rubbing the last vestiges of a troubled sleep from her eyes, Ma reluctantly opened the apartment door to Winnie who was laughing but holding me firmly in her arms. "Oh my God, Winnie!" Ma gasped. "Why is Herbie with you? What happened?"

"Well, Mabel", Winnie chuckled. " I couldn't sleep with all this heat, so I went out on the front porch to get some air and just as I sat down something caught my eye. I couldn't believe it, there's Herbie in his diaper. He looked like a baby duckling wobbling down the street, a cigarette butt hanging out his mouth. He was so cute, but then I realized I better get him quick before he falls into the road."

"Thank God, Winnie," Ma sighed. "If you weren't up, he could have been killed. For the life of me, I can't believe this could happen. I just checked on him around 4am and he was asleep in his crib. How he got out of that crib and down to the street without me knowing is beyond me."

"Damn door locks," Ma lamented. "I have been after old man Beckwith for months to fix them, but he just ignores me, the cheap son-of-a-bitch. You know, Winnie, he won't spend a dime on this dump and now look what happened. Boy, is he going to get a piece of my mind!" Ma exclaimed. "Thanks to him, I'll have to sleep with one eye open until those locks are fixed." The locks never got fixed, of course.

Grateful I was safe, Ma then took me from Winnie with a weary smile and gently scolded me, "Don't you ever do this to me again, you little shit pot," Ma whispered, "The next time you do something bold, I will really paddle your behind." She then hugged me tight, gently kissing me on the cheek. Although I didn't know what all the fuss was about, I nodded in agreement, babbling in my newly discovered voice, "Ok, Mama" then fell asleep in her arms.

An onerous August morning two weeks later, panic again rushed over Ma. This sweltering heat wave, which seemed endless, would continue for at least several more days in the unbearable tenement we called home. It was 6:30am as Ma rushed through the house, her heart in her throat, looking desperately for her wayward toddler. She searched every room, under every bed, in every closet but still no Herbie. How the hell could a tiny two year old go missing again, right under her nose?

Tears welled up in Ma's eyes as she yelled out for me and got no response. "Dorothy," Ma pleaded, "go out in the yard and see if he's there."

"Ok, Ma," Dorothy hollered back in a nervous response. Returning shortly with tears running down her cheeks, Dorothy screeched, "He's gone!"

"Quick, Dorothy," Ma yelled. "Go next door to Winnie's house and see if she's got him again."

Dorothy crawled through her bedroom window to Winnie's back porch and pounded on Winnie's door screaming, "Hurry, Winnie, open up. Herbie's missing again."

Winnie threw open her door and told Dorothy she didn't know where I was. They both panicked when Ma came to Dorothy's bedroom window in desperate hope that I was at Winnie's. "Oh my God," Ma screamed, tears flooding her cheeks. "Where can he be?" She then darted through our apartment, ripping open the door and careening down the stairs at breakneck speed. Despite her capacious body and poor health, she rushed frantically up and down the street hopelessly seeking her wayward toddler. Several neighbors flinched at this heart-wrenching sight.

She stopped and peered into the gangway which separated the Gibson and Koch houses, sanguinely calling my name, but to no avail. Suddenly, something terrifying caught her eye. Her heart in her throat, she instinctively covered her mouth to stymie a primal scream. What she saw would become seared into her memory forever. There I was, dangling upside down out of our apartment window. The only thing saving me from falling to my death were my tiny feet grasping the inside of the battered window sash. I sensed only the cool morning breeze lightly brushing my cheek as the blood continued rushing to my tiny head. I was bewitched by all those shiny, sparkling orbs dotting the sky.

As happened two weeks before, I woke up before the dawn and began padding about our apartment. However, this time I didn't wander down the stairs and into the street. Instead, I pulled myself up onto a torn, overstuffed chair next to the parlor window. A cool breeze was drifting into the parlor from the partially opened, screenless window. Being adventurous, I leaned over the chair seeking the source of that cool breeze. Eventually I squeezed my head through the slender opening. A narrow view of sparkling lights shining against the blackness of space enticed me to get an even closer look. I wiggled my body further out the window so that now my entire torso was draped over the outside of the window sill. I could delight in the awe of my own inspiring microcosm.

Suddenly, without warning, my sublime trance was violently shattered! Fear now gripped my quivering soul. What was happening to me? I was abruptly snatched from my ethereal world of beauty, feet first, and with a sense of foreboding I had never experienced in my short life. Huge appendages brutally clasping my feet and head whisked me back to reality through that same battered window that had led to my transcendent universe. My senses were now fixated on the laborious panting of my exasperated mother, who was crying and shaking uncontrollably, as she abruptly dumped me onto that dilapidated old chair.

Enraged by my frightening, near death experience, Ma lurched into a scathing diatribe. "God damn you, Herbie, why are you doing this to me? You're going to be the death of me, you little shit!" Then, suddenly and without warning, I again found myself dangling upside down, as Ma ripped me out of the chair and threw me over her knee. Within seconds, a stinging pain tore across my wet tush, and stars instantly reappeared before my tightly clenched eyes. Not beautiful stars like the ones in my earlier, ephemeral world but red and orange and scary ones! I didn't realize it at the time, but I had just experienced my first real spanking at the hands of my loving mother.

Needless to say, I never repeated my out of body, out of window, experience again. I had passed my inaugural class in "Lessons Learned 101," with flying colors. Nevertheless, my fascination with the astronomical light show of that early summer morning continues to this day. I still love staring up at the heavens on a quiet night and being engulfed by the all-encompassing universe. Although I really love looking at the heavenly universe, I never became an astronomer or an astronaut. Instead, I became a dreamer, day or otherwise. As you will see, dreaming took on a very different aura when I was a toddler.

A year or so later, I bolted out of my sopping bed, gasping for air, paralyzed from another frequent night terror. Ma rushed in and clutched my tiny, trembling body to her comforting bosom. Once again I had shaken her out of a tranquil sleep with my frightful scream. "Mommy's here, baby, mommy's here!" she soothed. "No one's going to hurt you now, I'm here. Open your eyes now, baby, you're ok." Hearing Ma's calming voice brought me back to the conscious world, as my rigid body relaxed from its torment. "What scared you this time, baby? Was it that mean man chasing you again?"

"No, Mommy, it was those big spiders hanging from the sky again."

Ma tenderly wiped the tears from my responsive blue eyes, calmly telling me, "It's just a bad dream, baby. Big spiders don't really hang from the sky, it's all your imagination. If they really did hang from the sky, it would mean they're your friends and will protect you and keep you safe, just like Mommy does."

"I don't like those dreams, Mommy. They scare me. But the ones I have when I'm swimming through the air make me feel safe and happy. They're pretty dreams, and I can do anything I want in those dreams. If someone is chasing me, I just flap my arms and up I go into the sky, away from all those meanies. Then I can fly anywhere I want—up to the park, down to the city, into our back yard—I even flew over all those pretty churches downtown. You know, Mommy! The big white one with that really, really, tall pointy thing sticking up in the air, and that big, gray one you took me to before."

"Oh, you mean St. Paul's? That's our church. Boy, little man, you certainly do have a vivid imagination," Ma chuckled, not totally believing me.

But those dreams were true. I still long to glide gracefully through the air, escaping all my troubles, floating wistfully over the tree-lined greenery of majestic Prospect Park and the gothic spires of the many magnificent churches dotting the landscape of this beautiful Victorian city.

Now that I had calmed down, Ma looked down and noticed that I had drenched my bed again. "OOPS! You pee'd your bed again, little man, didn't you?"

"I'm sorry, Mommy, I didn't know I was peeing, I was just so scared."

Because I would fall into such a deep sleep as a child, periodic bed wetting episodes dogged me through much of my early years, well after the point when most kids were able to sleep through the night without wetting. I guess that gives new meaning to the expression, "wet dream." Luckily, those bad dreams weren't a constant in my life and I outgrew them as I got a little older. However, to this day, I still long for those dreams of floating through the air. Although time seems to move slowly when you're very young, in reality, infancy speeds into toddler-hood in a nanosecond.

CHAPTER THREE

Sweet Smells and Ringing Bells

Each day was a new sensory adventure for me as a toddler. I might wake up to the sound of Ma bustling about the kitchen getting breakfast ready, the smell of hickory smoked bacon cooking in her cast iron skillet, and the aromatic fragrance of that "*Good to the last drop*" Maxwell House coffee percolating on the stove. If I slept late, I might awaken to the sweet smell of Ma's apple or mince meat pies wafting through my room. She'd make them quite often for us and give some to her special friends and neighbors. Because Ma was such a great cook, her pies and cakes were highly sought after. She'd happily make them for a certain few, and the little money she made would be used to pay off bills.

Other times I might be awakened by the clanging milk bottles being delivered by the Borden's milk man or the clanking of horses' hooves outside our window as the Freihofer's bread man made his rounds. (One of my earliest remembrances was seeing Ma take the cardboard cap off a bottle of milk, scoop out the sweet cream that had risen to the top, then indulge herself with that cholesterol-laden delicacy.)

On other days I might awaken to the chatter of Ma's best friend Winnie filling Ma in on the latest rumor about one of our impetuous neighbors who'd been seen carousing at Fox's bar and grill while her unsuspecting husband was out of town and probably doing the same thing. Even before the book came out in 1956, many small towns across America could easily be described as *Peyton Place* because of their sordid secrets.

Most times however, I'd be awakened by my bratty sisters who loved to tickle my feet in order to roust me out of bed. Once I was awake, they'd continue their torment in the kitchen until either Ma yelled at them to stop, or I'd start coughing and wheezing so badly that I'd have an asthma attack. (It's true, laughing can set off an asthma attack. It's called LIA, laughing induced asthma, but it's no laughing matter. Usually, these episodes weren't serious and didn't last long, but they were annoying and uncomfortable.)

Often times Ma would let us help with breakfast, either by making buttered toast or mixing up our special morning gruel, oatmeal. Yuk! Other times we'd make my favorite morning beverage, Hershey's cocoa. Occasionally, she'd even let one of the older girls, Dorothy or Patty, help make pancakes. However, our real treat was when Ma baked her famous cakes. Usually she'd pick one or two of us to help her mix the cake batter and, if you were really lucky, the yummy frosting. Of course, everything was made from scratch back then, no box mixes made it to our kitchen until many years later.

Ma tried to be fair in sharing the wealth and would rotate turns helping her, but if someone wasn't playing nice, usually me, then that person would have to sit by and watch as the others gobbled down the goodies with a big smirk on their chocolate-covered faces. Here's how the rules went: If you were special enough to be picked to stir the cake batter, you got to lick the spoon or bowl. If you were extra special enough to stir the frosting, you got to lick the frosting spoon or bowl.

One of the most hair-raising experiences I can remember in the kitchen was the time that my younger sister Jan wanted to help Ma make pancakes. It was a fuming hot Saturday morning. Ma hadn't gotten much sleep because of the dreadful heat and was in no mood to suffer fools or little snots for that matter, and Jan was being a little snot. I guess Jan didn't get the memo or much sleep either. It was actually pretty quiet in the kitchen that morning, except for Jan. My sister Brenda and I were quietly arm wrestling at the kitchen table and, of course, I was winning. My sister Patty and my brother Cliff had gone out in search of Mittens our newest kitten, who had gone missing two days earlier. In the meantime my older sister Dorothy was visiting with Helen Howard two doors up the street. Helen loved to kibitz with Ma and my older sisters and was also a regular customer for Ma's delicious pies. In fact, that's why Dorothy was there in the first place, delivering one of Ma's specialties—light and fluffy lemon meringue pie.

Although being just a little tot, Jan thought she was older at times and insisted this morning that she could flip pancakes like her older sisters. However, Ma was having none of that. She was at her wits end trying to making pancakes for us kids as well as cook bacon and eggs for our Dad who was lounging in bed, hung over from a night of carousing at Stickley's Grill.

Ma began to yell at Jan who was standing next to our decrepit stove, an open flame licking at her curly hair. "Get out of there, Jan, before you get burned! It's dangerous, go sit with your brother and sister."

"No, I won't!" Jan sniped, taking a tantrum, stamping her feet and whining. "I wanna to make pancakes! I wanna make pancakes."

Suddenly, Ma shrieked, "Oh, my God! Oh, my God!" Then started slapping Jan on the head with her dish towel and pushing her towards the sink. "Quick, get over here you two and help! Jan's hair's on fire!"

Glancing up, Brenda and I saw the pending disaster and immediately ran to help. Grabbing a couple of dingy pot holders from the table, we enthusiastically began whacking our helpless sister over the head. Swiftly, Ma grabbed Jan by her little bottom and flipped her head first into the sink which was half filled with dirty dishes and soapy water. The sizzling sound of her flaming head hitting the water was like a black smith's red hot iron entering a cooling bath. The pungent smell of burnt hair spread through the kitchen, a wispy trail of white smoke drifting towards our dingy tin ceiling.

Jan gasped for air as Ma yanked her drenched head out of the turgid water, bawling and coughing not yet realizing what had happened.

She was one lucky little girl. Lucky that Ma had seen her just in the nick of time to save her dimpled little face from being burned beyond recognition. Unbelievably, Jan didn't suffer any serious burns to her head or face just to her former Shirley Temple hair, which now stunk like my brother Cliff's dirty socks.

Hearing the commotion, Dad grudgingly dragged his sorry ass out to the kitchen to see what the screaming was about. "What the hell's all this racket?" Dad demanded.

A still frazzled Ma just looked at this sorry slug and cried, "Damn it, Frank, if you had gotten your ass out of bed earlier, this might not have happened. Jan caught her hair on fire!" Ma was still pissed at him for being his usual, hung over, uncaring self, having wasted another night at Stickley's Grill.

"Well, Jesus, Mabel, I would have helped if you asked," he lied. He'd have slept the rest of the morning away if given the chance.

Ma just threw her hands up in disgust and said, "Forget about it, Frank, it's done, it's over and I'm tired, so just eat your break-fast" as she slid a heaping plate of bacon and eggs in front of his disheveled self. "You want some coffee, too?"

"Yea."

So another eventful morning passed in our dysfunctional family and needless to say, a morning my little sister and the rest of us would not soon forget.

Me and my sisters fought like cats and dogs when we were young. We were constantly trying to outdo each other in a vain at-tempt to extract as much extra attention as we could from our be-leaguered mother. Ma was constantly besieged by our continuous conniving and childish antics. Usually, Ma seemed to have endless patience with our ranting. However, on those rare, bad days, she'd go off the wall a bit. These moments were brief, and, in my case, usually for good reason.

I remember when Jan whined to Ma about me one Saturday morning. "Herbie pulled my hair, Ma, and he stole my comb, too." The truth is, I did steal her comb and it was for a good reason. She had been whacking me in the back of my head with it when Ma wasn't looking! Ma was busy trying to make us breakfast at the time, and because she didn't see what was really going on, assumed that I was the culprit since I just happened to be holding the comb when she turned around. Now angry at all the commotion, Ma gave me a stern look, then ripped the comb from my hand. Believing I was now being treated unfairly, I tried to defend myself by grousing to Ma.

"Jan's the trouble maker, not me. She hit me first!"

Of course, Ma didn't believe a word I said by this time and yelled, "Damn it, Herbie. I don't want to hear anymore of this crap! I don't care who started it! Now stop picking on your sister. She's littler than you."

Being stupid, I of course spouted back at Ma in my lame defense. "I don't care if she is littler than me, she still hit me first!"

Bam! In a flash I felt this searing pain in the back of my head. Ma had finally blown. She had exploded in a rage of frustration at my stubbornness and had thrown that damned rat tailed comb at me for being such a snot. Miraculously, because I had such lightning fast reflexes, I was able to deftly turn my face away from the oncoming missile, preventing it from poking my eye out only to have it become impaled in the back of my head, instead. Just behind my right ear. (Maybe that's why I have bouts of tinitis today.)

I think Ma must have been a member of one of those weird carnival acts at one time. You know, the ones where they throw a meat cleaver at you and always miss. Well, this rattail cleaver sure didn't miss. Luckily, it turned out to be a minor cut. However, it looked horrendous at the time. There I was bleeding and crying like a little baby with a stupid, black comb sticking out of my head.

Now, totally calm, Ma walked over to me without saying a word and gently removed the comb as though it were a giant, plastic sliver, imbedded under my skin. She then cleaned out the cut with peroxide and put a small bandage on it. All of us kids sat there in stunned silence as Ma returned to cooking our breakfast, as if nothing happened.

Brenda, Herb (author) Jan; front row, Bonnie

CHAPTER FOUR

Childhood Pastimes and the Radio

Most of my early years were spent playing in the house or yard with my sisters. When I was really little, we used covers from Ma's soup pots as a merry-go-round; we'd take turns twirling on them endlessly in the parlor. As I got a little older, around four or so, I'd play with my sisters and their friends on the street. We'd play hopscotch, jacks and all those girlie games the guys hated. It was about that time when I realized I'd rather play with the guys in my neighborhood. So as I got a bit older, I'd play with other kids besides my sisters, occasionally going to the corner store for goodies.

The three-story red brick house on the northeast corner of College Avenue and Eighth Street housed Harry and Mae Moore's Store. The first floor housed the store, while the second floor, which was directly over the store, was a rental apartment and usually rented out. Harry and Mae with their four kids: Betty, Ellen, Marion and Ronnie lived on the third floor in a clean, modest apartment. One of their daughters, Marion, would become Sister Anne Pierre, while their son Ronnie would eventually become a New York State bureaucrat. As a youth he often worked in the store to help his parents out.

Ronnie, I was told, had the "hots" for my sister Patty. Of course, I wouldn't know what the "hots" meant until a much older age, at which time I too would get the "hots" for women, a genetic thing for guys I guess.

I remember Harry as a big, burly guy. Many years later, I was told that Harry had a great sense of humor, although I didn't recognize his humor at the tender age of four. I was usually scared shitless of him then. He was always playing practical jokes on the kids who'd come into his store, like threatening them from behind the meat counter with a large meat clever, then laughing his ass off as they ran out of the store screaming in terror.

I still remember the time he pretended to cut off his thumb in front of a bunch of us kids who'd come into his store to spend our nickel allowance on penny candy. As we approached the counter to purchase our goodies, we saw Harry with his back to us using the slicing machine. Suddenly he screamed and grabbed his hand pretending to be in severe pain yelling to his willing accomplice Mae, his wife. "Quick, pick up my thumb, Mae, before it goes down the sink!"

We stood frozen in place, mesmerized by this horrific sight. Dana Delachance in front with her hands covering her eyes, shaking and whimpering and me and Butchie Grillo in the back, not knowing whether to piss our pants, cry or run out of the store screaming, which was our usual reaction to Harry's antics. All the parents in the neighborhood knew Harry loved to scare the wits out of the kids, but in reality he was totally harmless and truly loved all the kids. Today he would probably be arrested for child abuse.

Mae shouted back in feigned terror, "I've got it, Harry! I've got it. Quick, stick it back on, before it's too late and starts to rot."

"Ouch, ouch, not so hard, Mae," Harry blurted back, as she mischievously tried to help Harry stick his thumb back on. "Aaa, finally," Harry sighed in feigned relief, " thanks, Mae, I think it's on straight now."

"Let me check, Harry" a complicit Mae bantered. "Yep, it looks pretty straight now," she quipped. "But you better see if it's locked in place." Taking his cue from Mae, Harry nonchalantly turned towards us stupefied kids with our mouths agape, pretending that we were not even there.

Gingerly holding his left hand in front of his chest, while keeping his left thumb bent downward at the joint (the tip hidden from sight), and adroitly holding his right thumb at a right angle with the first two fingers of his right hand, it appeared to us that he was actually holding his reattached thumb on with his right hand. Then, with a smirk on his face, Harry rapidly moved his right thumb back and forth. To our naive eyes, it looked like his thumb was snapping in and out of place as though it were attached by a thick rubber band.

Happy that his thumb was working again, Harry turned to Mae and quipped, "Boy, that feels great." He then quizzically looked up at us traumatized, speechless kids and groused, "What are you looking at?" Sardonically wisecracking, "You see a ghost or something? Well, I guess the cat's got your tongue." Then with a hearty guffaw, he laughingly admitted he really didn't cut off his thumb. He was only playing a little joke on us, but in doing so, also wanted to teach us a lesson about safety when playing with knives or other sharp objects.

Unbeknown to us, Harry had seen Butchie and me playing recklessly with a rusty pocket knife we had found the day before in front of Mr. Barton's house, which was located just north of Harry's store. We were trying to duplicate a game the older boys played called stretch. You stood opposite each other with your legs apart, then took turns throwing a knife outside your opponent's foot. If the knife stuck in the ground, your opponent had to move his foot next to the knife. (It took a bit of skill and experience to accomplish this feat.) Each player would alternate turns, until his opponent couldn't stretch any further, gave up in order to prevent getting sore nuts from stretching too far, was stuck by the knife, or just fell over because he was off-balance.

Luckily, before we were able to inflict any damage to ourselves, Peg-leg Pete, who lived in the basement of the Barton's house, unexpectedly emerged from his apartment and saw what we were doing. Fearing for our safety, he immediately screamed at the top of his lungs. "Stop it before you get hurt!" he then chastised us. "Get the hell away from my house with that damned thing or I'm going to tell your Ma."

His screeching had so startled and scared us that we dropped the knife on the sidewalk and scampered home like a couple of scared jack rabbits. We feared—with good reason—a major paddling from our moms if he ratted on us. However, Pete never followed up on his threat, so Butchie and I figured we were off the hook when we ventured into Moore's store the next day.

Nope! We weren't off the hook, because Harry had seen what had transpired and figured we needed to learn a lesson, then proceeded to teach us that frightening lesson. It's just too bad that poor, innocent Dana had to suffer through it with us. This little episode would become another of life's lessons learned the hard way. (Harry would eventually teach me this slight of hand trick when I was a few years older. Later in life, I would amaze my little daughters with this trick and eventually my precious grandkids.)

Peg-leg Pete was a World War II veteran who lost his right leg in the war. He was also suffering from shell-shock. He was extremely quiet and rarely ventured out of his basement apartment, unless it was to buy some beer at Harry's or down at Stickley's Grill. Sadly, Pete drowned up at Jack's Hole, just above the Poestenkill Gorge one hot summer evening. Rumor was that he was distraught, plastered and dived off the escarpment, never to surface again.

The only source of entertainment we kids had was the old hand-me-down radio Ma had in her bedroom. Knowing that I had a vivid imagination and that I was a very gullible little kid, my sister Patty conned me into believing that the people who were talking on the radio were actually *in* the radio. You see, I was not even five years old yet. That old wooden console radio was taller than I was. In fact, I remember that we pulled it out from the wall in Ma's room. Patty then had me peer at all the huge lighted tubes in the back.

"Look real close," she said, because she had actually seen people there inside those tubes. "Can't you see all those people in there?" she prodded. "Can't you see the fat guy with the beard and that skinny lady with the blue dress?"

I strained and strained my eyes as hard as I could. Trying my damnedest to see the tiny little people that Patty swore were in there, after much straining and brain washing, I finally yelled, "I see them now, I see them now!" And I did see them, at least in my mind.

Luckily I did not go blind staring at all those bright tubes or from masturbating when I got older. However, I do have macular degeneration now as I write this. Hum? Maybe there is some truth in those old wives tales about going blind if you diddle yourself. Anyhow, thank God Ma wasn't there when we did this. She was busy visiting with Winnie Koch next door. She would have smacked us alongside the head.

Needless to say, Patty didn't let this little episode go by without yapping to everybody about how gullible I was. She couldn't wait to tell Ma at supper time, with all my sisters sitting around the kitchen table. I still remember Ma laughing so hard that she almost pissed her pants, and my older sister Dorothy giggling at her end of the table, trying her damnedest to restrain herself.

Patty seemed so proud of herself for making an ass out of me. So there I was trying to defend my bruised little ego. My pleading to Ma that I did see those little people made them all laugh even more. That was when the tears welled up in my eyes. I was a sensitive little guy. Ma stopped her laughing and told all my sisters to cut it out. She could tell that I was hurt. She then picked me up and held me against her bosom, comforting me the way that only she could do with her warmth and motherly love. Patty was just playing a little joke on me, she said, but that I was not stupid for believing it. She then explained that there were no people in the radio. They were actually in a radio studio in New York, she said, and their voices were transmitted over telephone wires to our radio. It didn't matter that I didn't understand what the hell she just told me. All that mattered was that she loved me and was comforting me.

She then turned and yelled at my sister Patty. She cautioned her to stop playing stupid games with her little brother, or else she would get her ass whacked the next time. So here at the end is Patty running crying from the room and me being cradled in the safety of my Mom's arms, so sweet!

Our weekly treat as kids was listening to Ozzie and Harriet on the radio Friday nights and getting a candy bar from Ma as a reward for being "good" most of the week. "Good" was a relative term based on how much sanity remained for Ma after dealing with our tantrums all week long. She would usually send Patty and me down to Harry's store with a handful of nickels to pick up some Three Musketeers bars or O'Henry bars to munch on during our favorite show. We all loved Ozzie and Harriet because they had kids we could relate to somewhat. They were a semi-normal family. Although they weren't poor like us, they seemed to act like us, and they wanted the same things we did. Lucky for them, they had a father figure in their life, although Ozzie seemed like a bit of a screwball most of the time. Harriet was the calming influence in their family. So in that respect, they were like our family. In our house, like theirs, Ma was usually the calming person, always there to nurture and coddle us when we were sick and teach us right from wrong. However, we weren't necessarily good students at learning right from wrong when we were young.

CHAPTER FIVE

What's a Kinder?

Speaking of students, I would enter kindergarten around this time. Because of my birth date, I started school at age four. I was just getting to know my neighborhood buddies that summer when school abruptly intervened before I really became accepted by them. Frankie Brighton, Alan Sydner, Denny Barrow, Billy Finch and Butchie Grillo all hung out in my neighborhood. It's kind of funny how things go. Frankie, Denny, Alan, Billy, Butchie and I, as well as other neighborhood kids, played together or fought with each other on a daily basis. However, we would attend different schools. Most of the kids from Catholic families attended parochial schools, while the Protestant kids like me, who were mostly poor, attended public school. It was much less expensive back then to send kids to parochial schools than it is today. That may have been part of the reason why their parents sent them to St. Francis for elementary school and La Salle or Catholic Central for high school.

Sam's Barber Shop was where my brother Sonny brought me for my first "big boy haircut" that summer in preparation for school. This ritual served as a right of passage for preschool boys, having either their dads or older brothers take them for their first real haircut. Prior to this, their moms cut their hair, usually at the kitchen sink, with a dish towel wrapped around their shoulders and using common kitchen scissors. Some moms unceremoniously used small bowls to serve as a guide to cut the kid's hair. That could be why so many kids' hair looked like that of Moe from the Three Stooges movies. Luckily, Ma did my hair free style. So, although it didn't look professional, it usually had a few ragged edges and looked like a normal little boy's cut, not a caricature.

I remember being scared shitless that day, sitting in a booster seat at Sam's Barber Shop with a huge white sheet tied so tightly around my neck that I thought I'd choke to death. Sam said slyly to my smirking brother Sonny that he'd try his best not to cut an ear off if I moved my head, but he couldn't guarantee it. He then pointed to a glass bowl filled with fake rubber ears. Needless to say, I sat paralyzed with fear, tiny tears silently trickling down my cheeks, but managed to remain totally still and not make a sound, as Sam's monstrous machine and its long spikes buzzed rapidly around my head. I watched in terror as huge globs of my soft blond hair cascaded over the sheet, spilling onto the black and white tiled floor.

This was the same horrid trick Sam had used for years on youngsters who came to his shop for their "ritual" first haircut. For the most part, it worked quite successfully, guaranteeing a compliant, frightened child, and making Sam's job easier by keeping them from fidgeting in his chair. Ironically, at the end of the ordeal he'd reward each kid with a tootsie pop, then tell them that he was just kidding, but the trauma had already been inflicted. From Sam's perspective, the positive outcome from this trauma was that most of his young customers would always be well behaved, because in the back of their minds they would always wonder if he was lying.

The older neighborhood kids had nicknamed Sam the Barber, "Sam the Butcher" for his acumen of shaving most of them almost bald with his notorious brush cuts. When he finished, there was little brush left to cut. These hair cuts usually lasted the entire summer, thus saving parents some needed money. How ironic that his shop was located right next door to a real butcher shop, Helflick's.

My early school years were the source of many happy and often times humorous memories I cherish today. I can still remember my first day of school. I was supposed to go to half-day kindergarten at School 14 located at the top of College Avenue. My sister Dorothy was designated to take me that day. She was the oldest kid living home at the time, and being in eighth grade, Ma felt she was responsible enough to bring me. It turned out to be a daunting task for Dorothy.

Ma had tried to prepare me for the big day by having Dorothy do a couple of dry runs up to the school the weekend before classes started. However, that tactic didn't work very well, because when the day finally arrived, I was still scared to death. Shortly after Dorothy dropped me off with Mrs. McCann, my kindergarten teacher, she got called back to take me home. I was hysterical. Suffering from separation anxiety, I couldn't stop crying and had thrown myself on the floor in a tantrum, screaming for my Mommy. These little tirades would last a couple days before I was finally able to adjust and settle in. In the meantime, poor Dorothy was forced to drag me back home each day, then drag herself back up the steep grade that was College Avenue.

Eventually, kindergarten became fun with all the hustle and bustle going on in our basement classroom. We were located next to the home economics class where the girls in the upper grades would bake cookies and cakes that they shared with us. The swimming pool and gym were also located on this level. Along with learning the ABC's and finger painting, I also found some friends who would be with me all through my early school years.

Although Billy, Butchie and a new friend Carl Redmond, went to Public School 14 with me, Frankie, Denny and Alan went to St. Francis which was located a few blocks away on Congress Street. We developed a friendly rivalry starting in kindergarten over which school was better. Both schools celebrated various holidays together by having the day off, but the Catholic school kids got several religious holidays off that we didn't get, and boy, did they love to rub it in, especially Denny and Alan.

I'm not exactly sure which holiday it was that stands out in my memory, maybe it was All Saints Day, because it was in the fall. I remember it was a warm morning and we were finger painting near the open window that looked out onto the grass terrace that surrounded the building. Shrubs and bushes around the base of the building provided cover for my mischievous friends to hide.

Within seconds after Mrs. McCann left the room to get us some cookies from the home economics class next door, I heard what sounded like muted giggles coming from outside the window. Right after hearing those giggles I felt the sting from a hard stone that bounced off my right shoulder and onto the tiled floor. Shortly after hearing muffled laughter again I approached the window to see what was going on and up pops Denny and Alan, chanting *childishly*, "Nah, nah, nah, nah, nah...nah! We ain't got no school." They then proceeded to toss a few more stones into the classroom, hitting other kids who immediately started crying.

Just as Denny and Alan were about to toss more stones, Mrs. McCann abruptly burst into the room, a plate full of cookies firmly in hand. She had heard the wailing of her young pupils. Upon spotting the two antagonists squatting brazenly on the window sill, she quickly ran over to shoo them away admonishing them that if they didn't leave, she'd call the cops. Just as she neared the window, Denny reached down and grabbed a handful of the still warm cookies, stuffing one into his mouth as he pushed Alan out of the way and rolled onto the lawn out of the reach of Mrs. McCann. Denny had a big smirk on his freckled face, laughing at a flummoxed Mrs. McCann, "Thanks, you old bag!" he shouted, racing away with Alan as Mrs. McCann just stood there in stunned silence.

My year in kindergarten was pretty humdrum aside from that one incident, but as my early school years progressed things did become more stimulating and painful at times. One of my fondest memories from kindergarten was the hectic dash home for lunch each day. I was usually dragged along kicking and screaming by my sisters Dorothy and Patty as they scurried home to gobble Ma's gourmet goodies. Even though I didn't particularly enjoy being dragged along by my collar, I at least got to stay home the rest of the day and play, while they didn't. They only had forty-five minutes for lunch and had to rush back before afternoon classes started.

By the time they finished racing up three flights of stairs with me in tow, they'd collapse in their chairs, huffing and puffing. We then gorged ourselves on a huge pile of baloney salad sandwiches Ma had waiting for us. Baloney salad is a treat I still love today. It's inexpensive and simple to make. You just grind up a pound of Hembold's German style baloney, yellow onion and dill pickle, then mix it all together with Hellman's mayonnaise. Yummy! Occasionally, Ma might alternate by making a big pile of peanut butter and jelly sandwiches, which also went a long way and was inexpensive to make. The real treat for me each day was a huge glass of Borden's milk and handful of Ma's homemade oatmeal or peanut butter cookies. Those were the fun things. But, that year I also experienced some not so fun things.

Jack as a youth living in Derby Line, VT.

CHAPTER SIX

Tonsils Don't Tickle

I guess you could say I was a bit sickly as a young child. Nothing debilitating, just frequent bouts of sore throats and respiratory problems related to undiagnosed allergies, asthma and bad tonsils. Of course, all the smoke, animal dander and uncontrollable dirt may have played a part in my problems. When you walked into our kitchen, there always seemed to be a cloud of smoke hovering near the ceiling like the San Francisco fog. But this fog never lifted. It stained the paint on our walls and ceilings as well as the few remaining teeth Ma had left. I guess having so many kids had drained her of more than her youthful beauty. It also drained her of needed nutrients, minerals and health. The tin ceiling in our kitchen was also covered with untold numbers of fly traps, jam-packed with corpses. I guess the fly traps were a cheaper alternative to screens which Ma couldn't afford and which our slumlord never provided. As a result, Ma always kept her trusty fly swatter or rolled up newspaper nearby to whack those pesky critters unlucky enough to survive the fly traps.

Whenever I had one of these respiratory episodes, Ma would check for a fever by feeling my forehead. If I was wheezing, she'd slather Vick's Vapor Rub on my scrawny chest and send me to bed. I had to cover up by pulling blankets, sheets, coats or any other thing resembling bedding over my head. This was necessary in order for the Vapors to work their magic and *sweat* out my cold. That's how she cured my colds, sweating them out with Vick's Vapor Rub. Too bad Ma couldn't afford to buy Vick's stock because she'd have made a fortune on me alone.

Usually, the worst times for these episodes were in late summer, early fall or if I was playing out in the snowy cold of winter. I was so scrawny and sickly looking that Ma became very worried that something was terribly wrong. Puffing away on their unfiltered Chesterfield's one night, Ma said to Winnie Koch and Helen Howard, "Look at how scrawny Herbie is. I don't know what to do with him. He eats like a horse but is still so scrawny. Do you think he's ok, Helen?"

"Mabel, you worry too much," Helen said in her gravelly, smoker's voice. "He's probably just a little bit anemic. Call Dr. Kowlinger and have him come up and check him out." (Doctors made house calls when I was a child.)

"But the sore throats really worry me. It seems all my kids keep getting them. What do you think that could be?"

"Well, Mabel. Do you remember how my little girls had that problem a while back? It was their tonsils flaring up a little."

"Oh, yea Winnie, I remember that. What did the doctor do for them?"

"He just told me to have them gargle with salt and water and it seemed to help them. They have been pretty good ever since."

The next day Ma had Winnie make a phone call to Doctor Kowlinger for her. That night, right after supper, came a knock on the door. Ma asked me to answer it. So I did. Standing there was a tall, distinguished looking man in a dark suit, glasses, sporting a finely trimmed mustache and holding a black leather bag. While he had a comforting smile, there was something mysterious about him that made me wary. Who was this stranger, and why was he here? I'd soon find out.

"Hi, Dr. Kowlinger," Ma said as she came to the door wiping her hands with a dish towel. "Thank you for coming." She then led him into the kitchen where he sat down and asked her a series of questions I didn't understand. Ma then told me to go into the parlor with Brenda and Patty while she talked.

"Who is that?" I asked Patty.

"Oh, he's a doctor. Ma took me to him once for a sore throat."

"So why is he here now?"

"How do I know? Maybe Ma's not feeling good."

"I don't think so," Brenda blurted out. "I heard Ma say there is something wrong with Herbie."

"Me?"

"Yea, you."

"Why me?"

Now I was getting scared. I felt fine after the cold and sore throat Ma had me sweat out the week before. "I don't feel sick now so why is he here?" A few minutes later this tall, frightening looking man with the fraudulent smile and pencil thin mustache came into the room with Ma.

"Hello, kids," he said in his thick, Jewish accent. "I'm just going to give you all a little checkup. Don't be scared."

Scared! I was scared shitless. Especially when he opened that huge bag containing all kinds of tools I'd never seen before. He then took out a strange looking contraption that had what looked like ear plugs connected to a shiny metal sphere on the end of a long, black, plastic rope which he hung around his neck. It was his stethoscope. He also took out a glass thermometer along with wooden tongue depressors that looked like very wide popsicle sticks. I anxiously looked over at Patty and Brenda and now they looked scared too.

Always belligerent, Patty decried. "I thought he was here to check out Herbie? Not the rest of us."

"Since he was here for Herbie, I thought it would be a good idea to check out why you're all getting sore throats," Ma said.

"I don't have no sore throat, Ma!" Patty declared.

"Me either," Brenda, timidly whined.

"Well, you're getting checked anyway. So stop your whining. All of you!"

"But Cliff's not here to get checked. That's not fair." Patty pleaded in hopes she could forestall the inevitable.

"He'll get checked when he comes in," Ma asserted, opening the front window and yelling for him to come home. He was hanging out down by Alan Sydner's house with Alan and Denny Barrow. Reluctantly, he came running up the stairs a few minutes later right after the doctor had begun checking the rest of us out.

After almost gagging on the wooden plank the doctor shoved in my mouth, he then forced me to say ah. It was awful. In comparison, the cold stethoscope he placed against my shirtless chest almost felt refreshing, although I did begin to worry about what he was listening to with that thing plugged into his ears. When he told me to take deep breaths, I started feeling dizzy and almost passed out. Once he stopped, I could breathe again. Then without warning he started rapping me on the chest with his fists. To make things even worse, he took out a huge metal and rubber mallet. It reminded me of a tomahawk and felt like it when he started whacking me on my knees, elbows and anywhere else he felt like, making my legs , feet, elbows and hands bounce up and down uncontrollably. After almost blinding me by shining an *infrared* flash light into my eyes, the torture finally came to an end and he moved on to the next victim. Thank God!

After what seemed an eternity, the doctor finally completed his mission. With us kids sitting on the couch and the doctor and Ma sitting on our shabby, threadbare chairs across from us, the doctor gave Ma the news. All four of us kids sat there quietly but in a state of unease waiting for the bad news.

"Mrs. Hyde, the good news is that your children are in pretty good health."

"Thank God for that," Ma sighed.

"But, the little boy, um, is it, um Herbie?"

"Yes, doctor."

"Well, he appears to be a little bit small and skinny for his age. There is a chance he could be slightly anemic."

"Anemic!" I thought. That's what Helen said to Ma. "Oh, no. I must be very sick. Anemic! Oh, my God what's going to happen to me?"

But then the doctor said to Ma, "Not to worry, I will give you a prescription for a good iron tonic and he will be just fine."

"Phew," I thought. "I'm not going to die."

"Your other children are just fine too, except that all of them have swollen tonsils and adenoids. To avoid further sore throats and colds, they will have to be taken out."

"Out! How is he going to get them out?" I thought. "Oh no, I hope he doesn't have any more carpenter's tools in his bag. The plank was bad enough."

"Is it really necessary, doctor?" Ma questioned.

"In my professional opinion, Mrs. Hyde, I believe it is. They will be better for it if they're removed."

"Well, doctor, I have a lot of faith in you and I will agree to it. When should it be done and where?"

"It doesn't have to be done immediately—maybe in two or three weeks. I will schedule it with Dr. Davis who works out of Samaritan Hospital."

"One thing before you go, doctor. I don't have the money to pay to for the operations they need. I barely have enough to pay for this visit," Ma said meekly, tears beginning to well in her eyes.

"Don't you worry, Mrs. Hyde, it will get taken care of, I promise. Here is a prescription for that tonic. Two tablespoons twice a day and he will be fine."

"Thank you so much, doctor." Ma then handed him the crumbled three dollars she had in her grease-stained apron pocket. He gently smiled, patting us all on the head one at a time and quietly slipped out the door.

The next day I had to start drinking a thick, horridly disgusting, purple tonic that almost gagged me for three straight weeks. The fourth week after the doctor's visit would be the week all four of us kids went to the hospital to have our tonsils yanked out. It was not a fun experience, believe me. Brenda and I were in the same room while Patty and Cliff were in an adjacent room. Patty and Cliff had theirs done first and when they returned from the operating room Brenda and I could hear their muffled crying. "Oh, my God," I thought. "This is going to be painful!"

Suddenly, two masked men and a woman ominously entered our room with some kind of wagon with metal bars on it. Seeing the terror in our eyes the woman tried to calm us down with a soothing voice muffled by her mask. "Don't be afraid. Everything will be just fine," the masked woman said. I didn't buy it. Especially after one of the masked men violently grabbed my arm and held it down. "This will be just a tiny prick." The woman lied. "Just lay still."

"Tiny prick?" I thought, screaming out in pain. It felt like she stuck that needle right through my arm. However, within a few moments I started feeling groggy, relaxing as they dragged me onto that sterile wagon and pulled up the bars. As they pushed the wagon out of the room I could see blurry lights flashing by on the ceiling. It was cool now as metal doors loudly opened and we entered what seemed like a shiny, all white room. The wagon came to a sudden stop under a huge round light that looked like the sun through hazy eyes. Suddenly, a monster appeared, hovering over me with a mask and a big, shiny, metal orb on his forehead.

"Ok nurse, you can put him under now." Suddenly that same nurse who had stabbed me with that needle appeared above me with a hissing, triangular shaped device in her hand. She shoved this device over my nose and face. Now scared to death and unable to breathe, I struggled to break free from the grasp of those same two masked men who had entered my room earlier. Within seconds a noxious gas seeped into my mask and I slowly faded away.

I awoke to a horrible stabbing pain in my throat and immediately started crying, the smell of putrid ether still burning my nose. A calming voice and cool hand eased my pain. It was Ma, gently brushing my forehead. "You're going to be ok, Herbie," Ma soothed. She then gently brushed some ice chips across my dry lips. Just hearing Ma's voice and feeling her presence immediately started the healing process. Knowing she was near by was a comfort for all of us. Forty-five minutes later, after I had slowly regained my earthly bearings, Brenda was wheeled in. She, of course, was crying too. Ma immediately went to her aid as she had with the rest of us. Ma stayed late into the evening making sure we were all ok before she wearily headed home with my sister Kathleen.

We stayed for several days. The ice chips were soon replaced by delightful ice cream as the healing process moved swiftly along. Although the constant sore throats subsided in most of us, I didn't fatten up and still continued to have those nasty colds and asthma attacks. Of course, Ma continued to sweat them out of me with Vick's Vapor Rub right through grade school.

Unbeknown to us kids at the time we were having our tonsils out, our Dad was also in the hospital. He had been suffering for years with a chronic and debilitating disease (Burgers Disease) which cost him the loss of several fingers and toes. From what I heard years later, they tried various experimental therapies on him in order to find a cure. But in reality, he was used as a guinea pig. Huge scars on his side, back and legs stood in silent testimony.

Of course, none of the experimental therapies or surgeries worked. In the end, he would still lose his leg. I often wondered if that may have been part of the reason he could be so mean at times. However, not knowing exactly when these problems first surfaced clouds the issue of how long or why he acted the way he did. He wasn't always mean, just most of the time. I guess Dad was pretty self centered and narcissistic.

After all us kids were healed and back to normal, Dad wasn't. He was in the hospital for quite a while and when he did come home, he was a bear. He complained about everything. I guess he was feeling sorry for himself. He wanted Ma and the rest of us to wait on him hand and foot now that he only had one foot. (Pun intended.) I never realized until then how miserable he really was. He complained to Ma about everything.

"Damn it, Mabel, shut them kids up, I'm trying to sleep!" He usually slept half the day away when he first got home. The other half of the day he used for eating, complaining and peeing in the urinal that we had to dump for him as part of our chores. Thank God Ma emptied his bed pan when he took one of his frequent craps.

In the time right after his amputation, I'd see him take one of his crutches and whack my brother Cliff, for no good reason. Luckily, I can never remember my Dad ever hitting me. In fact, most of the time he just ignored me as though I wasn't there. In some ways, that was more painful than getting whacked with a crutch. At least Cliff got attention. Negative, but still attention.

Suffering through this dreadful disease all those years may have brought out the worst in him. It's hard to tell because it seemed most of the time he was mean and nasty and drunk. Maybe that was his way of coping? I guess I'll never really know the answer. But even if that was part of the reason, it's still sad that he had to take it out on Ma and others. My brother Cliff was his favorite whipping boy.

Eventually, Dad was fitted with a cumbersome artificial leg that he'd strap around his corpulent waist, then quickly hobble down to Stickley's Grill. This new device allowed him a sense of independence he hadn't had since well before his surgery. With this difficult but new found mobility, some of the older neighborhood kids Tony Fermetti and Babe Famundi coined a new nickname for Dad, "Hi-Speed," then laughed behind his back as he struggled to master his new prosthesis. Eventually, Dad was even able to drive his truck again like a maniac most of the time. It was quite impressive watching him do many of the same things he had done before his surgery—drive his truck, climb trees, and even swim. Dad managed to overcome his handicap in relatively short order and started working odd jobs and lumber jacking again. However, as he progressed, I began a series of mishaps I'd remember the rest of my life. Not long after getting our tonsils out, fate struck again.

CHAPTER SEVEN

Sliver Me Timbers!

As history would also show during my early years, I was like an accident waiting to happen. Because of that, I endured quite a bit of pain and have the scars to prove it. Of course, some of the pain was self inflicted, while some came at the hands of others. They were either mean and nasty, or in some cases, just careless. The one thing that didn't happen to me as a child though, I never broke an arm, leg or finger. However, I do think I may have broken my nose once when I whacked myself with a baseball I'd thrown into the air and caught with my big proboscis, instead of my glove. It wasn't a certified break because no one took me to the hospital, but it did bleed like a stuck pig and felt kind of squishy for several days.

Rug rats, the pejorative term for toddlers, would definitely apply to me and my sisters. The only problem with the term is that we didn't have any rugs or rats in our house, just decrepit wood floors in our living room, bedrooms, and what some might call our dining room, which also had a large piece of dilapidated linoleum with curled up edges. Our floors were not those highly polished polyurethane beauties you see today. No, ours looked more like grease-stained slabs of rough hewn lumber, straight from the saw mill. Because the floors hadn't been sanded or treated, it would lead to us kids being impaled with huge slivers in our bare feet or butts on occasion, depending on whether we were sliding on our feet or butts. Ma constantly reminded us not to slide, but I guess we never listened or were slow learners, because we slid on them constantly.

Removing those little buggers was often worse than getting them in the first place. Whenever we'd get one, Ma or Dad, if he were home on those rare occasions, would remove them with a red hot poker. Usually, Ma used one of her darning needles which was heated to about 1000 degrees with a match or, in some cases, on the kitchen stove. No anesthetics or sympathy were employed to ease the pain during these minor surgeries. For that reason, I have a lot of respect for what poor cattle must go through when they get branded, and why I never became a cattle rancher.

The most painful instance I can remember in my battles with slivers occurred when I was chasing my sister Brenda in a game of tag from the dining room into the kitchen, where Ma was preparing supper. The dining room contained a small wooden table, along with a few unfinished school house chairs and a cast-iron, coal burning stove. The dining room set rested on a tattered sheet of linoleum that also served as our skating rink. Bordering the table and our skating rink were those nasty wood planks, loaded with fiendish slivers. As usual, I slid my feet along the tattered edge of linoleum in hopes of catching Brenda before she escaped to the kitchen. Suddenly, the most excruciating pain I ever felt seared through me, causing me to black out for a second, before screeching at the top of my lungs for Ma.

"What happened? What happened?" Ma yelled, running in from the kitchen. Unable to catch my breath from the pain, I couldn't speak. All I could do was emit screech after screech, all the while grasping my right foot in hopes of easing the burning pain, tears cascading down my cheeks.

Ma held me tight, then screamed at Brenda, "What the hell happened here? What happened?"

Brenda was now crying too because Ma yelled at her. Thinking she had done something wrong, she sobbed, "I didn't do anything, Ma! We were just playing tag when Herbie slid along the linoleum and started screaming."

Immediately, Ma realized what happened: I had gotten another sliver in my foot, but this one was different than any I had ever gotten before. She immediately put me on her lap and gently removed my grungy sock, being careful not to hit the tip of this gnarly beast. This one was huge—bigger and nastier looking than anything she encountered before. It was a three inch long, wide, sullen dagger that had broken off that wretched floor and impaled itself deep into my tiny foot, punishing me for all my childish misdeeds.

"Brenda, quick, get the tweezers off my dresser!"

"Ok, Ma," Brenda yelled, racing into Ma's room and returning in the blink of an eye.

"Now, get me some peroxide from the medicine chest and get me a wash cloth, too."

Within seconds Brenda was back again with the needed tools. They didn't help! Still sitting on Ma's lap with my leg and foot turned sideways so she could get at the afflicted area, Ma told Brenda to hold my foot still as she applied the tweezers to the very end of the sliver, which was barely sticking out. I recoiled in pain, burying my face into Ma's bosom. This monster was dark and greasy looking, and you could see another two or three inches of it buried at a sharp angle, deep into the bottom of my foot. Each time she tried unsuccessfully to grab it, I'd scream, a slight trickle of blood oozing from the wound. Finally, she was able to get hold of it and began slowly pulling it out. However, as soon as she got about a half inch out, the end of the sliver snapped off, leaving the rest still imbedded deep into the bottom of my foot.

"Damn!" Ma cursed. "I almost had it." Now, there was nothing more to grab with the tweezers, because the remainder of the sliver had been sucked back into the bottom of my foot. If Ma couldn't squeeze out enough of the sliver to grasp with the tweezers, she'd have to get that damned red hot poker. Try as she might with that poker, Ma could not catch enough of that sliver to pop it through the opening. After twenty minutes of frustration for her and twenty minutes of agony for me, she decided to stop. Instead of proceeding, she would wait until my Dad got home and have him try to dig out the rest. In the meantime, she rinsed my foot with warm water and rubbed it down with peroxide to stem possible infection.

Even though I could still feel some pain, it was not as intense as it was, unless I tried to stand or walk. Ma made me a cup of hot cocoa and settled me on her bed to await my Dad's return from an odd job he was able to find that day, clearing some brush and trees up in Prospect Park.

An hour and a half later, Dad finally dragged himself through the front door, dirty and tired from a hard day's work. He was starved and just wanted to suck down a beer from the ice box and have a heaping bowl of Ma's goulash. However, after hearing the horror story of my accident, he decided to fix my foot before dinner. So the torture began, again.

This time, instead of Ma and Brenda working on me, it would be Ma and Dad, while my sisters looked on. I could feel the cold rush of peroxide on my foot as my Dad grabbed it and Ma poured. Dad squeezed the sides of my foot so hard that I thought I'd pass out again. Then he pushed his thumb deep into the base of my foot near the heel in hopes of forcing the remainder of the sliver to the surface. After what seemed an eternity, he declared to Ma, "It's coming, it's coming, I can see the end of it now. Give me the tweezers, Mabel, quick!"

"Here they are, Frank. Now just be careful you don't break it off again like I did," Ma warned.

"Jesus, Mabel, I'm not going to lose it," a sweating Dad complained.

Suddenly, even with my eyes tightly clenched, I could visualize and feel this long, filthy probe silently sliding out of my foot. With every inch the pain seemed to subside incrementally, almost to the point of having no pain at all.

"That's it," a triumphant Dad proclaimed, holding this three inch wooden trophy in his hand. "Shouldn't be any problems now, I got it all!"

A relieved Ma and an almost painless me professed our gratitude to Dad for getting that damned sliver out of my foot. As usual, I got another dire warning from Ma to stop sliding on those damned floors. So off I hobbled still not feeling totally pain free.

When things calmed down after my calamity, we all sat down to supper together for the first time in a long time. Boy, that goulash tasted so good. Ma was such a great cook with the uncanny ability to stretch whatever meager supplies she had into a gourmet delicacy. To me, homemade goulash was always a specialty. It was then that Dad popped the news he was going out of town for a while to do some work with his friend, Frank Lanquid. Ma was not too pleased about this because she would be the sole caregiver, plus the fact she thought Frank was a bad influence on Dad. On the other hand she knew we could use the extra money desperately, so it was a Catch 22 situation for her.

Two days later, around six in the morning, Dad left to meet his buddy Frank in Hoosick Falls before venturing up to Vermont. They'd be logging for a couple weeks as well as drinking and carousing when they got the chance. In the meantime, I was just beginning to wake from a hazy sleep. Drenched to the bone from sweating and peeing my bed again, I cried out, "Mommy, Mommy, I'm sick." The room was spinning out of control behind my clenched eyes. Hearing my moaning and crying, an exhausted Ma trudged dutifully in to see what was the matter, thinking I was still babying myself over the sliver episode or just looking for attention. However, once she saw me, she realized something was terribly wrong. Just as she was about to reach my bed, I lurched forward, projectile vomiting the remnants of last night's dinner, peas, Spam and potatoes on the floor.

"Oh my God, Herbie, what's the matter?"

Gasping and gagging I purged again, "I don't know, Mommy, I'm so sick." I then began to shiver, shaking uncontrollably as Ma felt my forehead.

"Oh my God, you're burning up!" Quickly sensing this was not a simple cold or flu, she immediately reached down and lifted my injured foot. It was hot and very red. She then turned it upward to look at where that nasty sliver had been and her heart sank. What she saw was disgusting. A putrid slime was oozing out of the bottom of my beleaguered foot. She now realized that they had not completely gotten the sliver out as Daddy proudly proclaimed, and now I had a raging infection.

Panicked about what to do next and no Dad to contact, she was at wits end. However, being a strong and resilient woman, she realized I had to be looked at and soon. However, with Brenda, Jan, and now the newest member of our little family, eighteen month old Bonnie to attend to, she realized she could not bring me to the emergency room herself. Instead, she woke up my older sister Dorothy and told her she had to take me to the hospital. Patty or my brother Cliff couldn't do it because they were too young and had to go to school in a couple hours. Normally she might have asked my oldest sister Kathleen, but she and her husband Steve had moved out of our apartment five months earlier. (Several of my older sisters and their spouses lived with us for short periods when they got married.) From that time on, Dorothy became our surrogate mom in times of crisis.

Before she let me go, Ma realized I was still in my stinky bed clothes and quickly cleaned me up, making sure that I had clean underwear on. God forbid you ever were rushed to the hospital and had dirty underwear on. The nurses would probably pass out from the egregious sight.

I was barely able to hobble around so when the cab arrived, Cliff and Patty helped Dorothy lug me down the two flights of stairs and into the cab.

Just before shipping me off to Samaritan Hospital, Ma handed Dorothy three of the five one dollar bills she had stashed under her mattress for emergencies. She wanted to make sure she had enough for the round trip cab fare and any other emergencies that might arise. Poor Dorothy was again charged to look after me and miss more school because of it. Ma, of course, would send a note to the principal explaining why she was not in class that day. Dorothy was a well behaved student, and knowing our family's circumstances the principal was usually very accommodating. (Not so much with my truant brother Cliff, however, who gave everyone fits.)

With all the pain and anguish I'd been through the past three days, having the emergency room doctor lance my foot and use an anesthetic to quell the pain was like a walk in the park. He was able to extract the last three quarter inch section of sliver that my Dad missed. After they cleaned me up and gave me a shot of penicillin, I was sent home and told to stay off my foot for another five days and to soak the foot in Epsom's salt twice a day until all the redness went away. Ten days later it did start healing dramatically, just in time for Dad to return without knowing what had transpired while he was gone. As a reward for taking me to the hospital, Ma let Dorothy keep the remaining money to use as she wanted. The rest of that school year passed without any major incidents. However, the following summer and school year didn't.

The Troy Record (circa, 1940).

CHAPTER EIGHT

Rats, Foiled Again

Even with school, my life up to that point in time revolved almost exclusively around what went on in our tenement home. It seems hard to believe that any house could be more dilapidated than ours, but the Koch's house was. It was a gray, three story, asphalt shingled apartment house, with many of its shingles missing. The paint on all the wood trim around the doors and windows was either peeling or non existent. Signs of rotting wood shown around the area where the shingles met the foundation. The foundation itself appeared to be crumbling from age or lack of maintenance.

On the north end of the house was a gray wooden stoop with two worn out steps, but no railings. On the left side near the front door, pieces of the siding were missing, exposing some of the broken wooden slats and tar paper. Basically there was about a ten inch hole in the side of the house.

The vacant lot between the Koch's and Barton's house was filled with weeds and discarded garbage, including condoms that passersby would toss after satisfying their licentious needs in the darkness of the overgrown lot. As innocent young kids we could never figure out what these latex devices were. Yes, there were slobs, even back in the good old days. That empty lot was a veritable haven for all kinds of vermin, animal and human.

We, on the other hand, lived in a veritable mansion—a six unit upscale condo (OOPS, I meant to say dump, hum...I mean tenement) three doors north of their house.

As was usual on our street, the neighborhood youth were busy either wreaking havoc on their neighbors, ringing door bells then running and hiding, playing baseball against the steps or pitching pennies or baseball cards against the foundation of Alan Sydner's house.

On an early summer evening just after dinner, a horrifying scream pierced the cool night. It was Hazel Koch! Hearing her scream was nothing unusual as she was always screaming or cursing at the neighborhood kids for whatever reason. We all thought she was half a whack job anyhow. But this time was different. She had been sitting on that beat-up stoop, pissing and moaning as usual about who knows what. I was in front of our house with my sister Patty when all hell broke loose with that blood curdling screech.

So we raced down toward the steps in front of the Gibson's house, which was next door to the Koch's house, in order to find out what the hell was going on. By the time we got there the guys had encircled a parked car by the steps. They had sticks and red murphys in their hands pondering what to do as Hazel kept screeching, "There's a fucking giant rat under the car." True it was! There was a fucking giant rat trapped under a beat up 1940 Chevy sedan, surrounded by a herd of "varmint" hunting youths, who had nothing better to do but to scare it out of its wits. It could not make its way to the sewer for meals or safely back to its nest in the house. It was cowering under the car, and if you got on your knees, you could see its red eyes peering out, ready to strike at any time.

The older boys were so brave and daring. "Big Game Urban Hunters" in search of the ultimate prey, the giant Ratilla the Hun! Now they had their prey in their sights, all gung ho and full of piss and vinegar. But who would be the most daring hunter of them all? Who would be the hero to save our endangered neighborhood?

Would it be Denny Barrow, the Leo Gorsky of the gang, or Alan Sydner his willing follower? Would it be Frankie Brighton, the elder statesman of the gang? No, it would not be any of these brave warriors who would risk their lives and limbs. It would be Herbie. Yea, he can do it! It was sort of like those old cereal commercials when the kids needed a guinea pig to try out some new brand. Hey! Mikey can do it. In this case it was Hey! Herbie can do it. And so I did.

Thus I got volunteered to be the bravest of them all, the one who would reach underneath that dilapidated car and rid the world of this deadly beast. What an honor for a scrawny little kid. I bravely reached under that car and snagged the rat's tail, yanking him out from under his safe haven as I exalted, "I got him, I got him." However, I didn't realize how painful this little adventure would be for me. I felt like a big kid now, proud as hell, holding this scraggly sewer rat by its long tail. I thought that I was now a part of the gang of older kids, sure I'd earned my way into the club.

However, within a few seconds elation turned to terror as everyone around me screamed. I didn't yet feel the pain. The rat had swung around during my glee in capturing him and had taken a chunk out of my right index finger (I still carry that jagged scar today).

Blood was streaming down my hand, yet I didn't even feel the pain of that razor sharp excision. I was a hero, I saved the world, so why were they all still scared? This was my moment of glory. Then suddenly, reality hit home as I looked down and saw what had happened.

Instantaneously, pain erupted as I dropped my trophy and grabbed my finger as some adult swooped down and pulled me away. The rat met his demise with a stoning from those red murphys the older boys had been carrying. He was splattered dead by the curb. Thankfully, the rat was tested for rabies and the test came back negative. However, those results would not ease my pain.

I would become a public celebrity, a future folk hero for my bravery, or so I thought. If I was older, I would have been cited for my stupidity. I remember my older sister Kathleen being with me in the emergency room, holding me down as the doctors and nurses pulled down my tiny, hand-me-down farmer jeans and underpants. They then viciously plunged a gigantic syringe filled with antibio-tics into my tender, virgin butt. That pain was greater than anything I had ever experienced before—even worse than being bitten by that damn rat.

Sadly for my tender young ego, the morning newspapers and radio newscasts would report that a little five year boy had been viciously attacked by a sewer rat, and he had to be rushed to the hospital for tests and treatment after being rescued by friends and neighbors.

Hey! Where was the testimony of my great heroism in saving the neighborhood and the world from this dangerous beast. No! I would not get the acclaim for my feat of bravery; the neighborhood adults and my supposed friends would be proclaimed heroes for saving me. So ironic. I learned a life lesson early on. Don't believe everything you read in the papers or hear on the news. After I survived that beastly attack, things should have been much easier for me the rest of the year. Hum! I wonder?

My sister Dorothy worshipped my older brother Sonny when they were kids. She always tried to tag along with him and his friends whenever she could. But Ma used to force Dorothy to watch me and my younger sisters when she needed a break from all the lunacy. Since I was the one most often out of hand, with no boys to play with usually, Ma would pawn me off on poor Dorothy much more often than she pawned off my sisters. Dorothy even took me for my haircuts after a while. But, instead of taking me to Sam the Barber, like my brother Sonny did, she'd take me to Charlie Markan, the black barber near Seventh Avenue, because he only charged a quarter, and Sam charged fifty cents. She came out ahead of the game that way with an extra quarter she could use for spending money. Ma never found out of course, no harm no foul.

Sonny, Louie Fermetti and Babe Famundi would often climb the barbed wire fence just south of the Sydner's house and onto a large overhanging tree branch they used as a shortcut to the Day

Home compound, where they hung out and played ball. On this day, Dorothy decided to tag along, with me in tow. Since Sonny and his friends were already over the fence and headed for the Day Home, she decided to boost me up onto the limb, so she and I could go down and watch them play.

I felt like a feather to her because I was so scrawny. But just as I was about to grasp that oak branch and climb aboard, I lost my grip, fell backwards towards Dorothy, and impaled my scrawny right arm onto the barbed wire fence.

Hysterical, Dorothy grabbed me and held me tight against the fence, screeching for my brother's help, as I writhed in pain. "Sonny! Sonny! Help me! Quick!" Dorothy screamed.

Hearing Dorothy's frantic plea, Sonny raced back up the hill, climbed onto the branch and lifted me up, carefully handing me down to Luke Howard, who had raced over from Harry's store after seeing what happened. Now safely back on the ground, you could see a gaping hole in my forearm with what looked like a tiny, peeled tomato sticking out. I was crying and bleeding profusely as everyone stood by in a state of panic over what to do next.

Luckily, within a few short minutes I was being attended to by Virginia Perrault, a nurse, who was on her day off and had raced down the street to help out when she heard all the commotion. She stanched the bleeding, then gently pushed the bloodied muscle back into my forearm and held it closed until we reached her apartment, which was next door to ours. Ma nervously watched as Virginia adeptly cleaned out the wound, closed it with butterfly bandages, then wrapped it in sterile gauze.

Since I had a recent tetanus shot, having been chomped on by a toothy, recalcitrant, rodent earlier that summer, I didn't have to go the hospital for any additional treatment. Today you can see a perfectly straight scar, about three inches long, on my forearm. To look at it, you'd think it was done by a highly skilled plastic surgeon, not a practical nurse. Luckily my arm healed quickly. With that trauma out of the way, I again tried to establish friendships with the guys who lived near me. Enter the Pelhams who lived on College Avenue right around the corner from us. We had moved to the Koch's shortly after they moved out. In fact, the Pelham's house was located just up the hill from Moore's store. Because the houses were built into the side of the hills in our neighborhood, our backyards were adjacent to each other. In fact, I could look down into their back yard from a tree I used to climb in our yard. I think I must have been part monkey, because I was always climbing trees or fences or poles.

That used to piss off our backyard neighbor, Mrs. Pelham. She would see me looking into her yard from my perch in our tree and yell at me, especially when she was pulling in clothes from her clothesline. I remember she did have lots of bloomers on her line. I was too young to be a peeping tom yet, if that's what she thought I was doing. I couldn't understand why she yelled at me. Never crossed my mind that she might be concerned about me falling out of the tree. I guess she never gave it a second thought that her clothesline was hooked onto our tree. Apparently she also never heard of the good neighbor rule: be nice, respect your neighbors and their kids, or else they could knock your clothesline down to the ground while accidentally falling from a tree.

Ma used to say Mrs. Pelham was a snooty bitch, looking down her nose at our family because we were poor. In fact, Ma used to tell me that Mrs. Pelham thought her shit didn't stink. I never really understood what that meant. But I bet her shit did stink, because mine sure did.

Time after time I would ask if I could play with her sons Donnie and Dougie, who were about my age. She would either ignore me or say that they had better things to do than play with me. So time and again I would return home to my house crying. I guess she thought I would infect them with some deadly disease. Or, God forbid, they might become infected with...poverty.

The Pelhams usually kept to themselves and were not very friendly to any of their neighbors. However, when they did talk to the neighbors, it was usually to brag about how special their sons Donnie, Dougie and Tommy were. They were the best behaved, the smartest, the best at anything they did. Bullshit! They were spoiled monsters. Mr. Pelham was a cop, and it was rumored that he was always drunk and very mean. The kids were behaved at home because he probably kicked the crap out of them for no good reason.

However, on the rare times that they did go out on the street to play with other kids, they would always instigate trouble. Like the time they decided to play with Butchie Grillo, my best friend at the time. They ended up breaking Mrs. Pinachie's window when Donnie hurled a stick through it. However, confronted by Mrs. Pinachie, they blamed Butchie, who had left five minutes earlier to go home for supper. It was at that time that Mrs. Ravono, who lived next door to Mrs. Pinachie, challenged what the little monsters said. She had witnessed the whole thing and told Mrs. Pinachie exactly what happened. Sensing that they were now in deep shit, Donnie and Dougie ran home crying, scheming how to save their asses from getting kicked by their old man.

So instead of approaching Butchie's father about the broken window, Mrs. Pinachie marched down to the Pelham house to get restitution for her broken window. Mr. Pelham answered the door, his breath reeking of stale beer. Immediately he became belligerent toward Mrs. Pinachie. When she tried to explain that his boys had been seen by her neighbor throwing a stick through her window, he continued his harangue, insisting that his boys would never do anything like that and that they had already told him the entire story. Apparently, in a preemptive strike to save their fat little asses, Donnie and Dougie had rushed home and lied through their teeth to their old man. He said that his boys came home crying about how they were going to be blamed for something they didn't do—breaking Mrs. Pinachie's window. They claimed Butchie Grillo did it, not them. Mr. Pelham was adamant that his sons would never lie to him.

Shouting in Mrs. Pinachie's face that Mrs. Ravono was a damned liar, he then slammed the door in her face. The rotten little bastards got off scott free while poor Mrs. Pinachie had to pay to replace her own window. Luckily, she had a good neighbor in Walt Howard, who worked for the local paint company. He replaced her window for cost and a bottle of Fitzie's beer. Walt loved his booze too, but he was a good, friendly drunk, always looking out for his family and neighbors.

My misadventure with the Pelham boys would occur shortly after Butchie Grillo's. However, mine would have a much different outcome than Butchie's. I had just walked back from Moore's store with a little pack of paper caps to put in the shiny cap gun I had gotten for Christmas. It felt like a real cowboy gun to me. It was made out of white metal, with a little compartment in which to load your caps on a tiny spool which fed them to the trigger. I'd pretend to be Roy Rogers or the Lone Ranger hiding behind trees or cars and shooting at the make believe outlaws I'd seen in movies down at the State Theater on Fourth Street.

I was sitting on Mrs. Gibson's front steps after filling my gun, daydreaming about my next adventure. Suddenly, I caught a glimpse of Donnie and Dougie Pelham walking up the road towards me. I aimed my gun at a bird perched on the telephone wire across the street and snapped off a shot just to get their attention. The Pelham boys usually just ignored me, but this time the sound of my gun got their attention. They looked at each other quizzically, whispered something, then slowly walked up to me with big smirks on their faces.

"Wow, Herbie, that's some gun you got there!" said Dougie.

"Sure is shiny," chirped Donnie.

"Yea, it is pretty shiny, I got it for Christmas."

"You ever play cowboys and Indians with it?" spouted Dougie.

"Nah, never have anybody to play with."

"Really?" Dougie said.

"Nope."

"Well, me and Donnie will play with you if you want."

"Really?"

"Yep. But we got to have rules."

"Ok. What's the rules?"

"Well, you will be the Indians and we will be the cowboys."

"Hum?" I thought. "That seems strange, but at least I have someone to play with for a change."

"Ok, you can be the cowboys and I'll be the Indians."

"Great!" blurted Dougie.

"Now, give us the gun and go hide behind one of the trees. Then, when we give you the signal you come out and we'll fight."

"But, I won't have a gun to shoot if I give it to you."

"Dummy! Indians don't have guns, remember?"

"Oh, yeah, that's right, they have bows and arrows. But I don't have a bow and arrow, either. "

"Yep, I know, but that's ok," said Dougie. "You just pretend you have a bow and arrow when we call you and remember this is only make believe, right?"

"Oh, yea, right."

Excited about having some real friends to play with, I gleefully waited behind a huge elm tree in front of our house until it was time for the battle to begin. While waiting, which seemed like an eternity, I was lucky enough to find a long, thin, green switch lying on the ground, right next to a dirty piece of twine. I was then able to neatly tie the twine around one end of the switch to the other end, creating a makeshift bow to play with. After searching the weeds a bit longer I found a brittle, straight, skinny broken tree branch which was about eighteen inches long. I could use that as an arrow. Boy, was I lucky. Now I could defend myself against them evil cowboys when they come-a-fighting, and come-a-fighting they did.

"Hey, Tonto! Get out here and fight or were going to shoot the Lone Ranger!" screamed Dougie, as he and Donnie emerged from between two parked cars with their hands behind their backs.

"Don't you dare or I'll shoot you with my bow and arrow," I blurted in gleeful defiance. I flew down the steps in front of the Gibson's house to fight the evildoers, shouting, "I'll save you Kemo Sabe, I'll save you!"

Whack! Within an instant, searing pain coursed through my head and ugly stars began their orbit around my brain. Within a few minutes I regained consciousness with the gentle prodding of Mrs. Gibson who had rushed to my aid. She held a damp cloth to my bleeding head as an irate and upset Ma angrily denounced what those villainous Pelham kids had done to me. They had feigned being my friend in order to pummel me over the head with the very same gun I let them borrow. The impact of those blows knocked me momentarily unconscious and carved a gash in the top of my skull which bled copiously, matting my hair as it slowly coagulated.

Those little monsters had taken my gun, broken it in half and whacked me over the head with it because they thought it was fun. Being cowards and thinking they wouldn't be caught, they quickly raced up College Avenue pretending that they had been playing in their back yard when it happened. Unlike what happened the time before when they broke Mrs. Pinachie's window, this time they wouldn't go unpunished. Mrs. Gibson, one of the most revered of all our neighbors including the Pelhams, had seen the entire episode from her gangway.

Although being one of the few black families in the neighborhood, the Gibsons were highly respected because they were good, church-going people who always treated others with respect and had often helped neighbors in distress. Mrs. Gibson also was known for keeping a watchful eye on us kids when our parents weren't around or were busy. Nothing got by Mrs. Gibson's eagle eye. Often she would reprimand us kids personally instead of going to our parents if she were to catch us doing something dangerous or wrong. But she always did so with a demeanor of caring and respect, knowing full well the challenges many of our parents faced.

In addition, her home was one of the most well-kept homes on the street, with a beautiful back yard filled with rose bushes, peony bushes and several grape arbors. She would often share those grapes with her neighbors but would not tolerate any of us kids stealing them from her yard. That was the one time when she would go to the parents to report it because she felt that it's better to ask for things than to steal. Being a woman of faith she felt that kids should honor the Ten Commandments and stealing was the one that she always enforced, even if it was just fruit.

Luckily, Virginia Perrault was home from her nursing job that afternoon and ran over to make sure I wasn't seriously hurt or that I should go to the emergency room. She was also one of Ma's best friends, often lending her professional care during several of my childhood traumas. Luckily this one turned out to be a minor trauma with me ending up with a headache for a couple of hours. Once the bleeding stopped and peroxide and a bandage applied, I was fine. However, the trauma for the Pelham boys was about to begin.

Realizing I was ok, and with her emotions now in check and armed with the facts, Ma and Mrs. Gibson marched side by side up College Avenue to confront the Pelhams about what their sons had done to me. Mrs. Pelham did a double take when she opened the door and saw Ma and Mrs. Gibson solemnly standing there.

"Oh! What can I do for you, Mrs. Gibson?" a stunned Mrs. Pelham asked, totally ignoring Ma.

Looking supportively at Ma who was quietly seething now, Mrs. Gibson tersely asked, "Is your husband home? This is important."

Confused, Mrs. Pelham replied, "Well, actually he is home today, it's his off day from duty. Can I ask why you want to speak to him and not me?"

"Sure you can, but we really want to talk to both of you about something your sons have done."

With that said, Mrs. Pelham abruptly turned and looked disdainfully at Ma then turned back to Mrs. Gibson and uttered, "Does this involve them?" nodding her head towards Ma. By this time Ma had all she could do to contain herself from slapping the arrogant bitch in the face. But she was able to control herself as an understanding Mrs. Gibson gently placed a calming hand on her shoulder.

"We will discuss the details when Mr. Pelham is here, so please go get him for us," Mrs. Gibson said, pithiness dripping from every word.

Begrudgingly Mrs. Pelham turned and went back into the house returning a few minutes later with her weary looking husband by her side.

"Hello, Mrs. Gibson and Mrs. Hyde" an unusually respectful Mr. Pelham greeted, unlike his obnoxious wife. "What seems to be the problem?"

Taking the lead, knowing that Mrs. Pelham had no respect for Ma or our family, Mrs. Gibson spelled out in detail right down to the pooling blood on the road what their sons had done to me.

Screeching in disbelief, Mrs. Pelham adamantly defended her sons. "My boys would never do that, in fact I forbid them to play with those dirty kids. So I know this couldn't have happened."

"Damn it, you're a fool," Ma shot back. "Those damned kids of yours did do it and for no good reason. They split my Herbie's head wide open with his toy gun, then left him to bleed in the street. Go ask the little bastards yourself if you don't believe us."

"Calm down, Mabel, calm down," Mrs. Gibson soothed. "I'll handle this."

A shocked Mrs. Pelham tearfully asserted to her husband, "This can't be true, Tom, it can't! Our boys would never do something like that. Herbie must have made this all up."

"Mrs. Pelham, it's true." Mrs. Gibson countered. "I saw the whole thing myself, Herbie did nothing wrong, he was the victim. It was your sons who took advantage of him, then used the gun he let them play with to brutally attack him."

"Oh no, oh no, I can't believe it, Tom, even if Mrs. Gibson say so."

"Edith, be quiet!" Tom shouted. "I want to hear this. I know Mrs. Gibson would never lie and so do you, so listen."

"Now, Tom," Mrs. Gibson said, "Mabel could have just as easily called the police department to report this incident and you being a policeman know how that goes. I also know that Mabel doesn't want to report it. That is why I came with her, because she thought you would never believe her if she came alone. I have no reason to lie to you or Edith about this, none whatsoever. I just believe the truth has to be told and they have to be held accountable for their actions."

"Tom," Ma said earnestly, "I don't want your sons to go to juvenile court. God knows I've been through that myself. I just want them to know how hurt and upset Herbie is. He was so excited thinking that they were being his friend, and then this happened. He could have been seriously injured or ended up in the hospital or worse. Luckily, Virginia was around to tend to him. Thank God he's ok, but he could have been killed." Tears welled up in Ma's eyes as Mr. Pelham put an understanding hand on her shoulder.

"I believe you, Mrs. Hyde, even though it breaks my heart to think my kids could do something like this. I assure you both that I will deal with them sternly, they won't go unpunished." Mrs. Pelham now quietly whimpering in despair stood by her husband as Ma and Mrs. Gibson said their thanks and headed back home, satisfied that justice would be served and it was, in short order. Within minutes of Ma's return I could hear yelling and screaming coming from the Pelham's back yard as Mr. Pelham meted out his own justice at the end of his thick, leather, policeman's belt.

Although I was never allowed to play with the Pelham boys on the street again, I was able to forgive Donnie several years later when we played Little League baseball together. Summers seemed to last forever for me as a kid. That's not always a good thing because I could end up having more unwanted misadventures.

My cute, bratty sisters in our back yard. Brenda and Patty in the back row and Bonnie and Jan in the front row.

CHAPTER NINE

The Boys Club Years

As you can see, my life experiences would meander along several intertwined paths during my youthful development. These paths encompassed my family, neighborhood buddies and new friendships that evolved in school and the Troy Boys Club. The Boys Club played a pivotal role in guiding me through the pitfalls and snares of growing up without a strong male presence at home. It offered me an opportunity to grow and bond with boys my own age, yet still have adult males nearby to mentor and guide me during those formative years.

Ma enlisted our neighbor Dom Greco to get me into the Boys Club at age five, two years earlier than normally allowed. Being the assistant club director at the time and understanding Ma's concerns, Dom graciously bent the rules. Ma rightfully feared that I wasn't getting enough positive male interaction at home, and she knew the older kids loved to pick on me. She believed it would allow me to escape the torment neighborhood kids inflicted on me. What she didn't realize—those same tormentors also went to the Boys Club. Yep! Denny, Alan, Frankie, Billy and Carl along with a new tormentor she didn't know, were members too.

Dom lived in the Barrow's basement apartment and knew all the neighborhood kids, the good ones and the trouble makers. He was a very tough task master and didn't take crap from any kid. Stuff you might get away with at home wouldn't happen under Dom's tutelage at the Boys Club. For many kids who went there, Dom was a father figure but a tough one. It was not unusual for some to get a slap alongside the head if they stupidly stepped over the line.

By default, Dom became their disciplinarian. (I think his philosophy, although not necessarily from the Bible was:
Spare the rod, create a juvenile delinquent!) What he did back then would not be tolerated today. It was rare when someone got whacked, but when it happened, it was usually well deserved. To the best of my knowledge, no one ever suffered lasting injury or trauma from Dom's discipline. In fact, many guys I have talked to since look back with fondness towards him and express gratitude that he was there to help them get through those formative years. It was at the Boys Club where I learned to play ping-pong, pool, basketball and develop overall physical fitness.

Additionally, during my years at the Club, I also learned arts and crafts. After school sessions were taught by Mrs. Boone, wife of the RPI football coach, who volunteered her time. A thin, pretty woman with short blond hair, blue eyes, glasses, and a ready smile, she took me under her wing. I think she looked after me because I was so much smaller than the other kids, and she felt I needed an older sister to look after me, sort of like Dorothy and Patty did. She would often give me a ride home because I lived right near the campus, and it was on her way. However, her taking an interest in me also created one of the scariest periods in my life.

There was a new kid on the block named Richie Spooner, whose family had recently moved into the basement apartment of the Mayes's house. They only lived there for a couple months, thankfully, but those months would be months of sheer terror I'd remember the rest of my life. One afternoon, while walking to the Boys Club by myself ensconced in my usual daydreaming, I was startled back to reality by a painful thump on my shoulder. It was Richie pounding me with his fist.

"Hey, kid! Where you headed?" he eerily asked, evil dripping off his pointed tongue. His brilliant, emerald green eyes had a satanic tinge of redness to them, making the hair on the back of my neck stand on end and sending shivers down my spine. There was an aura surrounding him that seemed surreal and immediately gave me a feeling of unease in my gut. That primeval dread would soon be validated.

Stunned by the sudden, painful poke, I answered warily. "I, um, I'm going down to the Boys Club."

"Great," he said. "So am I. We'll be friends and walk together, every day!" His terse statement sounded more like a threat than an offer of friendship. Even though I didn't have many friends my age and wished for more, I had reservations as to whether I wanted *this* stranger to be my friend. "I know your name! It's Herbie. I'm Richie."

"How do you know my name?" I asked.

"I know a lot about you, and everything else that goes on around here," he bragged. Listening to that scary retort led me to never question anything he said or did. I was totally petrified of him and meekly acquiesced to anything he said, fearing that challenging him would result in immediate retribution. Now being *his* new best friend, Richie joined my crafts class.

For several weeks he coerced me into walking to and from the Boys Club each afternoon, turning down rides home with Mrs. Boone. It seems Richie hated the attention she was giving me. He apparently was envious and complained to me about it daily. "You little brown-noser," he screeched. "The only reason she likes you and gave you all those rides home is because you kiss up to her. You stink at crafts! Look," he said, pointing to the completed, black and red lanyard hanging around his neck. "Mine is great, but yours isn't even half done yet and looks like crap." He had a point, I wasn't very good at crafts, and I was very slow completing my projects. I think that's why she gave me so much attention and not him.

Thankfully, he wasn't allowed to go to the Boys Club at night. However, Ma let me go a couple nights each week because I was in the harmonica band, having recently joined at the urging of Tony Fermetti. Tony had been a member for several years when he was younger and thought that it would be fun for me as well as keep me away from my tormentors. Being like a fourth brother (he always seemed to be at our house), he was also aware of my breathing problems. He felt playing in the band would be helpful in combating my asthma attacks.

Even though I knew Richie wasn't supposed to be out, I still ran to the Club every night. I feared he might see me, sneak out of his house and torture me. You might think this irrational fear was unwarranted, but as time would tell, it wasn't.

He was extremely jealous of me and his attitude toward me quickly took on an ominous tone. He'd laughingly taunt me about how he wanted to kill me.

On our way home one day, we stopped near a vacant lot on Seventh Avenue to toss pebbles at a passing train that was billowing thick, black smoke as it chugged its way out of the Sixth Avenue tunnel. The cacophony of wheels rumbling, bells clanging and horns blowing filled the air as it headed towards its final destination: Union Station. That's where returning soldiers and weary travelers would soon be reunited with their waiting loved ones.

Out of the blue, Richie lunged forward, grabbing my arm so hard that it felt like it was being crushed by a vice. He then tore into my soul in an unearthly voice, "I'm going to stab you to death some day." His Satanic eyes pierced my heart as he began laughing like a hyena. (Where's an exorcist when you need one?)

"Ha, ha," I laughed back, frightened to death. "Don't kid like that, Richie, please! You're scaring the crap out of me." Slowly, his eyes cleared and he returned to the conscious world, released from the angry grasp of some evil being hiding deep inside him.

"I scared the shit out of you, didn't I? You little prick."

Luckily, as his tirades began to grow in intensity and frequency over the next couple weeks, his family abruptly moved out of their apartment, leaving the city. I never saw him again. However, I never forgot him and the fear and terror he subjected me to.

Many years later, a local nightclub owner was stabbed to death by an employee. He was killed over the affections of a woman. The killer's name? Richard Spooner, the same Richie who had threatened to kill me over the affection of our crafts teacher.

Although the trauma that Richie imposed on me eased when he moved away, I still struggled to find my identity and my niche among my buddies. Growing up pretty much as the lone boy in a household of strong female personalities, I faced unique challenges my buddies didn't have. I was at an awkward age; being several years younger than most of my friends, I didn't quite fit in with this little band of rascals. However, that didn't stop me from trying.

Being small and scrawny made me an easy target for teasing and bullying, especially since my older brothers weren't around to protect me or teach me how to fight. It's not unusual for smaller kids to get picked on by older, bigger kids. Being picked on affects a young boy's fragile psyche. I know how it affected mine. I was forced to learn how defend myself and fight back, often getting the snot kicked out of me in the process.

Eventually, the teasing and taunting would turn into respect and equality, but that didn't come quickly or easily. I had to fight for it and earn it in various ways over many years.

Because my brothers weren't around for large portions of my early life, I became very close to my sisters. That's why I can laugh at myself today and rightfully declare: I'm in touch with my feminine side. I had no choice but to be in touch with it, because my sisters had such an influence on my life as a kid and still do today. As you can probably surmise, because of that relationship I am a very sensitive, emotional person in many respects, but I also don't take any crap when someone challenges my dignity or manhood.

Additionally, complicating matters for me while trying to establish my male identity was my sister Patty, who became my surrogate older brother in some respects. This was both a blessing and a curse. She could often be seen duking it out with Denny Barrow and others when they got carried away pummeling me. However, when she was not around to protect me, I'd get the snot kicked out of me again anyway because she had kicked the snot out of them for beating me up before. It was an unending cycle.

Patty was a tomboy who was as tough or tougher than most boys in my neighborhood. She and her best friend Mickey Brighten were known as the two toughest girls on the block. They were like fighting sisters, joined at the hip. Rarely would any guy or, for that matter, any girl challenge them to a fight. If they did, they'd end up on the short end of the stick, with either a bloody nose, swollen lip, or in some cases for the guys, sore nuts. Neither of them fought like ladies. They were a couple of street fighters, and for street fighters, anything goes.

Because girls seemed to mature at a younger age, Patty and Mickey were always beating up the boys. They seemed stronger and tougher than the boys their age. However, when they began to blossom into budding young maidens, I think the older boys who had reached or were approaching puberty would try to take advantage of them. They would purposely instigate a wrestling match in order to cop a cheap feel. Of course, these guys would get slapped in the puss when they did, all the while laughingly asserting their innocence. The guys could never admit what they were up to because they would get turned in to their parents in a heartbeat. I guess you could say, it was all part of the "feeling out process" known as male adolescence. I don't think it ever got beyond that stage with Mickey or Patty, because they lived too close to the guys. So, out of respect for their families and fear for their lives, the guys would meander out of the neighborhood in search of girls who might be willing to help them sow their wild oats.

CHAPTER TEN

Trying to Know Dad

E ven with all the newness of school, the Boys Club and relationships I was trying to develop with neighborhood kids, things at home remained constant with my Dad. He never changed. When I was a toddler, I hardly recognized him when he'd come. He was usually half in the bag when he arrived, and if he wasn't, he'd manage to be by the end of the night. Other times he'd head straight down to Stickley's Grill to carouse with his buddies.

My toddler's thoughts must have been, "Hum! Here's that strange man again, and Ma's crying. Why?" I could never understand how that happened—because he never hit her—they just yelled all the time. Now, as an adult, I can reasonably surmise the yelling was because Ma was having such a hard time keeping our house clean while raising us brats. Although looking like a bum himself, he always managed to complain about the house being a mess and being a sluggard much of the time, he, of course, never offered to help.

Now that I was several years older, Dad would sidle home thirsting for a cold beer and send me down to Stickley's Grill to buy a pail. (You could buy a pail of beer for about fifty cents back then.) When I returned with his amber libation, I'd watch him sit there at the kitchen table acting like some triumphant potentate. However, that image was belied by his dirty tee shirt and the acrid smell of chain saw oil he had spilled on his trousers permeating the air. Now ensconced in the rickety kitchen chair that served as his illusory throne, he commanded Ma to get him a raw egg which he cracked open and dropped into his beer. Once it sunk to the bottom of the glass, he'd guzzle it down with gusto. I guess this was some macho, fertility thing. Other times he'd pour salt in his beer to keep it from going flat.

After downing about four glasses of this witch's brew, he began to hold court at our kitchen table attempting to regale a beleaguered Ma, Winnie and us kids with tales of how hard he worked felling trees. He'd dwell on how he struggled to hoist those heavy logs onto his dilapidated truck, and how he transported them over muddy, rut-filled back roads, only to be stiffed by the local saw mill owner. He complained to a disbelieving Ma that he was paid only half of what the logs were worth, and because of that he didn't have much left to give her. What he conveniently failed to mention was that he probably had pissed most of it away during the week carousing at some backwoods, sleazy, watering hole. Ma was expecting that money so she could put it on her monthly tab at Harry Moore's store. Sadly, she would now be short and would have to beg Harry for more time in order to come up with the delinquent funds.

Half in the bag and cocksure he'd snookered Ma with his disingenuous malarkey, he blithely launched into a bombastic rehash of his daring adventures working as a Customs Inspector on the Canadian border. During those bucolic days before me and my younger sisters were born, the family had lived in the tiny border town of Derby Line, Vermont. (In fact, my sister Dorothy was born there.) He quickly regurgitated chapter and verse, the many times he and his partners had chased bootleggers through the snow-covered woods along the Canadian border, describing how they would lay in waiting, wearing camouflaged clothing in a tree-covered hunting blind.

Ironically, one time, while they were lying in wait for bootleggers, they ran across an old farmer trying to smuggle pigs across the border. Who knows? Maybe the old codger was hungering for some Canadian bacon? I imagine our family must have eaten pretty high off the hog when Dad brought home his share of the contraband livestock they commandeered.

Now possessed by his own blithering narrative, Dad condescendingly laughed as he described the time he and his partner Doug furtively watched their prey drag a sled full of illegal whisky through a narrow opening in the dense woods. Deftly, he detailed how he could hear their labored breathing some twenty feet away as they struggled to pull their stash towards a rarely used section of road and their waiting accomplices. However, unbeknown to the culprits, their accomplices had already been handcuffed and were sitting in the back of the Customs van, guarded by a third officer.

Dad then boasted, "It was so hilarious watching those dumb Canucks do all the heavy lifting for us. They dragged the booze right up next to the road for us. Then, just when they thought they were safe, me and Doug jumped out of woods with our guns drawn and scared the living shit out of the poor bastards. They looked stupefied, and that's when I screamed at em. 'Get down on your hands and knees, you dumb, French ticklers! This is the border patrol!'" His partner then forced the culprits to lie in the snow face down, with arms and legs spread.

Dad continued his derogatory canard and laughingly smirked, "They looked like a couple of idiotic, snow angels when we cuffed em!" He then noted that after forcing them back to their feet, they were unceremoniously marched to the waiting van and justice.

With the bootleggers now secured, he and Doug went back and pulled the overflowing sled the short distance to the road. In the meantime, their partner had backed the van up to the edge of the woods to make it easier for them to load the hooch. Dad noted that once the contraband and the car were impounded, they would drive to the local town magistrate and have the bootleggers arraigned. Once that was completed, almost all of the unstamped liquor was placed securely in the holding area. However, several bottles (twenty, thirty or so) of the higher quality liquors would have to be retained by the agents and the local magistrate—the "rationale" being the liquor had to be taste-tested for quality assurance purposes before trial. Funny, how the criminal justice system works.

Sadly, from what I was able to glean from listening to later conversations between Ma and my older sisters regarding my Father's fatuous behavior, he apparently didn't last too many years as a Customs agent. He was relieved of his duties for some undisclosed reason. I wonder how things might have turned out for our family if he'd hadn't blown his career in the U.S. Customs Service.

Even with all the bad things that occurred because of my Father's infatuation with illegal booze, it apparently didn't end after he lost his job. Discouraged and disgruntled after losing the best job he would ever have, Dad apparently had one more somewhat humorous but extremely dangerous flirtation with illegal booze.

Ma recounted how the family remained in the second floor apartment on Derby Line for a short period after Dad lost his job. Now unemployed and drinking quite heavily (not the same high quality hooch he'd become accustomed to, of course), he hatched a hair- brained scheme whereby he would easily make his own hooch. He thought he might even be able to make some money, too. So, with a book he obtained from the local library on how to make your own vodka, he now fancied himself a chemist. Better yet, a Master Brewer.

Using a bushel of potatoes he had obtained from a local farmers' market and figuring he could create a high quality vodka, he stupidly lurched along a dangerous path he thought would lead to fiscal solvency. He was going to create a market winner, Hyde's Premier Vodka, right on his own back porch. So, off he blithely went firing up his cobbled still, against the better wishes of Ma, of course, who thought it was a dangerous folly. It turned out to be just that. Dangerous and full of folly.

With the putrid smell of potato mash permeating the apartment for several days, Ma repeatedly warned Dad that he was playing a dangerous game. However, he dismissed those warnings. His ego still bruised from losing his job but secure in his arrogance, he continued to plod along with his nimrod scheme. However, being who he was, he didn't give this project the proper respect and attention it deserved.

Late one afternoon, off he strolled down to the corner grill to guzzle some beer in hopes of drowning his lethargy. He carelessly had left his frothing brew unattended. Unwittingly, he failed to vent the area properly to prevent methane gas from building up in that small space and causing an explosion. I guess in his state of apathy, he never gave it a thought. Within twenty minutes it *did* explode, knocking Ma to the floor in the kitchen and blowing the glass out of one of the windows on the back porch. Luckily, Ma wasn't hurt, just stunned. She and my brother Jack were able to quickly extinguish the small fire spawned by the explosion. However, our neighbors were not happy about what happened. While all this pandemonium had broken lose, Dad was blissfully frittering away the afternoon getting loaded, while his silly pipe dream went up in smoke. Needless to say, the family didn't live in Derby Line much longer.

Soon after, our family moved to Winooski, Vermont, located near Burlington. There Dad apparently got at least one more decent job working at the local munitions factory. But with the war beginning to draw to a close and Dad's inability to keep a decent job, the family moved to Swanton, Vermont, where I was born. We lived there until I was a year old then moved to Troy.

CHAPTER ELEVEN

Primary Grades

First grade offered a different set of challenges and experiences for me. My sister Dorothy would no longer take me to school or drag me home for lunch; that became my responsibility. However, she became our mentor and surrogate mom if and when problems arose in class for me or my siblings. She was always being called down to the principal's office to get reports on how my brother Cliff was either missing from class or causing problems.

She often recounted the times she was forced to stand by and watch Cliff get whacked on the knuckles with a ruler by Mr. Damnesian for his transgressions. Cliff would stand there with a pained smile on his face, take it like a trooper and never cry. Instead, he'd just laugh it off, pissing Mr. Damnesium off even more. Cliff was irreverent and tough as nails even at this young age and would remain that way the rest of his life.

I moved up from the basement to the first floor for first grade. Upon entering the building from the south side you had to walk up two flights of black granite steps to reach my classroom, which was the first one on the left.

Mrs. Polechek was my first grade teacher and was very matronly looking. Although relatively young, she dressed like a much older woman, always keeping her hair in a bun and usually wearing bland, colorless dresses and thick, high-heeled, black shoes. It's kind of ironic that her youngest daughter Cindy and Cindy's cousin, Jimmy Polechek, would become my classmates later in grade school, along with Carl Redmond, Butchie Grillo, Billy Finch and Linda Bissell.

A day in first grade seemed like an eternity after kindergarten. Classes were full-day, and if you didn't bring a brown bag lunch to school, you would have to go home for lunch. Our mom insisted we come home for lunch.

In the front of our classroom was a large blackboard, with broken pieces of chalk and erasers sitting on a narrow, wooden railing. There were also several pull-down charts, one containing maps while another had various letters that resembled hieroglyphics. They were the letters of our alphabet and would be used to teach us the "Palmer Method" of writing.

Our one-piece desks had ink wells in them, and each day along with selecting one lucky kid to clean the dirty erasers, another would be selected to fill the ink wells, using a rickety looking ink can, similar to the one the Tin Man carried around in "The Wizard of Oz."

We did a lot of fun, science things in first grade, like making butter from heavy cream. Mrs. Polechek filled a large Mason jar with the cream then fastened the metal cap on top. Starting with the first seat near the window, she would have each kid shake it until they got tired then pass it to the kid in back of them. The jar continued around the room until the butter started to form. It was really tiring to most kids, as it took about thirty minutes and two trips around the class before it actually became butter. Once the butter was complete, she drained off the buttermilk into a smaller jar, mixed in a small amount of salt, then spread our fresh butter on crackers she'd brought for our morning snack.

Other times she had us bring in our pet bugs in a jar: caterpillars, worms or even butterflies, and sometimes kids were allowed to bring in their pet turtles for show and tell. In the spring, she brought in an incubator so we could watch baby chicks being hatched. However, the three R's (reading, 'riting and 'rithmetic) took precedence over everything else we did in class. We also had to be disciplined in the things we were working on in class, and we had to learn how to behave. That was a real challenge for most five year olds, especially me.

One of the first things we had to learn in first grade was to control our bodily functions. So, to keep some semblance of order, Mrs. Polachek set specific "potty" rules you had to adhere to. You had to raise your hand and be acknowledged by her before she'd let you go, and you had to be back in a reasonable time. (Five minutes or less, otherwise she'd come looking for you.) Only one kid could go at a time, and she didn't tolerate kids whom she felt were trying to take advantage of the "potty privilege."

From past experience, she knew some kids would raise their hands every hour, just to get out of class. It became a game to them. It seemed as though every kid in class had a case of the grip (diarrhea) or an overactive bladder, resulting in a steady stream of kids holding up their hands at once. I rarely raised my hand.

However, one day my stomach was grumbling, and since I didn't want to take a chance and fart in class, I put my hand up to go to the bathroom. Mrs. Polachek looked up, saw me, and said, "You can go, Herbie, but make sure you're not gone too long, and make sure you wash your hands when you're done."

"Ok, Mrs. Polachek, I will." My stomach was still grumbling and I was having some minor cramps when I headed off to the boys' room, located at the other end of the floor. However, by the time I sat down to poop, I couldn't go. I was only able to let out one, stinky fart. So I quickly finished up, washed my hands and quickly headed back to class.

Soon after I returned, a steady stream of kids began heading off to the bathroom. I apparently opened the floodgates that morning. However, within a few minutes of my return, my stomach still didn't feel right. With little warning, the cramps I had experienced earlier came back with a vengeance. I soon felt this horrible urge to go again, so I quickly raised my hand hoping Mrs. Polachek would see me. She didn't at first. But, right after Billy Brazier returned from his trip to the boys' room, Mrs. Polachek saw me frantically waving my hand.

"Why are you waving your hand like that, Herbie? You just came back from the bathroom."

"I'm sorry, but I couldn't go the last time, but now I *really* have to go, bad!"

"Well, you're going to have to hold it," she retorted with sarcasm, not believing me. "You'll have to wait your turn, because Marianne and Julie had their hands up first, and you know I only allow one person to go at a time."

"But, they're girls, Mrs. Polachek!"

"Don't be bold young man. Get back in your seat."

"But, I really have to go, Mrs. Polachek."

"That does it, young man. Don't you say another word. You go out and stand in the hall until I come out and tell you when to go."

"But!"

"No buts about it. I'm tired of these games you kids are always playing."

Not wanting to aggravate Mrs. Polachek any further and doubled over in pain, I somberly headed out into the hall with my head down, clenching my stomach. I tried my best to hold it as long as I could, struggling not to cry. I hoped against hope that she would come out soon and tell me I could go. The minutes ticked by like hours, and still no Mrs. Polachek.

One by one, the girls trotted past me on their way to-and-from the girls' room, giggling as they watched me hunched over in pain, thinking I was faking it. I wasn't. After about five minutes of exquisite pain, I couldn't hold back any longer. Sadly, I pooped my britches, sending an explosive cloud of toxic fumes throughout the hallway.

Within seconds, Mrs. Grantham, the fourth grade teacher, rushed out of her room, located directly across from ours and saw me standing there all red in the face. "Oh, my God, what is that awful smell?" Looking straight at me, she sternly asked, "Is that you, young man? I thought there was a dead animal out here. God, you smell awful." Holding her handkerchief to her mouth she quickly rushed into my classroom, and within seconds a stunned and embarrassed Mrs. Polachek came out and upbraided me for crapping my pants.

"Couldn't you wait, like I told you?"

Confused, I began crying. "I'm sorry. I told you I had to go, but you didn't believe me—I couldn't hold it anymore."

"Well!" Mrs. Polachek fumed in a huff over the incident and knowing full well she was partly to blame. She then groused, "Now, I'll have to get your sister Dorothy to take you home. There's no way you can stay in class in this condition!"

Dorothy was immediately summoned to bring me home. Irate, Mrs. Polachek told her, "Tell your Mother what happened!" She also gave her a nasty note to give to Ma, demanding Ma keep us home if we're sick. (I wasn't sick when I went to school.)

Needless to say, Ma was upset when I got home. But after I told her what happened, and reading that nasty note, she was more angry at Mrs. Polachek than me, calling her an old witch for forcing me to stand in the hall. Thankfully, that was the last time I ever had one of those accidents in school. Ironically, Mrs. Polachek never refused to let me go to the boys' room again.

As usual, when I began second grade, my sisters and I continued to find ways to harass and tease each other. Patty began teasing me about girls. That was the year she wrote Susan Selnick's name on my sneakers in red ink because she thought I had a crush on her. I didn't—I had a crush on my second grade teacher Ms. Hancock, who was pretty and always treated me nice. I was so distracted and infatuated by her that I managed to fail second grade. (At least, that's my excuse.)

Ma, of course, yelled at me for ruining my sneakers when she saw them. I tried to tell her it was Patty's fault, but she didn't buy it—especially when Patty lied to her and adamantly denied doing it. Wouldn't you know, the first new pair of sneakers I ever owned would end up scuzzy-looking for the rest of the school year. (I usually wore used ones from the Boys Club.)

Ma told me to just wash the ink off, which I tried to do. But instead of it washing off like Ma thought it would, it smeared. Seeing how that didn't work out so well, Ma then told me to polish them with white shoe polish. Surprise! That didn't work either. It just turned them a light shade of pink and pink is not a fun color for a "macho" second grader's sneakers.

Even though they were now pink, Ma still insisted that I wear them because all my other shoes had holes in them or were falling apart. One pair had pieces of cardboard covering gaping holes where the soles used to be. The soles on my other pair were cracked in the middle and were held together by thin strands of a glue-like material. Several times Ma tied shoe laces around them to hold them together, but to no avail. They didn't survive the grueling trek up College Avenue to school each day and soon were shredded and useless. Whenever I went anywhere, you knew I was coming because you could hear the soles slapping the ground like some giant dinosaur's tongue.

The other kids teased the crap out of me for wearing pink sneakers. One day before school started, Billy Finch pointed to my sneakers and yelled, "Herbie's a little sissy!" Everyone laughed, while I cringed. This went on relentlessly for several days both in and out of school. In order to stop the constant taunting, I decided to soak my sneakers in a mud puddle one rainy day. From that time on, instead of being pink, they were just grungy looking, much like the rest of my hand-me-down clothes.

Thankfully, Ma never complained about the sneakers again once they became filthy looking. Apparently she'd heard about the teasing I was getting from my friends and figured I'd been punished enough. Plus, my other shoes weren't fit to wear.

Most of my other remembrances of second grade are vague. However, I do remember how shy I was around Ms. Hancock, and would fidget excessively if she called me to her desk. She knew I was struggling with the Palmer Method and simple math, something that haunted me all the way through grade school, but she was determined to help me out. However, I apparently was unteachable that year. The good news—now I'd have her as my teacher for one more year. The bad news! Ma was really pissed at me for flunking. Well, I guess the second year's always the charm—I apparently got over my infatuation with Ms. Hancock and passed on my second try.

During my first year in second grade, I still continued to go to the Boys Club, playing basketball in the house leagues and running endlessly on the rubberized track that hung from the ceiling rafters. Playing so much basketball at the Club would serve me well that following summer. When the older kids let me play street basketball, I surprisingly held my own.

View overlooking Troy from Prospect Park.

CHAPTER TWELVE

The Chicken Man

Every Saturday morning around ten o'clock we'd hear this beat up old flatbed truck, with its noisy muffler and fumes spewing out the tailpipe and making its way up Eighth Street from Harrison Place. The driver yelled in his deep base drone, "Chickens for sale. Get yur live chickens, he'ah!" as he sputtered to a stop in front of Old Man Manino's, which was located next to Denny Barrow's house on the west side of the street. We nicknamed this guy "Chicken Man."

I'd hear the older guys talking and laughing about choking the chicken, but I never realized what it meant until this one Saturday, when it hit me. This guy apparently was really choking his chickens with all those fumes. I didn't see the humor in it, though.

The back of his dilapidated truck was stacked three high, four wide and six deep, with wooden chicken cages filled with scrawny, white and brown chickens, coughing and squawking at the top of their puny lungs. This racket and the stench that accompanied these little beasts drew the attention of the whole neighborhood, especially us kids.

Chicken Man would hop out of his truck, in his disheveled farmer jeans, scraggly beard, work boots and billed hat. His breath reeked from the smell of booze that he had overindulged in the night before at Gainor's Gay Spot, a bar located on Broadway near the old Union Railway Station. It was notorious for what Ma used to say was its disgusting goings on. It was a strip club and a home for local ladies of the night.

The Chicken Man's visits had become one of the weekly rituals we kids looked forward to. On rare occasions a few neighbors would purchase these critters. However, most would get their chickens all ready to cook from the Helflick Brothers Meat and Grocery Store in the old Basset Building on Congress Street.

A regular customer of the Chicken Man, Old Man Manino was mysterious and scary and mean. He would often swear at us in his broken English with that gnarly cigar hanging out of his mouth. Thank God we rarely saw him leave his basement apartment, but Denny Barrow told us plenty of stories about all the racket erupting from his back yard. Every week, shortly after Chicken Man left, Denny would hear unearthly screeching in Old Man Manino's yard and feared someone or something was being killed. "It's a death chamber over there," he'd say. Little did he know that he was to learn it was a "death chamber" for chickens.

Having heard these ungodly sounds week after week, Denny finally summoned enough courage one Saturday to investigate what was really going on, and he climbed up the old maple tree that hung over Old Man Manino's fence. In one corner of the yard Denny could see a huge pot of rapidly boiling water, the smoke from the apple wood fire permeating the air. He could see the back of Old Man Manino, clad in a red plaid shirt and dark blue suspenders. His arm was raised menacingly, holding what looked like a huge ax. In his other hand was a pitiful, scrawny chicken, screeching and flailing about on an old tree stump. The next thing Denny heard was the eerie sound of air swishing and a horrid thump.

Suddenly, the screeching ceased, followed by deadly silence. Moments later Old Man Manino began cursing in unintelligible Italian. "Ah fungule," he yelled, as blood splattered on his gray work pants. Then Denny saw a sight he would never forget: A headless chicken, dashing around the yard. Denny struggled to hold back a stream of vomit rising up his throat. He desperately shimmied down the tree, trying not to be heard. He feared that if Old Man

Manino knew he had witnessed the slaughter, he would kidnap Denny and chop his head off too in order to protect his deadly, murderous secret.

Being only eight years old and frightened beyond belief, what could Denny do? Could he tell his parents about this monster? Would Old Man Manino deny it? Then what? The old man would seek his revenge. No, Denny would need to seek guidance from someone more mature than he, but not his parents. He decided to consult Frankie Brighton, his mentor and the oldest of the neighborhood boys. Frankie was ten years old.

One typical Saturday morning, Frankie was shooting hoops with Pat Mcavoy, Yummie Kiley and Bobby Vittner up the street where they had rigged a basketball hoop and backboard, fastened to an old telephone pole. Pat, Yummie and Bobby were several years older than us kids and lived on Ferry Street but would often play basketball or stick ball with us younger kids. Denny raced to tell Frankie what he had just witnessed. Out of breath he gasped, "I just saw Old Man Marino murder a chicken in his yard."

"That's bullshit," Frankie said.

Yummie snapped, "You're a futtin asshole, Denny." Yummie had a few teeth missing, as well as a slight speech impediment, causing him to omit various letters of certain words when he got excited. Yummie laughed, "Everyone knows he just buys those chittins for dur futtin eggs, right?"

Pat and Bobby chimed in laughing, "Yea, Yummie, right."

"No, Yummie!" Denny cried. "I saw it with my own eyes. Old Man Manino chopped the head off and I almost puked out my guts on his shed. I'm just glad he didn't see me in that tree. I mean I hope he didn't see me in that tree. Now I'm really scared," whined Denny.

"If what you're telling us is true, Denny," Frankie opined, "then we can't let this go on."

"I always thought the old bastard was some kind of weird pervert anyway, always hiding down in his basement. Who knows what he'd do if he really got pissed off at one of youz guys sometime," Yummie slyly chimed in. "He might even try to futtin kill one of youz, just like he does those futtin chittins."

"Did you tell your old man?" Frankie asked.

"No, because I don't think he'd believe me and I know old fart Manino would deny it. Then what? I'm really up shit creek without a paddle," responded Denny.

"Thank God you didn't tell your old man," replied Frankie. "We gotta plan a way to stop the old peckerhead from slaughtering any more of those poor birds."

"Jesus, Frankie! You're a stupid asshole too," Yummie shouted. "They're not birds, they're futtin chittins. Come on you guys," Yummie yelled to Pat and Bobby. "Let's get away from these futtin idiots." So off they trotted, laughing and snickering all the way down Eighth Street toward Ferry Street, where they lived.

"Boy," Pat yelled to Yummie, "these jerks wouldn't survive a day in the boondocks, would they?"

"Can you believe they actually think Old Man Manino murders chittins?" chortled Yummie. "He's a mean old perverted bastard, but not a futtin chittin murderer. I can't wait to see what those clowns do next week when Chittin Man comes around again".

The next Friday, around 6:30pm, me and Butchie Grillo decided to go up the street and see who was shooting hoops. To our surprise, sitting on the wall that looks down to where the guys were playing, was fat-so Billy Mayes. (Guys picked on poor Billy even more than they picked on me; to my dismay, I picked on him too.) Frankie Brighten, Denny Barrow, and Bobby Vittner were playing "Outs," a game which is similar to the one played by kids today called "Horse." The only time these guys ever let me play ball with them was when they were short players for a pickup game. So it wasn't surprising to me that Frankie asked us if we wanted to play, since they were short a couple of players.

Frankie was shrewd. He would pick the teams. He gave Billy, who was totally inept at any sport, to Denny and Bobby, much to their chagrin; then he picked me and Butchie for his team. Although I was small, Frankie knew that I could shoot and pass, while Butchie, who was bigger than me, would be used to bludgeon Billy and Denny when they got the ball. Since there are no referees in a pickup game, you could foul the shit out of your opponent without a getting a foul, unless the leader, in this case Frankie, called a foul. It was pretty much assured we would win this game.

As predicted, Butchie hammered the shit out of Billy and Denny every time they got the ball, pissing Denny off to no end and making Billy whimper every time he got an elbow to the gut. This game became a battle between Frankie and me and Bobby. Bobby was a great player, even better than Frankie. As the game progressed, I would feed Frankie the ball under the basket, usually after Butchie had cleared the way. This allowed Frankie to make several easy lay-ups. However, each time I had the ball and ran into trouble, Frankie would call a foul on either Denny or Billy, which allowed me to shoot free throws, which I was very good at. All complaints of cheating fell on deaf ears since Frankie was the boss. The only time Frankie wouldn't get away with this crap was if Yummie was playing, then, of course, Yummie would be the boss, because he was older than Frankie. Yummie cheated even more than Frankie did. Ain't seniority great!

Even with all our cheating, Bobby kept the score close, making several outside jump shots and a couple of sneaky lay-ups. We were leading by the score of 19 to 18 when I got the ball and drove to the basket unimpeded. I blew the lay-up but Frankie called a critical foul on Denny, which sent him into an uncontrollable rant. "You cheating son-of-a-fucking-bitch, Frankie! I never touched him and you know it, you peckerhead." Frankie pushed his hand into Denny's chest and sternly admonished him that he did foul me, and to stop his whining or he'd slap the shit out of him.

There I stood at the foul line shooting what was to be the winning two points of the game. I would be the star, the hero! I bounced the ball my usual four times, then calmly sank my first shot giving us 20 points in a game of 21. Now with the game on the line, my nerves took over. I began with my usual routine but this time when I hoisted my "winning shot" for some ungodly reason the only thing that sank was my heart, as the ball bounced off the rim. "Oh shit," I thought, "I blew it and Frankie's going to kill me." He didn't though, because lucky for me the rebound went right to Frankie, and with Butchie clearing the way, wiping out both Denny and Billy, Frankie was able to lay in the winning basket just beyond the outstretched hands of a hurtling Bobby Vittner.

As expected after we won, Denny continued his pissing and moaning about getting screwed, and how we only won by cheating. Frankie just laughed it off and called Denny a loser, then told him that the next time they played he could be on Frankie's team, shutting Denny up.

After the game we were all hot and sweaty, so we hopped up onto the wall to cool off. Frankie then offered us a swig of Coke from one of the half dozen bottles he and Bobby had swiped from Eddie Morris's store earlier in the day. Nobody liked Eddie because he was so cantankerous, nothing like easygoing Harry Moore. Eddie was always nagging us for hanging out in front of his store; so whenever they got a chance, the older guys would pilfer stuff from Eddie's store, to get even with him for being such a peckerhead. His store was located a block south of Harry's store where Eighth Street dead-ends into Congress Street.

Ferry Street (where Yummie and Pat, both members of the Ferry Street gang lived) runs parallel to Congress Street and could only be reached through several alleys and gangways, or at the southeastern point near Prospect Park and Spy Hill. The Point was where Ferry Street merged into Congress Street.

After we cooled down for a few minutes Denny began ranting to Frankie again about what he saw Old Man Manino do the week before. Butchie and I had not heard this horrifying story, so when Frankie took over the gory details of Denny's tale, (being naive six year olds), we were mortified. That's when Frankie enlisted us to help in his nefarious scheme to liberate the innocent chickens from the carnage we envisioned happening to them.

Chicken Man usually spent around ten to fifteen minutes at Old Man Manino's taking his order, bullshitting, and guzzling some of Old Man Manino's homemade dandelion wine. So, we'd only have a short window of opportunity to free the chickens before he came back to his truck. We had to be quick and efficient in order to pull off this caper.

Frankie laid out his plan. We would all meet at the wall the next morning around nine and shoot hoops until we heard the Chicken Man's truck coming up the hill. Denny would then run down the street and station himself across from his house, sitting on the Mill sisters' porch; he'd be our scout. Once Denny gave the signal that the Chicken Man was on his way down to Old Man Manino's basement, we'd spring into action.

As planned, we assembled at the wall promptly at 9am: Frankie, Denny, fat Billy, Butchie, and me. However, Bobby Vittner didn't show. He thought we were idiots, and after relating our plan to Yummie, Yummie just laughed, telling Bobby, "Don't get involved." Instead, Yummie, Pat and Bobby would hide down by the Koch's house that morning and watch the goings on from a distance, just so they could laugh their asses off, then taunt us if we got caught.

After waiting about fifteen minutes for Bobby to show, Frankie angrily muttered, "Screw Bobby, we can do this without him." We started playing a few games of "Outs" while awaiting Chicken Man's arrival. Just like clockwork, around five minutes to ten, Chicken Man's truck sputtered and weaved its way past us, almost sideswiping Frankie, who had to jump out of the way to avoid getting whacked. Frankie was so pissed, he grabbed a nearby rock and hurled it at Chicken Man's truck, smacking one of the cages and sending the doomed chickens into a screaming, shit fit. "You crazy son-of-a-bitch," Frankie screamed at Chicken Man as he got out of his truck. Chicken Man just glared up the street at us. He then gave Frankie the finger and began laughing loudly, while meandering down the gangway toward Old Man Manino's apartment.

When Denny gave the go ahead, a flustered Frankie screamed at us, "Get moving before the peckerhead gets back to his truck!" We raced like hell down the street, tripping over ourselves in a vain effort to get the deed done before Chicken Man returned.

By the time we got there, Denny had already undone one of the cages. The chicken it housed had tumbled unceremoniously onto the curb after Denny threw it in the air, squawking and flailing its wings. But, instead of flying off to freedom as Denny expected, it stayed right where it landed, pecking at bread crumbs neighbors had thrown out for the many pigeons who inhabited the neighborhood. Flummoxed, Denny couldn't understand why the damned chicken didn't fly away. However, even with this strange turn of events Denny continued to open more cages—a daunting task, as many of the metal latches were rusted shut. Sadly, each chicken he released also began to feast on the savory tidbits found by the curb instead of flying to safety. Denny must have been thinking to himself, "Hum, that damn Chicken Man must be starving these poor little bastards."

As soon as the rest of us got to the truck, Frankie realized he was not tall enough to reach the top layer of cages, so he and Butchie boosted me onto their shoulders where I could then open the cages. In the meantime, Billy would be our spotter, making sure we knew when the Chicken Man was on his way back.

Lucky, or maybe not so lucky for one chicken, I was able to force open its cage, pinching my fingers in the process. After prying open the wooden gate, I reached in and grabbed the chicken by its thorny feet, but the dodo started pecking at my hand. Damn! That hurt like hell. This little escapade was fast becoming a very painful experience for me, as well as for the doomed chickens.

Now, I was more pissed at the chickens than I was at Old Man Manino. Finally, I was able to grasp the emaciated beast by its neck, rip it out of its cage and throw it into the air, assuming, like Denny, that it would gratefully fly away. Nope! Instead, the friggin shit bird plummeted into the middle of the road, squawking and running around in circles like a chicken with its head cut off. Seconds later, it became the unwanted hood ornament for a sleek, black, Buick sedan which was racing up Eighth Street like it was in the Daytona 500! The loud thud it made when it hit, plus the sound of screeching brakes, sent cold chills down my spine. That feeling intensified as Billy began to bawl in his whiny voice, "The Chicken Man's coming! The Chicken Man's coming!" I knew then we were in really deep shit. Not only had I just impaled a stupid chicken on the hood of a car, probably killing it, but the friggin Chicken Man was on his way back up to his truck, and he was going to be really, really pissed at us.

Thanks to Frankie's stupid plan backfiring, not only didn't we free the useless chickens, we may have killed one of them, and in the process messed up some stranger's hotshot car. In a panic, we now realized that we had to abandon our plan immediately. "Scram, you guys," Frankie blared, "or we're going to get busted." (By the way, Frankie's father was a cop, so he knew all about being busted.)

Within a split second of that frightening admonition by Frankie, we all scurried off in different directions, like terrified vermin jumping off a burning ship. We were trying our damnedest to avoid getting caught by either the pissed off race driver or the even more pissed off Chicken Man and Old Man Manino.

Frankie, Denny and Butchie raced like hell up the street past the Stroski's house, which was the last one on the west side of the street. Careening to safety down the worn, brush-lined path to the alley in back of Seventh Avenue, only then did they realize that neither the Chicken Man nor the race car driver would be able to catch them. Breathing a collective sigh of relief, they figured they would spend the rest of the day downtown, taking time to fabricate an alibi for their bungled stunt, if later questioned by their parents.

On the other hand, Billy and I were in a dire predicament. Since both of us headed off in the opposite direction from the rest of the guys, we had limited escape routes. Luckily, I was so thin that I could almost become invisible to the naked eye, However, poor Billy wasn't. His circumstance seemed even more dire than mine.

The Howards had gone out for the day, and thinking no one had seen me yet, I opted to hide in the big oak tree that stood by their house, which was directly across the street from this frenzied debacle. This tree had huge, curved roots, extending out onto the sidewalk creating a semicircular vestibule in which to hide. Although now out of site, I was still trembling with fear of being caught. My mind raced ahead, figuring that if nobody saw me I could escape punishment. That was, unless Chicken Man, Old Man Manino or that pissed off race driver found me hunkered down in that old tree. I struggled for what seemed an eternity to keep my heart from jumping out of my scrawny chest, while this melodrama played itself out.

Billy, on the other hand, became the target of all the vile language and venom that spewed from the mouths of Old Man Manino, Chicken Man, and the race driver. "You're going to pay for this you fat, little fucker!" Chicken Man screamed at Billy, while darting around his truck, trying to ensnare as many of his recalcitrant chickens as possible, before they got splattered by either the Ice Man's truck or several cars which were now streaming up Eighth Street.

This was turning out to be a frightening yet uproarious spectacle. I could hear Old Man Manino cursing, half in broken English and half in Italian as he chased poor Billy down the street, spittle and his gnarly cigar flying from his mouth.

"I gonna killa you poca, scopata, bastardo," he screeched.

Luckily, just as Old Man Marino was about to grab him by his blubbery neck, Billy was able to squeeze his corpulent torso through the narrow gangway that separated his house from the Famundi's house, slamming the gate shut in Old Man Manino's face in the process, and locking it so the old bastard couldn't reach him. Billy then ran out of the backyard and up the alley to where he thought the other guys would be hiding out, the cacophony of venomous invective fading into the distance.

With his chest heaving from all that unwanted exertion, Billy was finally able to catch up to Frankie and the other guys as they meandered down Broadway toward Mancinelli's, a luncheonette located at the southern corner of Fifth Avenue and Broadway.

"Where's Herbie?" Frankie demanded of Billy.

Breathless, Billy mused, "I think he was hiding in back of the Howard's tree."

"Shit!" said Frankie, "he's screwed if he gets caught, but ain't nothing we can do about it now." So off they trotted, leaving me to my own devices.

After listening to all the venom and threats being spewed at Billy, I began shaking with trepidation, tormented and ruminating about how the hell I was going to escape from this nightmare. Just as I was about to burst into tears from fear and foreboding, I heard a commotion down by the Koch's house. It was Yummie, yelling at the Chicken Man.

"How da futt do I know how them chittins got out, you futtin asshole? You must be futtin blind or just plain stupid? You were just chasin the guys who did it when we got here. Now get the futt out of our way so we can play some hoops, or I'll whack you with this futtin red murphy!" (a brick, which Yummie held menacingly in his hand). The Chicken Man anxiously backed away, swearing that somebody was going to pay. Someone would pay, but it definitely wasn't going to be Yummie.

So Yummie, Pat and Bobby continued their march up the street to shoot hoops, laughing and snickering all the way. When they got to where I was hiding, Yummie signaled for me to get in line between the three of them, shielding me from sight as they continued their brazen hike up the street. When we got to the wall and began shooting hoops, Yummie chastised me for being so gullible, then lambasted Frankie and the other guys for hanging me out to dry.

"You never leave your buddies behind, never," Yummie proclaimed.

So, it turned out that it was Yummie and his buddies from the Ferry Street gang, and not my buddies, who saved me from what could have been a ghastly fate.

As was usual during most of our hair-brained escapades, some neighbors saw what happened and dutifully turned us in to our parents. So even with our best efforts and alibis, we couldn't avoid punishment for our stupid misdeeds. In the end, our altruistic stunt turned sour, caused pain not just to the chickens but also to our parents, who had to make restitution to the Chicken Man for his maimed and mangled chickens. Luckily for me, there was little or no major damage to the hood of the car my chicken adorned. The owner just had to clean up a mess of giblets and feathers. Although the financial cost to our parents was relatively minimal, the cost to my sore ass was priceless. Even so, my seemingly endless summer continued to march on.

CHAPTER THIRTEEN

Eddie Barrow's Bike

Denny Barrow had a younger brother Eddie who was about my age. He was a tough, freckled face kid who, like Denny, loved to pick on other kids. However, unlike Denny who used to pick on me because I was smaller than he was, Eddie would pick on kids who were usually bigger than he was. Luckily, I was not bigger than him. I guess little kids like me weren't a challenge to him, plus he knew how much crap I had taken from older kids like Alan Sydner, Frankie Brighten and his brother Denny. They tried to pull the same crap on him but they never got away with it, because, unlike me, Eddie wouldn't take crap from anybody, especially his brother Denny. It was quite a sight to watch those redheaded Tasmanian devils go at each other, until their Dad would break it up, usually before Eddie hurt Denny by kicking him in the nuts or hitting him with a brick.

I was thankful that for a time Eddie and I were friends and not enemies. In fact, he was like my own personal bodyguard. If someone tried to pick on me, they had to deal with him. You remember the old expression, "Sticks 'n stones may break my bones but names can never hurt me"? With Eddie, if you called him names, he would definitely hurt you...with sticks, stones, rocks, cans or anything else he could get his hands on.

It was also kind of nice to finally have another kid my age in addition to Butchie Grillo to hang out with. More importantly, Eddie also had more stuff than me. He had a new baseball glove plus a shiny new red bike Santa had brought him for Christmas that year, and a neat wooden scooter his father had fashioned for him using two by sixes and roller skate wheels. (Although Ma tried to explain it, I could never understand why Santa brought Eddie a bike but never brought me one too. Especially since everybody knew I had been so good all year while Eddie was a devil.)

Like his older brother, Eddie was on steroids when it came to picking on kids. His favorite victim was the biggest, fattest and wimpiest kid on the block, Billy Mayes. I can't remember how many times I saw Eddie pounding the crap out of Billy in back of the large maple tree near the Barrow's house. If Billy sneezed the wrong way, that was an excuse for Eddie to pop him one.

If some strange kid came strolling through the neighborhood and looked at him cross-eyed, he'd go ballistic. I can't remember how many times I would see kids running for their lives as Eddie peppered them with rocks. If he was really mad at them, he'd hop on his bike and continue to chase them all the way to the RPI Approach where they could escape by sliding down the granite railing to Seventh Avenue. When they knew they were safely beyond Eddie's rock-zone, they'd bravely give him the finger, but then never returned to our neighborhood.

The Approach was like the red line in our neighborhood. You could occasionally go a block further without getting too much hell from your parents if they found out, but no further, because only a few more blocks was Harrison Place—totally off limits for all us kids. Few kids our age had ever been there and it would remain a mysterious place to us. About the only thing we knew for sure about this place was that the Chicken Man always came up from there to sell chickens. What our parents would not tell us was that Harrison Place was considered a "black ghetto," a term I would not understand until many years later, long after all its homes and businesses were demolished in order to build a senior citizen high rise.

One summer day I headed over to Eddie's house to see his new bike. "Hey! That's some bike you got there, Eddie," I said. "I wish Santa had brought me one too, so I could learn to ride like you."

"You don't know how to ride a bike?" Eddie snickered. He then popped a wheelie in front of me to show off.

I thought to myself, "Now that's a stupid question! How the hell could I know how to ride? I'd only been on a bike once before, and that was as a passenger on back of Dickey Finch's bike when he almost killed me." Still thinking, I pondered, "Boy! I'd sure love to try riding a bike sometime." Then, responding to Eddie's show-boating, I sarcastically retorted, "Boy! Popping wheelies sure looks like fun, Eddie, and I bet it was so hard to learn."

"Nah, it was simple." Eddie gloated, "Boy, you must have been really bad last year or Santa would have brought you a bike like me."

Eddie's taunting really hurt my feelings, and because I was upset and angry, I unwittingly blurted out, "Damn you, Eddie! That's not true. I was good last year." However, quickly realizing that my outburst may have pissed him off and fearing he might pop me one, I wimpishly stammered, "Uh, my Ma told me I was very good last year and, uh, the only reason I didn't get a bike was because there was a shortage of materials due to the war (the Korean War hadn't ended yet). Santa could only make a few bikes this year and he must have run out of them just before he got to our side of the street, and my Ma also promised me that if I was good all this year, she'd make sure I was the first on Santa's list to get one come next Christmas. That's why I'm going to be extra good so I can get a bike just like yours. Boy, Eddie", I cajoled, "you must have been really good and lucky, because you got yours just before Santa ran out."

"Phew!" I thought to myself. "I hope he bought it?" However, still fearing the worst might happen, I steeled myself for the Tasmanian devil's onslaught. However, it never came. I guess Eddie bought my cock-and-bull story, because he didn't get pissed and he didn't pop me.

Instead, he grinned at me and said, "It's really lots of fun riding and I know I could teach you how to ride, real easy." So being in an uncharacteristically friendly and jovial mood, Eddie offered to teach me the basics of bike riding, suggesting that we go up the street to practice by the wall where we usually shoot hoops.

"Great!" I shrieked in the excitement of the moment. Then, thinking to myself. "Wow, I'm finally going to ride a bike. I'm sure glad Eddie turned out to be such a great friend." Then, in the blink of an eye Eddie was off, hopping on his bike like he was in the Pony Express and racing off into the distance. Spraying a cloud of dust in the air, he screeched to a stop at the spot where we played hoops. From past experience I knew his mood could change in a flash and I didn't want to risk that happening. As soon as I saw him speed away, I quickly bolted after him, fearing that if I didn't get there immediately he'd say, "Screw you," and not teach me how to ride.

As I was racing to meet Eddie, I remembered how several guys who lived in the neighborhood and had bikes thought they were daredevils like "Evil" Knieval. They would ride their bikes on top of the concrete wall that ran from the last house on the east side of Eighth Street, until it ended in a ramp at the entrance to the Sisters of Saint Joseph Motherhouse, which stood on a hill overlooking the street. They would then race their bikes down that narrow ramp onto Eighth Street by the RPI Approach. This took a steady hand and a lot of skill but to my knowledge no one had been killed or crippled pulling this dumb stunt. However, several careless bikers had gotten banged up pretty good, because they were riding too fast and lost their balance. They ended up sliding on their butts along the dusty road leading to the Motherhouse.

Luckily, those guys were off playing stick ball on Ferry Street that day. If they were around watching me, they'd surely bust my balls as I struggled to stay on Eddie's bike without falling and trying to avoid getting hit by the occasional car that raced past. As I continued my struggle, I discovered that this wasn't going to be as easy as I thought. Learning to ride a bike was really tough, and I proved to be a slow learner as Eddie tried his best to teach me the basics. It was so hard pushing those pedals in a smooth motion while trying to keep my balance. After a dozen attempts, it became obvious that Eddie was starting to get mad at me, and that's not a good thing because he could "blow" at any time. Now, fearing for my life, I forced myself to really concentrate in order to prevent this mini-demon from exploding into his usual rage when frustrated. Luckily, after a few more painful attempts I was finally able to keep going, eventually being able to make turns in the middle of the road. I was really confident now and thought I was an expert. But as time would tell, I was far from being an expert, even as I screeched to a dusty stop like Eddie had done earlier.

Smug with a sense of accomplishment, my miniature mentor pulled me off his bike and demanded I meet him on his front porch so he could kick my ass in a game of cards. Before he darted back to his house and knowing he was still in a good mood, I asked Eddie if I could ride his bike again sometime. Still being in a relative state of exaltation, Eddie quipped with mock sincerity, "Sure, you can use it anytime you want, you little twerp, as long as I'm not using it." He then admonished me, "If you ever do use it again, you damned better well take care of it and make sure it's returned safe and sound, otherwise I'll kick your scrawny ass."

Unctuously, I thanked Eddie, even though I had the feeling that I was becoming a sycophant, and not really liking that feeling. However, in retrospect, I guess sometimes you gotta do what you gotta do in order to get what you want. So, off I trotted after Eddie as he raced down the street bringing his bike to a screeching stop in front of his house, hopping off and leaning it against a staid old maple tree.

Eddie and I played cards for a good hour and a half on his front porch before his Dad yelled out the window, "Supper's ready, so you'd better get in here otherwise you're gonna miss Howdy Doody." Since Eddie was leading me in a game of "Slap the Jack" and wanted to whip me badly, he chose to ignore his dad's first warning. Big mistake, because within a few minutes his Dad would be glaring out the window, yelling, "Get in here now or you're going to go bed without supper, and no Howdy Doody!"

Eddie's Dad was a tough task master, but he was also a decent, hard working man who was a great role model for us kids. Even though we were poor, he never looked down his nose at us. He often took me under his wing like a surrogate father, similar to the way that Harry Moore did.

"Shit," Eddie, muttered under his breath to me, "I'm kicking the crap out you and now I gotta quit." Pointing his finger at me, he chided, "I'll finish you off tomorrow."

In a flash, Eddie's Dad was out the door and hovering over us, ensuring that we picked all the cards up off the porch. Once we had completed that task, Eddie grudgingly headed into the house for supper, grousing all the way. I was about to head home when out of the blue, Eddie's Dad blurted, "Hey, Herbie, you hungry? You have supper yet?"

"Nope, Ma ain't called me in yet. Why?"

"Well, I thought you might want to have supper with us to-night. That is, if you can behave yourself and your Ma says it's ok." My heart was racing because I had never been invited to Eddie's house for supper before. Wow! This was like a dream come true.

"Gee, Mr. Barrow, can I really come for supper?"

"Of course you can, Herbie, or I wouldn't have asked you in the first place, but remember you have to be good, and you have to check with your Ma first."

Ecstatic, I darted across the street to my house, raced up three flights of stairs then breathlessly blared to Ma. "Hey, Ma! Eddie's Dad said I can have supper with them if I'm good, and you say it's ok. Can I go Ma, please, can I go?"

Weary from the summer's heat and chasing after my bratty sis-ters all day, Ma looked at me scornfully, "No, Herbie," she moaned, "I'm just getting supper ready for you kids now and I don't have time to worry about you misbehaving at the Barrow's house."

With tears welling in my eyes, I pleaded, "Please, Ma, please, can I go? I promise I'll be good, cross my heart and hope to die."

Between tending a simmering pot of my favorite Irish stew in her sweltering kitchen and chasing her simmering brood around our apartment all afternoon, Ma's energy and patience had been sucked right out of her. She was just about at wit's end with my sisters when I had walked in, so of course I got the brunt of her frustration. However, when she looked up and saw the tears and the dejected look on my face, she had a sudden change of heart. Sensing I was about to burst into a full blubber, she decided she couldn't deal with it and gave in to my whining plea.

"Ok, Herbie, you can go but you have to be home by 7:30, and if I get a bad report back, you'll never be able to play with Eddie again." Ma had a lot of respect for Mr. Barrow both as a dad and a man. She rightly assumed she'd have one less headache for a couple of hours with me over at Eddie's house and also knew I'd be in good hands.

My disappointment was immediately replaced with elation as I ran to Ma and wrapped my arms around her opulent waist, hugging her tightly in order to show my gratitude. "Thanks, Ma, I won't let you down. I promise."

As quickly as I had dashed up the stairs, I darted back down. Luckily, despite my glee I grasped the railing as I stumbled over the worn top step. Sure as shittin, if I hadn't grabbed it, I'd have been tumbling ass-over-teakettle down three flights of stairs, and my glee at going to Eddie's house might have turned into another unwelcome trip to the emergency room.

When I reached the Barrow's house, I noticed that Eddie's bike was still resting against the large maple tree which stood like a giant beacon. Being a good Samaritan, I figured I would tell him he left his bike outside before someone came along and stole it from him. (Eddie had this bad habit of leaving his stuff outside unattended, and occasionally some of it had been swiped.)

Although short of breath and wheezing from all that exertion, I was still able to hurriedly ring the Barrow's front doorbell, eagerly anticipating the fun that lay ahead. (The reason I was short of breath and wheezing was because I was having a mild asthma attack, a condition that wasn't diagnosed until I was an adult. Ma just thought I was anemic and susceptible to lots of colds.)

Just as I was about to ring the bell again, Eddie whipped open the door and led me into his house, poking me in the side as he laughingly whispered, "I'm gonna kick your ass tomorrow playing cards, and don't you forget it, you little twerp."

I gingerly poked him back and laughed, "Right, Eddie," as we headed into his kitchen for supper. I knew in the back of my mind that I had better finish losing that game the next day or I'd really be facing the "wrath of Eddie." However, in the midst of all this bantering I forgot to tell Eddie that his bike was still outside.

"Hi, Herbie" Mrs. Barrow smiled. "I hope you're hungry, because I just made a big batch of Irish stew for supper tonight."

I thought to myself, "Irish stew? Oh shit. I should have stayed home." I then mused. "Um, either Tuesday was Irish stew night on Eighth Street or lamb was on sale this week at Helflick's market."

Of course, out of respect to Mrs. Barrow for inviting me to supper, I told her that I was starved, and that Irish stew was my favorite. It was my favorite, because my Ma was a great cook and whenever she made Irish stew it was delicious. On the other hand, Mrs. Barrow's stew, um? Not so delicious. So even though her stew wasn't up to my Ma's standards, I still ate a lot, and besides, I really was starved.

During the meal, I was having a great time laughing and joking with Eddie and his sister Peggy until Denny started his crap, pulling my ears when his Mom and Dad weren't looking, then whispering to me that I looked like "Dumbo the Elephant." I couldn't fight back, of course, because if I got caught, Eddie's Dad would never invite me back again. So I just laughed it off and whispered back to Denny that I'd get even someday. Looking back on it now, I realize that I actually *did* have big ears which tended to stick out, and being so scrawny, well, that only served to exacerbate the "Elephant Ears" effect. But I was no "Dumbo the Elephant" and Denny didn't have to rub it in all the time. If I were mean like him, I could have called him "Dennis the Menace" because of his freckles and red hair. Hey! he looked more like "Dennis the Menace" than I looked like "Dumbo the Elephant." Better still, I could have called him "Dennis the peckerhead" because he was a peckerhead for teasing me all the time.

Eating supper at the Barrow's house felt different than eating supper at my house. The food sure didn't taste better, but there was a male presence with Eddie's Dad being home every night. It felt like their family was more of a whole, a complete family unit. I know that Ma really strived to make us feel that way as a family. My sisters and I were very close, but my Dad was rarely home, and my older brothers were either away in the service, juvenile detention, or in the case of my oldest brother Jack, married and raising his own family. It would be impossible for us to have that same environment as the Barrows. Mr. Barrow seemed to evoke a sense of order, discipline, and respect in his kids, at least while they were in his presence. Maybe if my family had that strong supportive male presence at home, we might have had that same sense of security.

After dinner, Mrs. Barrow and her daughter did the dishes while Mr. Barrow told Denny to take out the garbage, one of Denny's weekly chores being the oldest boy. All Eddie and I had to do was bring our dirty dishes to the sink, then go into the parlor and behave ourselves.

After a few minutes, Eddie's Dad yelled into us that we could turn on the TV and watch "Howdy Doody," and that Eddie's Ma was making us a couple of root beer floats for dessert.

"Wow," I yelled back, "Thanks, Mr. Barrow, I've never had a rootbeer float before and I've never seen Howdy Doody either."

During the early 1950s a new entertainment medium began to pop up in our neighborhood living rooms. The *Television* would insidiously change our lives forever in ways that few could have foreseen. Only "rich" families could afford this luxury. How ironic, along with Eddie's other cool stuff, he also had a brand new television sitting in his parlor. In fact, the Barrows were the first on the street to have one, and, being nice people, they would invite many of their neighbors over to watch this newfangled contraption. Of course, only the adults were allowed to watch at first, with us kids being relegated to sneaking peeks through the front window. However, as the novelty wore off for the adults, kids were then allowed to watch selected shows like "Howdy Doody," "Freddie Freihofer" and various cartoon shows.

"Howdy Doody" featured several live characters: Buffalo Bob Smith, the host, and Clarabell the clown, who was a mute and communicated by using a horn and squirting people with a seltzer bottle. Several other characters were marionettes: Howdy, Phineous T. Bluster and Princess Summer-Fall-Winter-Spring (who would eventually be played as a live character on the show). Howdy Doody was a national show for kids, while "Freddie Freihofer" was a local kids' show produced by WRGB in Schenectady. The male host Uncle Jim Fisk, dressed as a Freihofer delivery man, sketched cartoons of Freddie the rabbit, along with other characters drawn from "squiggles" that kids in the audience would also draw using pens on a large sheet of white paper. There was always at least one kid celebrating his or her birthday that day on the show; as a treat, each kid in the studio audience would receive some of Freihofer's famous chocolate chip cookies along with a slice of birthday cake.

In the not too distant future, outdoor activities like shooting hoops, playing baseball, riding bikes or just playing tag would become a thing of the past. They would be replaced by families sitting passively in their living rooms and getting fat watching the "Boob Tube." Everyone, it seemed, would become mesmerized by this new electronic marvel. If only they could have peered into the future and seen the impending health scourge hovering on the horizon, "The Obesity Crisis." Luckily for my waistline at the time, my family's only source of entertainment remained that old radio in Ma's room, so I still spent most of my free time playing outdoors or at the Troy Boys Club.

"Boy!" This was turning into one of the most fun days I could remember. First, learning how to ride Eddie's bike then eating supper at his house and watching Howdy, Buffalo Bob, Clarabell, Mr. Bluster and Princess Summer-Fall-Winter-Spring. The day seemed to fly right by and before I knew it, we had devoured our delicious root beer floats and were watching John Cameron Swayzie and the news. Luckily I looked up and saw that it was 7:15 already. Remembering what Ma told me, I knew damned well that I'd better be home by 7:30 or I'd never be able to come over again. So, I hurriedly thanked Eddie's Ma and Dad for supper and headed home. Eddie walked me to the front door and warned me again that I would get my ass kicked the next day playing cards. Then, with a devilish smile on his face, he slugged me lightly on the arm as I ran off the porch.

By the time I finished racing up the stairs, I was huffing and puffing like an old locomotive running out of steam, barely beating Ma's deadline. As expected, Ma was standing there holding open the door. She realized, of course, that I just made it in by the skin of my teeth but decided not to chastise me for cutting it so close. Instead, she asked me how things went.

"So did you have a good time over at Eddie's house?" Ma said.

"I had so much fun, Ma. It was great! Hey, Ma, I bet you can't guess what we had for supper?" I giggled.

Playing along, Ma pondered. "Um, baked macaroni?"

"Nope", I teased, "guess again"

"Um, steak?" she mused, with her eyes looking up, and her thumb and first finger pressed against her cheek.

"Wrong again, Ma," I laughed out loud. "Guess again!"

"Chipped beef on mashed potatoes?" (another one of my favorites, and a staple at our house).

"Nope, keep trying," I insisted.

Now, tired of being the "foil" in my little game of twenty questions, Ma declared impatiently, "Ok, Herbie, enough is enough! What the hell did you have for supper?"

Confused by Ma's sudden change of mood, I impishly whispered, "We had Irish stew."

"Did I hear you right, young man? You had *Irish stew* for supper?"

Sensing she was getting upset with me, I confessed. "Yes, Ma, we had Irish stew for supper, but I didn't know it until I sat down at the table." Then in a desperate attempt to rationalize what happened and to brownie Ma up, I spouted. "If I knew she was having stew for supper, I wouldn't have gone, Ma, because yours is so much better than hers! Uh, and I couldn't tell her yours was better, uh, because if I did, she might get mad and send me home, and I didn't want to miss Howdy Doody. I'm sorry, Ma! Please don't be mad at me. I won't do it again, Ma! I promise. I won't go again if I know they're having Irish stew!"

With a thunderous roar, Ma burst into uncontrollable fit of laughter, gasping for air. After finally catching her breath, Ma saw the perplexed look on my face "Herbie! You didn't do anything wrong, so stop apologizing." Then, with a huge smile on her face she chortled, "It's just so hilarious that the first time you get invited to Eddie's house for supper they have the same thing as us. I guess Mrs. Barrow bought her lamb from Helflick's like I did this week, because it was on sale." (Boy! Where did I hear that before?)

Phew! Now I felt better knowing Ma wasn't mad at me. However, still feeling the adrenaline rush from my experiences that day, I continued to ramble on about all the fun things I did with Eddie. Ma patiently listened as I told her how Eddie taught me how to ride his bide and how he told me I could use it anytime, even if he wasn't around, as long as I took good care of it and brought it back safe and sound.

Dubious of what I was saying about Eddie's promise, Ma cynically warned that it might not be the wise thing to do unless Eddie's Dad had agreed to it. Always the wily one, I of course told Ma that I was sure I saw Eddie talking to his Dad about his bike and me. However, after telling Ma what I thought I heard, I began to have second thoughts. Maybe his Dad had given Eddie the ok to give me more lessons. But, Eddie did tell me himself that I could use his bike anytime. So in my twisted logic I really wasn't lying to Ma, I was just interpreting what I thought I heard Eddie say. No harm, no foul.

I think Ma bought my little opus because she then began to expound about the dangers of bike riding. Noting emphatically that I was far from being an expert, she dutifully reminded me of the painful accident I had while riding on the back of Dickey Finch's bike the previous summer. Ugh! That painful misadventure was one I definitely wanted to forget, especially since Ma had warned me never to ride with Dickey in the first place. (Dickey was one of the craziest kids in the neighborhood and totally fearless about doing anything dangerous or daring.)

My mind painfully raced back to that afternoon when Dickey and I were playing in front of the Wagner's house, which was located four houses up the hill on the north side of College Avenue. It was around 12:30 when I told Dickey I was hungry and that Ma wanted me home for lunch. So he offered to ride me home on the back of his bike. Remembering how Ma had warned me never to ride with him but not wanting to get him upset or angry, I fibbed. "Ma warned me not to ride on the back of anyone's bike because I could get hurt." However, Dickey insisted he'd be very careful and would get me home safely.

By this time I was starving and succumbed to Dickey's con job, bravely hopping on the back of his bike. With a villainous smirk on his face and me perched precariously on the back, Dickey tore off like a bat out of hell. We went careening down College Avenue on his wobbling bike, me holding on for dear life and screaming at the top of my lungs for him to stop. As we approached the bottom of the hill, Dickey abruptly turned his bike to the right so that we could go up Eighth Street toward my house. Suddenly, both tires went out beneath the bike and it slid along on its side, with me in tow, for about twenty feet, ending in a painful cloud of dust and stones. I felt an excruciating pain in my right forearm and leg and blood was now streaming down my side as I lay there in pain.

Suddenly I heard my sister Patty cursing at Dickey, who was standing there unscathed with a stupefied look on his face. He had safely leaped from his bike before it came to a screeching halt with me trapped underneath it. "You crazy son-of-a-bitch, Dickey! What are you trying to do, kill my little brother?"

Patty ran down the embankment and tried to pull the bike off me as an unfazed Dickey looked on. By then I was crying like a baby from the pain, while Dickey pleaded that he didn't do it on purpose, that it was just an accident, that the bike had just slipped on some dirt and rocks by the sewer. Patty didn't buy it. She gave him a shove and screamed, "I saw what you did, you little bastard! You bailed out and jumped off the bike and that's why it crashed." She tried to pull me up just as Harry Moore reached the scene. He helped Patty get me up on my feet, then sat me on the curb to calm me down. He had raced out of his store after hearing the commotion of the crash. Harry told Patty to go into the store and ask Mae for a bottle of hydrogen peroxide and some gauze. He then told her to bring them to Ma so that she could clean out all the dirt and crud that was ground into my torn skin.

Harry then yelled at Dickey. "Get your damn bike and go home, you little instigator, before you get into more trouble!" Wow! Harry must have been really mad for him to use a cuss word, because he rarely swore. I think Dickey sensed the anger and realized he'd better get out of there quick, because if Harry was that pissed at what happened, then he'd surely get his ass kicked when my sister Patty got back. He knew she was already mad at him and would kick the crap out of him. So he wisely decided to grab his bike and hightail it up College Avenue to avoid an old fashioned asswhupping. Luckily, I didn't suffer any broken bones, just those nasty cuts and abrasions which hurt even worse. Ma scrubbed them hard to clean out all the dirt and gunk, all the while bemoaning the fact that I didn't heed her earlier warning.

Thankfully, my mind soon eased back to the present and away from all those painful memories. Now with those vivid recollections behind me, I began to conjure up various schemes to ride Eddie's bike again. After tossing and turning most of this dreadfully hot night, I was finally able to drift off into a groggy sleep. Visions of the fun I had with Eddie and his bike danced in my head along with hazy dreams of more fun to come.

Early the next morning after that fitful night's sleep, I awoke to the sound of a June bug's mating call. (I may have mistaken the omnipresent June bugs that inhabit our region for the periodical cicadas who had invaded the northeastern states at the end of their seventeen year life cycle.) Thankfully, the high pitched bleating would only last for a short period that early morning as their mating rituals were usually conducted under the cover of darkness, and daylight was rapidly approaching. I guess their rituals were pretty much the same as humans. The apartment seemed eerily quiet that morning, and soon the sound of chirping birds replaced the high pitched whir of the June bugs.

It seems that I was the only one awake at this time so I quietly went into the steamy kitchen and made myself a bowl of cereal, which I quickly gobbled down along with a couple of soggy peanut butter cookies from the bottom of Ma's cracked, ceramic cookie jar. I then glanced into Ma's room. I heard her snoring lightly and rightly figured she was exhausted from all the heat and needed her sleep, so I made sure that I didn't wake her, and besides, I had already made my own breakfast.

Now being wide awake, my mind, of course, returned to all the fun I had the day before, along with thoughts of riding Eddie's bike again. To insure that I didn't wake Ma or my sisters, I tiptoed into the parlor and glanced out the front window, peering up the street at Eddie's house. To my surprise, I saw Eddie's shiny red bike still leaning against the tree. The sight of it unattended there jolted me back to the fact that I had forgotten to tell Eddie that he'd left it outside when I was at his house the night before. So in the altruistic spirit of friendship, I decided that I better go out and put Eddie's bike on his porch before someone came along and stole it. Not wanting to wake Ma or my sisters from their sleep, I got dressed, snuck out of our apartment, and went over to Eddie's house with every good intention of saving his bike. As I left our house, I was struck by the fact that no one else in the neighborhood seemed to be out and about that hazy morning.

When I finally reached Eddie's bike, I carefully grasped the handlebars and began to push it along toward his front porch. Boy, it felt so good just holding this shiny red hotrod in my sweaty little hands. Suddenly, my mind raced back to the day before when Eddie *enthusiastically* told me that I could use his bike at any time, or so I subconsciously chose to remember. Now I faced a dilemma! Should I immediately put the bike on the porch and tell him it's there, or take it for a short test ride to hone my riding skills? I was tortured as to what I should do for what seemed an eternity. However, within about five seconds, I made my fateful decision and decided that it wouldn't do any harm if I took Eddie's bike for a little spin before he got up for the day. Besides, I was protecting it for him so that no one could steal it, and it was definitely in good hands, mine! So off I blithely went with Eddie's bike safely in tow, ready to enjoy the rapture of bike riding.

I quickly walked it up a slight incline until I reached the flat section of road. I confidently threw my right leg over the center post of Eddie's bike with my right foot landing on the pedal. Now straining to remember the lessons I learned the day before, I pushed down hard on the right pedal and, with all the strength I could summon, lifted myself up and plopped my scrawny ass on the bike's seat. I then slid my left foot onto the other pedal. I figured it would be cinch to get the bike moving again but I quickly realized it wasn't, as I immediately started to fall. Luckily, I was able to hop off before it crashed to the ground.

So now the learning ritual had to start all over again, however, this time without Eddie's assistance. Just like the day before, it took numerous attempts to ride with some degree of stability. After about twenty minutes I was comfortably riding up and down the street and making turns with relative ease. Ah! Now my ersatz confidence was fully restored, I felt I could do anything with this amazing machine. Believing I was a riding expert, my ego forged ahead. I would seek more adventurous challenges. My mind quickly shot back to the times I had seen the older, experienced kids, ride their bikes effortlessly on the wall that ran along Eighth Street. Feeling euphoric, I decided that I too could traverse this rarely used thoroughfare. So I confidently walked Eddie's bike up the embankment at the beginning of the wall. I set out to race along this narrow by-way to the end, then down the speed ramp and back into the road. I could already feel the adrenaline rush.

Slowly I started walking along the narrow ledge as a sense of angst crept into my psyche. Although I was still filled with a sense of overwhelming self confidence, that tiny, nagging sensation of self doubt was beginning to build an undercurrent that threatened my plan. Blocking out any quivering doubts, I decided it was time to take the challenge. I hopped onto Eddie's pride and joy and started my enigmatic journey. Now with my confidence brimming, I raced forward along this narrow route to disaster, oblivious to any impending obstacles on my race to glory. Sadly, I didn't see the shallow crack in the concrete wall that lay ahead. Without warning, I hit this rut and the bike wobbled out of control. "Oh, shit!" I screamed. Scared out of my wits, I tried desperately to keep the bike on the wall but didn't have enough strength to straighten it out. The bike lurched toward the edge of the wall and in an instant of sheer panic, I made the decision to jump off or risk being mangled in a tragic fall. Pushing off the bike, I tumbled into a tangle of coarse weeds and grass and watched the bike go flying into the abyss.

As I lay safely in a thicket of grass and weeds with just a few minor scrapes and bruises, my mind raced to the obvious. What happened to Eddie's bike? I quickly lifted myself and looked below, praying that the bike wasn't smashed to bits. To my surprise, there didn't appear to be any damage at all. It was just lying on the side of the road in a little section of grass and weeds that separated the wall from the curb. "Wow," I thought! "The grass must have broken its fall. Phew! I lucked out again." Relieved that everything was ok, I hopped down off the wall to retrieve Eddie's bike. When I grabbed the handlebars, something didn't feel quite right. When I tried to turn the bike around, the handlebars and front wheel fell off the frame and into the road. "Oh!" I screeched. "I'm screwed! What the hell am I going to do now? Eddie's going to kill me because I broke his bike in half." Desperately, I tried to reattach the bike but to no avail. All my options rapidly faded into the morning haze. I had to find a way to save my ass before Eddie found out what happened or I'd be toast.

Too panicked to even cry, I fell back into the high weeds in despair. Confused and dismayed, I watched the early morning sun begin filtering through the tree tops. Suddenly, a devious idea seized my mind. "Hey! I haven't seen a single soul out this morning. So nobody saw what happened, right? So?" I argued to myself. "The bike kinda disappeared; Eddie's stuff had been stolen before and he left it out overnight. Wouldn't it be logical that some strange kid could've come along and hijacked it? He could've taken it for a joy ride then ditched it in the high grass at the bottom of the wall."

So, that's what I did! I picked up the bike and put it gently in the high weeds where it sunk out of sight, unless you happened to be walking along the top of the wall and looked down. Once I thought it was sufficiently hidden, I took off as fast as I could, running back to my house in hopes of sneaking back in before anyone could see me.

By the time I made it back, I was gasping for air as I quietly shut the door behind me. To make sure I was home free, I peeked out the cracked front door window but saw nobody on the street. Just as I was about to slink my way upstairs, I glimpsed fat Billy Mayes with a basketball in hand, heading up the street to shoot some hoops. At least I knew that he didn't see me. Luckily, I was able to slither into our apartment unnoticed, get undressed, and silently slip back into bed, pretending to be asleep.

Within a few minutes, things began to stir in the apartment. I could hear Ma filling up the coffee pot, while my sisters Patty and Brenda argued over who would help Ma make toast for breakfast. Ma yelled at them both to stop fighting, because Brenda was going to make the toast that morning. She told Patty to go wake me up because she wanted me to run an errand down to Harry Moore's store when it opened, while Patty was to help make the beds.

Usually when I had to do this one particular errand, Ma would give me a hand written note for Mae, for a box of something called Modess. (It seems to me that this chore was bestowed on me about once a month, for God knows what reason, and was usually accompanied by gales of laughter when my older sister Kathleen or Winnie Koch were there.) As a reward, Ma always gave me a few pennies so I could buy some candy. I never complained, even though I couldn't understand what all the laughter was about. To my chagrin I found out years later what the laughter was all about.

When Patty came into my bedroom and shook me, I pretended to be angry at her for waking me out of a sound sleep. She yelled at me to stop whining and get up, because Ma needed me for an errand. So I got back into my wrinkled clothes and slowly meandered out to the kitchen rubbing my eyes as though I had just woken, my tousled blond hair askew. Ma was just finishing sautéing a couple of eggs in butter and Crisco and put them on an old melamine plate along with a couple pieces of toast. She handed that to me along with a glass of milk. I told her that I wasn't really hungry. I didn't mention that I had already eaten a bowl of cereal and cookies earlier.

"Eat your eggs, Herbie," Ma admonished. "We can't afford to waste food and you need to put some meat on your bones, because you're so damned scrawny."

"Ok, Ma," I whined back and wolfed them down. I guess I was hungry after all. When I finished, Ma told me to bring my dirty dishes to the sink so she could wash them.

It was then that Ma that noticed the scratches on my arm. "Where did you get those scratches, Herbie? I didn't see them before."

Uh, oh! Now I had to think fast or my little morning disaster might be exposed and all hell would break loose. Quickly, I conjured up a response and stammered. "Uh, I forgot all about them, Ma. I, um, had a little fall when I was riding Eddie's bike, but it didn't hurt so I didn't think to tell you." Of course I didn't tell her *when* I had that little fall, letting her assume it was yesterday, because if I told her it was yesterday then that would be lying, and Ma frowned on lying.

"Well, you better go into the bathroom and clean them with some peroxide before you get a nasty infection," Ma warned. "When you get done, I want you to take this note down to Moore's store for me. So be quick about it."

Relieved that Ma bought my little disingenuous tale, I quickly went into the bathroom and cleaned out my minor wounds. Although the peroxide burnt a little, that discomfort would be nothing compared to the pain my scrawny ass would suffer if the truth came out. When I came out of the bathroom, Ma handed me a note, along with eight pennies for candy. She then told me again to go down to the store and give Mae the note, as was the usual custom. Relieved, I gleefully skipped down the stairs and headed to the store, secure that my dreadful secret was still intact.

As I made my way back from my errand, happily chewing on some Squirrel Nut Zippers and Necco Wafers, I heard a commotion in front Maggie O'Brien's house on the other side of the street. It was Billy Mayes, running for his life as Eddie and his brother Denny were chasing him and screaming at the top of their lungs that they were going to kill him for wrecking Eddie's bike.

Gulp! I almost choked on my candy when I heard those harrowing words. "Damn!" I thought. "They found Eddie's bike, and because Billy was shooting hoops near where I dumped it, they assumed he did it and were going to kick the crap out of him."

Billy kept screaming that he was innocent as the pelting of sticks and rocks continued. Now scared shitless myself, I raced back to our apartment, breathlessly handed Ma the paper sack Mae had given me, then ran to the front window to see what was going on. Bewildered by my actions, Ma followed me and asked what was going on. I stood quivering in my sneakers as I saw Billy being pounded until his Dad came to the door and pulled him to safety. He yelled at the two demons to go the hell home and leave Billy alone or he was going tell their Dad what they'd done. Eddie kept screaming that Billy had broken his bike while a still whimpering Billy kept crying to his Dad that he didn't.

After hearing all the screaming and seeing the goings on outside, my Ma—intuitive as always and now smelling a rat—turned to me and said: "Herbie, do you know anything about this? Did you have anything to do with what happened? I remember you talking about riding Eddie's bike when you came home last night and now I have a bad feeling that this involves you for some reason."

I was trapped. I knew I couldn't go any further with my charade, especially after Billy almost had the snot kicked out of him. I broke down and cried, confessing to Ma all the whiny details and justifications of why I did what I did. She didn't show any mercy as she took out a strap and whacked my ass until her arms got tired. She admonished me never to lie to her or try to deceive her about my misdeeds, even though they may have been out of my control or just innocent mistakes. Misdeeds have consequences, and now someone innocent has paid the consequences for my misdeeds and stupidity.

Needless to say, Ma dragged me by my elephant ears over to see Mr. Barrow and apologize for what I had done. She told him that she would find some way to pay for the damages I had caused. Mr. Barrow told Ma not to worry, as he was easily able to fix the bike by replacing a shear pin that had snapped. But he also reprimanded me for what I'd done and told me that as a consequence, I couldn't play with Eddie again at his house until Mr. Barrow felt sufficient time had passed as punishment, and until he was sure he could trust me to tell the truth when things went wrong, even innocent things. He explained to me that the crime was not that I had the accident, but that I tried to cover it up and that I had not asked for permission to use the bike. He also told me, and Ma agreed, that I should go down and apologize to Billy Mayes and his Dad for what happened, the same as he made Eddie and Denny do.

So Ma dragged me down to Billy Mayes's house where I would repeat my mantra, explaining exactly what happened. Being good neighbors, they accepted my apology, even though I wasn't the one who tried to beat up Billy. They were just thankful that Billy didn't really get hurt.

And so, another life's lesson learned. Needless to say, Santa didn't bring me a bike that next Christmas, and needless to say Denny didn't stop picking on me. The good thing, however, was Mr. Barrow did let me come over again after a few weeks to play with Eddie and watch Howdy Doody. In the interim, Eddie continued to kick the crap out of me in Slap the Jack, a game I still love to hate.

CHAPTER FOURTEEN

Games We Played

As a young kid, I don't remember many of my friends being fat except for Billy Mayes and Tommy Pelham. I guess the reason most of us weren't fat was because we were always physically active. If we weren't fighting or horsing around, we were playing various street games. Some of the more notable games I remember were: stickball, baseball against the steps, One-Two-Three-Spud, It, pitching pennies or baseball cards, and Monkey in the Middle.

My sisters and other girls on the street would play: hopscotch, jump rope, jacks, and hide and seek. Other times the girls would roller skate up and down the street. (At that time, roller skates were metal contraptions that strapped on shoes or sneakers with a skate key to tighten them up.)

My personal favorite street games were stickball, baseball against the steps, pitching pennies and One-Two-Three Spud. In spite of the fact I enjoyed Spud, it could be very painful. If you lost, which I usually did, you had to stand facing a wall, and the winners would take turns throwing a rubber ball at your back as hard as they could. Stickball was much less painful and much more fun to play. In stickball, bats were constructed from broomstick handles.

The rules were pretty much the same as in regular baseball, except there was no catcher, no bunting, and no bases to run. Although a game, it was really an exercise in honing your pitching, hitting and catching skills. In order to play the game, you had to find a wall or side of a building and draw a "strike zone" in chalk. The batter then stood in front of the strike zone. Standing across the street about thirty-five or forty feet away, the pitcher then pitched to the batter using a soft but firm ball, usually a Spaldeen or tennis ball, not a real baseball. Spaldeens were either bought or swiped from Cahill's Sporting Goods store downtown. Whether they were swiped or not depended on whether you had the fifty cents to pay for them. They were a precious commodity for us, and if you lost one down a sewer or to a passing car because of your ineptitude, it was your responsibility to get a replacement.

The boundaries for the field could be a telephone pole or fire hydrant on the other side of the street. Hits were determined by the distance the ball traveled in the air. No grounders were allowed. The players determined what would be a single, double, triple or home run.

Most times I played stickball with either Frankie, Denny, Alan, Billy or Pat on Ferry Street near the Point. I was usually relegated to playing in the outfield while the older guys were either hitters or pitchers. Since most of the older guys fancied themselves super stars, they got to pitch or hit. Rarely was I allowed to do either. Pat, who was a huge Brooklyn Dodger fan, always wanted to pitch and pretended that he was Carl Erskine or Clem Labine. Meanwhile Frankie and Denny, both Yankee fans, pretended to be Mickey Mantle or Hank Bauer. Billy, on the other hand, had no favorite team and just played.

Being so tiny and a Dodger fan, I, of course, imagined myself as Pee Wee Reese, playing shortstop and catching hard line drives. When I was able to pluck a long fly ball out the air and thus save a home run, I imagined myself as Duke Snyder, the great Dodgers outfielder. I would rarely get a chance to bat, but when I did I was usually whacked with the hardest fastball Pat or Denny could throw. They, of course, claimed they were just trying to brush me back. If that were the case, they were pretty lousy pitchers because good pitchers didn't hit you. Surprisingly, I got my fair share of hits. They were mostly singles, though, because I didn't yet have the reflexes or strength needed to hit long fly balls like the older guys. However, when I got a little older and had more experience playing, I could hit the ball pretty good and with surprising power for a little guy.

The one street game I hated the most was Monkey in the Middle. You guessed it. I usually ended up being the monkey in the middle. One particular episode stands out among them all. It happened on an unusually cool, late summer morning. I had just finished breakfast and was headed down to Moore's store to do an errand for Ma. On the way to the store I was kind of dawdling along, daydreaming. Just for the fun of it I ripped off a switch from a tiny elm tree that was sprouting out of the weeds near the Koch's house. It was then that I heard a commotion coming from across the street. I looked over and spotted Alan, Denny and Frankie playing Monkey in the Middle in front of Alan's house. Unfortunately, there was Denny pissing and moaning, the current and not too happy, monkey in the middle.

Suddenly, Denny spotted me. With a big grin on his face, he shouted in a solicitous voice, "Hey, Herbie, want to play?" Sensing they had a new victim, all three stopped what they were doing and waited in rapt anticipation for my answer, especially Denny. I was a bit addled about what to do. I knew I had to finish my errand but was really thrilled that they wanted me to play.

Perplexed, I shouted, "I, uh, would love to play, but I have an errand to do for my Ma right now."

"Ah! Don't worry about it," Frankie conned. "You can do your errand later. We're not gonna be here much longer so you better get over here quick if you wanna play."

Now faced with a dilemma, I pondered what to do. "Geez." I thought. "This is the first time they asked me to play in a long time, but on the other hand Ma might get mad if I didn't get back soon." After a brief moment of self doubt, I rationalized that Ma didn't say I had to be back right away so what's the harm if I played for a few minutes.

"Ok, you guys. I'll play for a little while, but I have to get this errand done soon. If you goof around with me, I'll have to leave."

In my six-year-old mind I figured that Denny would still be the monkey in the middle and not me. I also naively thought they'd honor my request not to goof with me. So, with Ma's note safely tucked away in my pocket, off I blithely trotted to join in the fun. Big mistake!

It being so cool that morning, Ma insisted that I wear a ratty old sweater and knit cap to the store. She didn't want me to catch a chill. Well, that knit cap would become the bane of my existence that morning as well as the switch I brought with me. Immediately, when I got to the other side of the street, Denny snatched the cap off my head and Frankie grabbed the switch out of my hand and handed it to Alan. It was then that my torture began.

A smirking Denny gloated, "Ok, you little twerp, now you're the monkey in the middle!"

In Monkey in the Middle, there were usually just three players and a ball. The one chosen to be the monkey would have to jump up and try to catch the ball as it was tossed over his head. If you caught it, the one who tossed it would then become the monkey in the middle. A reasonable game of sorts, in theory, unless you were tiny like me. Then the chances of catching the ball were slim to none.

On this particular day the rules were insidiously changed, just for me. Instead of tossing a ball, they had rolled up my cap into a ball and began tossing it between the three of them. So now I was surrounded by three nemeses who I thought were friends. They threw my hat so high that I could never reach it, and they also disparagingly laughed at me and called me stupid names.

"Jump, scurvy Herbie, jump!" an exhilarated Denny crowed.

Alan then took his turn mocking my big ears, blurting to Denny, "You're right, Denny, he does look like Dumbo the Elephant with that cap off."

They treated me like a trained seal jumping for my meals. But even worse than that, when I asked them to stop, they wouldn't. I was getting tired and scared. I was afraid that if I didn't get back from my errand soon, Ma would kill me. Just when I was at my wits end they ratcheted this torment to a new level.

Frankie, acting as if he was the ring master in a three ring circus, began whacking me on my arms and legs every time he threw my hat over my head with the switch he had taken back from Alan. He then laughed and shouted at me as I pleaded for him to stop. "What's the matter, Fido? Can't you jump any higher?" He then handed the switch to Denny who did the same thing. Laughing and mocking me at each turn, he then handed the switch back to Frankie while Alan looked on, stupefied at what they were doing.

This torment continued for several minutes. They seemed fixated to make me feel miserable, small and helpless. I don't think they even realized how much it was hurting me or how scared and upset I was becoming. They couldn't see the welts forming on my arms and legs. I guess they thought it was all just innocent fun. It may have been for them, but not for me.

Suddenly I was somehow able to snag the switch from Frankie's hand, and in one swift motion, blindly struck back at my tormentors. In an instant I heard this God awful screech coming from Frankie, who was now writhing in pain on the ground and holding his face.

"My eye, my eye! He stabbed me in the eye!"

In pure shock at what happened, I quickly dropped the switch. It was then that Denny started screaming at me. "Look what you did now, you little bastard. You poked Frankie's eye out. Wait until his father gets ahold of you, he's gonna put you in jail!"

I was confused and petrified beyond belief that I had committed the heinous crime Denny said I committed. My cluttered mind tried to decipher what to do next, before they could cart me off to jail. I'd never see Ma again or my bratty sisters. I'd never again eat her famous macaroni and cheese or chipped beef on toast. What could I to do to escape this horrible fix? I envisioned Frankie's Dad who was a big guy and a cop to boot, racing down the street and hauling me off to jail. I saw him grab me by the scruff of my neck and throw me into the paddy wagon with all those murderers and crooks.

I had to escape before it was too late. I would soon become an unlikely six-year-old fugitive, running away from the law, justice and home. Glancing down, I saw my crumpled cap, grabbed it, and took off up the street. I knew I had to get away before they noticed my absence during the tumult. As I raced away, I briefly glanced at Alan's Mom and Dad trying to console poor Frankie. I never looked back again. I knew I had to find a place to hide and escape the angry mob I was sure would hang me.

As I reached the Lempki's house, I spotted the underside of the Barrow's front porch and the basement apartment located on the lower level. My mind raced back to the time I was playing hide and seek with Eddie and discovered a tiny cubbyhole sequestered in back of the support beams under his porch.

Using the sturdy, metal, Borden's milk carton that sat by the front door of the basement apartment, I quickly hoisted myself up onto the concrete ledge by holding the support beams and then slithering my way back to my hideaway. Huddled in this dank alcove with my desperate thoughts, I was now acutely grateful that Ma had dressed me the way she did that morning. If she didn't, I think I might have succumbed to hypothermia even though it was still summer.

Suddenly, out of nowhere I heard footsteps thundering down the street towards Alan's house. I could only surmise it was Frankie's Dad running off to render aid to his stricken son. Minutes later I could hear the muffled hullabaloo. Additionally, I could vaguely hear what sounded like the muted pleadings of my sister Dorothy and Mrs. Gibson trying to explain what happened to an irate Frankie's Dad. I timorously pulled my cap tightly over my ears, blocking out all the wild neighborhood ranting. Scared and depressed, I drifted off into a coma-like sleep, waking up to darkness many hours later. I was unaware of the turmoil and anguish Ma had been through for the past ten hours while everyone in the neighborhood was futilely searching for me.

A slight drizzle was coming down as I climbed down from my protective cocoon, cold and starving, not having eaten in over twelve hours. No one was in sight as I crossed over to my house and silently glided up the worn wooden stairs leading to our sorrowful apartment. My mind was still in a state of murkiness. As the door creaked open, an hysterical screech emanated from my fraught and tearful Mom. Still weeping, she ran over and hugged me.

"Where have you been, Herbie? We've been worried sick searching for you!"

The protective fog that had enveloped my fragile mind suddenly lifted when I saw the anguished expression on Ma's weary face as she held me tight. It was then that I pleaded, crying uncontrollably, "I didn't do it on purpose, Ma, I didn't mean to poke Frankie's eye out." I couldn't stop sobbing. "They were picking on me and wouldn't stop. They took my cap and started hitting me with a switch. It hurt so bad and they wouldn't stop. They just kept laughing at me and calling me stupid names."

"Oh, poor Herbie," Ma sighed, tears rolling down her cheeks. "You thought you poked Frankie's eye out?"

"Yea, Denny said I did, and he said Frankie's Dad was going to put me in jail."

"Oh my," Ma soothed. "That's why you ran away?"

"Yes. I was so scared that Frankie's Dad would put me in the paddy wagon with all the bad people and take me to jail. Denny said he would, plus, I thought you would be mad at me because I didn't do your errand."

"I wasn't mad, I was just so worried that you were hurt or got lost somewhere."

"I got so scared that I ran and hid under Eddie's porch and fell asleep. When I woke up, I couldn't remember what happened until just now. Am I going to jail, Ma? I'm so afraid. Am I?"

"Herbie, Herbie, Herbie, you're not going to jail. Frankie's Dad was upset at first, but I think he realized what happened when Mrs. Gibson told him she saw the whole thing from her front porch. She told him how they were picking on you and hitting you.

"But, did Frankie's eye fall out like Denny said?"

"No, silly, but it was scratched with that stick. I think he's going to be ok."

"I'm so happy I didn't poke it out. I only swung because I wanted to make them stop hitting me and give my cap back."

Relieved that I wasn't going to jail, my tears finally stopped. "I'm starving! Can I please have something to eat, Ma?"

"I bet you're starved by now since you only ate breakfast. What do you want?"

"Do you have any leftover baked macaroni?"

"I can heat you up some. How about some bread and butter too?"

"Yep."

"How about some hot cocoa, too?"

"Mmmm, yes, please."

So, that's how the rest of the evening went, tranquilly. Ma was finally able to relax, knowing I was home safe, and I was able to shake off the burden of fear that had engulfed me. I was back home, secure in thinking I wasn't going to jail or be ripped away from my loving Ma. Even though I had slept through all the hullabaloo that day, I was able to peacefully sleep through the night. The next morning gone were those dreadful fears of the previous day.

After eating a huge breakfast of pancakes covered in butter and maple syrup, I asked Ma if I could go up the street and shoot some hoops. "Ok, Herbie, but if those guys try to start anything with you again, I want you to come right back home. We don't need a repeat of what happened yesterday. You understand?"

"Yes, Ma, I do. If they even get near me, I'm going to run right home."

"Ok, then. You can go, but be sure you come home for lunch."

"I will, I promise"

So, off I went with my brother Cliff's basketball in hand. I dribbled the ball past the Howard's house, pretending to be Marcus Haines of the Harlem Globetrotters. I'd start and stop like him, switch hands then try unsuccessfully to dribble between my scrawny, knock-kneed legs. Just as I was reaching the last house on our side of the street, Frankie and his Dad abruptly appeared on the second floor landing of their house. I stood mesmerized, hoping that they didn't see me. No such luck.

"Hey, Hydie! I want you to get over here, now!" Frankie's Dad commanded. "I want to talk to you."

Petrified, I meekly replied, "Yes, sir, I'll be right there." I suddenly felt doomed. My heart raced. The thoughts of being dragged away to jail again engulfed me. How could Ma be so wrong? She had said everything was ok. Resigned to my fate, I slowly trekked across the street. I looked up to see a sullen Frankie, his right eye covered in a thick gauze bandage, staring at the sidewalk.

"Do you see this, kid?" Frankie's Dad said, pointing at Frankie's battered and bruised eye.

"Yes, sir," I bleakly replied. "I didn't mean to do it, I really didn't. It was an accident. Please don't put me in jail!"

"Listen, kid. You're not going to jail. I found out the whole story. He deserved what he got for what he did to you yesterday. You had every right to fight back." He then turned to Frankie and demanded he apologize for picking on me.

A glum-faced Frankie, biting his tongue sputtered out a constrained apology. "I, um, I'm sorry," Frankie whispered, a hangdog expression on his face.

"What did you say? What did you say, son?" his perturbed Dad reiterated. "I could barely hear you."

"I'm sorry for picking on you and hitting you," Frankie reluctantly blurted out.

"That's better, son." Now, turning to me, Frankie's Dad commanded, "If Frankie ever treats you like that again, you're to come see me, and if I'm not around, you have your Mom call and leave a message for me. You understand, Hydie?" (Geez, I hated being called Hydie, but I wasn't about to complain to a cop.)

"Yes, sir, Mr. Brighton," I saluted back. "I will."

"Ok, you can go now." So, off I scooted up the street to shoot hoops as Frankie's Dad took him back to the eye doctor for a check-up.

Frankie never hit me again as he promised his dad. Teasing however, well that's a different story. Although Frankie never really teased me like he did before, that didn't stop Denny from his appointed rounds. I think Frankie actually might have given me a little more respect for fighting back. One thing I learned from that incident is that at some point in your life you may have to take a stand and fight, even if it becomes painful to one party or the other.

CHAPTER FIFTEEN

Third Grade

Summer finally ended and third grade began. I had Mrs. Lenox that year. Luckily, I didn't have a crush on her like I did with Ms. Hancock. Although third grade was boring, we did start having gym classes three times a week, which was fun. We played a lot of dodge ball, but also learned other things like gymnastics, rope climbing and agility skills.

More importantly, we discovered that we could peek at the older girls, who were swimming in the pool that was adjacent to the gym, separated by what looked like a corrugated metal, garage door. Billy Finch, of course, was the one who noticed the crack underneath the garage door where we peeped when Mr. Latito wasn't looking. Peeping was fun but, unlike the older boys, who swam in the nude starting in sixth grade, the girls wore bathing suits. However, being pre-hormonal at this age, we didn't really care about nudity. It was just fun peeking at them because they didn't know it, and we could tease them about it later. We found out in later years that the older girls used to peek too, and they saw more of the boys than we ever saw of them.

Third grade was also the year that I sat behind Billy Brazier, who always came to school dirty. His hair stuck out in all directions like porcupine quills, plus he smelled like a skunk. I guess his Ma didn't give him a weekly bath like my Ma did.

I almost threw up the day I noticed a bedbug on his shirt. He had smelled especially bad that day, with a familiar, pungent aroma I hated. That "bedbug" smell. He got a little upset when I whacked him on the shoulder with my wooden ruler, squishing the beast into a bloody pulp.

Turning angrily toward me, he yelled, "Hey, why did you hit me?"

"Shush," I whispered back. "You had a bedbug on your shoulder, and if Ms Lenox saw it, she'd send you to the nurse."

"Oh, Ok. I thought you wanted to beat me up."

"Nah, I'd never do that." He then turned around and that's when I noticed the cooties scurrying around his neck. "Hey, Billy! You got cooties, too." Hearing a commotion, Ms Lenox looked up and noticed us arguing. She quickly came over to calm us down.

"Ok, you two, what's going on?"

"Herbie hit me and said I had cooties."

"You do have cooties, I saw them, and I just smushed that bedbug with my ruler so it wouldn't bite you."

"Herbie, you never hit anyone, you hear me?" Ms. Lenox warned.

"But he does have cooties, Ms. Lenox, and I did kill a bedbug, you can see it smushed on his shirt. I'm scared of bedbugs, and my Ma told me she'd kill me if I came home with cooties again."

Getting a bit flustered, Ms. Lenox promised, "If I find lice on either of you, you're going to the nurse and she'll send both of you home." She then stomped back to her desk. When she returned with her ruler, she had Billy lean forward and scraped the ruler slowly up the back of his neck. Scores of cooties skittered out of his hair and around his neck, causing her to gasp in shock. "Go to the nurse, Billy, right now!"

"Yes, M'am" Billy sheepishly replied.

"Ok, Herbie, it's your turn, I want to check you out, too." Being cootie free for several weeks now, I felt safe. But, I shouldn't have because she found a few in my head too. So, off I trotted to the nurse's office to be sent home like Billy.

Needless to say, when I got home, Ma wasn't too happy. "Not again, Herbie. When will this ever end?"

"It was Billy Brazier's fault, he gave them to me."

"I told you to stay away from him."

"I can't, Ma, he sits right in front of me."

"Well then, I'm going to send a note to Ms. Lenox to have your seat moved, this can't keep happening."

Out came the newspapers, fine comb, and a small jug containing a disgusting, yellow toxin (kerosene) which she poured over my head. After thoroughly rubbing it into my scalp, she let it sit for a minute. That's when the burning started, soon to be followed by more exquisite pain, as she scraped the fine comb through my hair, forcing dozens of dazed and weakened cooties onto the newspaper she had spread out on the kitchen table.

She killed the larger ones with her thumb, then snapped the *nits* with her thumb nail, fracturing their fragile skeletons. After she was sure there were none left, she crumpled up the newspaper and threw it into the garbage. She then dragged me over to the kitchen sink, where she washed my hair with Lifebuoy soap, until she felt comfortable that all the toxins were gone. She repeated that process for the next three days until she was positive I was cootie free.

Luckily, that was the last major cootie flare-up of my grade school years. It seems like back in those days, cooties and ringworm were a major problem. Kids with ringworm would be seen wearing their moms' silk stockings pulled tightly over their shaved heads. I guess that was to protect others from getting infected.

Wearing those stockings was like having a scarlet letter plastered on their foreheads. They were often shunned like lepers. Whenever you saw a kid with a stocking pulled over his head, you hightailed it as quickly as you could. Ma insisted that we could catch it too if we got too close. Thank God, nobody in my family ever caught it. Cooties were bad enough.

In the early summer of that same year I experienced my first and last trip to Camp Barker, the Troy Boys Club sleep-away camp. The camp was located a few miles out of town on Forest Lake and was staffed by volunteers from RPI who served as counselors. The kids were housed in a series of small wooden buildings set on concrete blocks. The uninsulated cabins were set in two rows of five or six each, separated by a grassy field. The field served as the parade ground and each morning after reveille, we'd stand outside as the flag was raised. Two lucky campers were selected each morning to help raise the flag. For most kids it was a time to have fun in the great outdoors. Each night at dusk the counselors started a huge bonfire and would tell scary stories like the "Monkey's Claw" right before we went to bed. Just as we were about to drift off to sleep, someone would run around and bang on the walls of each cabin, making us believe it was the monkey's claw trying to kill us.

Billy Finch and his brother Dickie were in the same cabin as me that year, along with Bobby Mathers. Billy was a wild man as usual and would play games at night when we were ready for bed. He snuck some matches into the cabin one night. The same night we had hot dogs and beans at the mess-hall. We all had gas that night and after lights out, Billy whispered to Dickie to rip one. Just as he did, Billy lit a match and a burst of light shot out of Dickie's butt, like you'd see come out of the exhaust on a hot rod. We all laughed at this hilarious site. Of course, Billy got caught and had to do laps around the parade ground in his bare feet.

For me, being at camp was a dreadful experience because I was homesick the entire two weeks. Plus, I still wet the bed occasionally. Luckily, I wasn't the only one who wet the bed that year, Bobby Mather's did too. Since our mattresses were made out of cotton ticks stuffed with grass and hay, flea and tick bites were abundant. And if you wet the bed, like we did, then you had to take the straw stuffing out of your tick. You then had to sleep on top of the metal grating which was strung across each bunk with just the wet mattress cover. Not fun! But, it sure helped us to break our bed wetting habit.

The initiation for first year kids? Cleaning the *Kybowl*. The kybowl was a large, outhouse type bathroom, located at the far end of the parade grounds, directly across from the mess hall. My specific chore: cleaning around the base of the porcelain toilets with a bucket of soapy water and used toothbrushes. I gained a tremendous appreciation for school custodians after working the Kybowl that year.

Every weekend, family members could visit the camp for an hour to make sure the kids were behaving. They usually would meet in the mess hall for breakfast. The counselors also handed out the mail each Saturday. I never received any letters from my family during my ordeal, and since Ma had no way of coming to visit me, I was heartsick the entire two weeks.

The only benefit that came out of this misadventure was that one of my counselors took me under his wing. That next winter, he invited me to his fraternity's annual Christmas party for kids. He made sure that I got some really nice gifts too, including a new, corduroy winter coat and a Radio Flyer sled. I couldn't believe my good fortune. Especially the sled, because it was the first and last one I ever owned.

In addition, that summer all the neighborhood kids got invited to the Emerald Club's field day at the Methodist Farm located a few miles outside town. The Club provided yellow school buses to transport us all out to a day of fun: sack races, pie eating contests, ball games, swimming and lots of food. The field day became a wonderful summer event that we all looked forward to each year. Another annual event we all looked forward to was Manory Restaurant's ice cream giveaway for city kids. Kids lined up around the block for this annual treat.

Summer seemed to fly by that year with Camp Barker, the Emerald Club's field day, and the annual picnic sponsored by Dana Delechance's father and Ed Barrow. One Sunday each summer, they loaded all us neighborhood kids on the back of Mr. Delechance's flatbed vegetable truck, then brought us out to White Bridge. There we had a cookout and went swimming. That was part of the goodness of the neighborhood. Rich or poor, everyone was invited.

One of Troy's many parades on Broadway near Union Station and Gainor's.

CHAPTER SIXTEEN

The Old Saw Mill

As quickly as summer seemed to fly by, several other events would touch my life like no other. Even though I began to see Dad for who he was during this period, it was also when he first seemed to notice I existed.

Now, several years after getting fitted with his artificial leg, Dad decided to take me along with him while he cut down a tree in Grafton. I think that was the only time I ever remember him taking me anywhere by myself. I played in a grassy field nearby, listening to the whir of his chain saw in the distance as he dangled from the top of the tallest tree in the woods. When he finished, he loaded several large logs onto the back of his truck. He then came over to me and with a big smile on his face said, "Hey, Herbie, you want to go fishing?"

"Really, Daddy, can I?" I had never fished in my life.

"Hop in the truck!" So off we went to a small pond I'd never been to before. Dad took out his fishing gear from the back of the truck and placed it into a small rowboat that was tethered to a rickety wooden dock. He had me climb into the boat then rowed out past the middle of this placid pond. Once we reached an area near the other side, he began casting his line toward the shore. After a few casts he pulled in a shiny, reddish, gold fish. He gently unhooked it and threw it back. He then handed me the fishing pole. Taking my hand, he then showed me how to cast. It was the first time in my entire life that my Dad had ever done anything that personal with me. Ever!

I got a few nibbles but didn't catch anything, and soon Dad put the pole away. Without uttering a word, Dad then removed his shirt, work boots, pants and artificial leg and, without warning, dove into the lake. Luckily, I was able to steady the boat with the oars, otherwise it might have capsized. I watched in amazement as he swam about the lake for a good ten minutes before lumbering back into the boat in his drenched underwear. Thank God the boat didn't capsize because I didn't know how to swim very well. That small interaction with a man I barely knew as a father made a profound impression upon me for the rest of my life. I felt a closeness to him that I'd never felt before or again.

We headed back to shore where Dad got dressed. After loading his fishing gear and me back into the truck, we headed off to Buskirk and the saw mill where his friend Frank Languid worked part-time. Pulling his rickety truck up to the loading dock, he pounded his horn until a bedraggled Frank sauntered out to greet him.

"Hey, how the hell are you, Skinner?" asked Frank.

"Good but pretty thirsty," Dad offered back. "Could use a cold one. By the way, how the hell is that sweet wife of yours after last weekend?" Dad asked, a knowing smirk on his face.

Smirking back, Frank remarked, "She's always good, you old coot! You know that." Looking knowingly at each other and laughing, they quickly changed the subject when they noticed me sitting in the cab, all ears.

"Get out here, Herbie. I want you to meet my best friend, Frank."

"Ok, Dad." I pushed open the door, hopped out of the truck, then headed over towards Dad and his grungy looking friend with the blood shot eyes. I yanked my head away as Frank rubbed my brush cut with his calloused, smoke stained fingers. I almost gagged from the stench of untold weeks of B.O. wafting from his unwashed body.

"Hey, kid, I ain't gonna bite," he snarled. "Boy, Skinner, he's definitely a Hyde. Funny, how he's got them blue eyes and blond hair—like my Johnny. Seems like both our families have lots of blond hair, blue eyed kids."

"Yea, ain't it," Dad laughed. "Ok, enough socializing, Frank. I got to get these logs unloaded.

Soon they had loaded all Dad's logs onto a large steel table, located just inside the rusted, double doors that led in to the saw mill. You could tell this mill had seen better days. Many of the broken wooden panels on the aging building had been replaced by rusting, corrugated metal panels. Standing outside, I could smell odious fumes spewing from the sputtering, diesel engine powering the long conveyor belts. At the end of the conveyor table was the ominous, metal blade that rose menacingly. As the rough logs were fed into the saw blade, thick black smoke rose to the rafters as unearthly screeching pulverized my senses. Instinctively, I grasped my ears in hopes of stilling those hideous howls.

Twenty minutes later, when all the rough planks had been stacked on a pallet, I saw Frank hand Dad what appeared to be two, ten dollar bills.

"Christ, Frank, is that all this hard work is worth?"

"Sorry, Skinner. These fucking owners are clamping down on me. I got to be careful about what I'm paying out—they don't want to pay nothing anymore. I wish I could do better, but I can't. Can't afford to lose this job. You know how rough it is out there finding work."

"Yea, I know, Frank. Damn it!" Dad complained, still agitated about the meager payoff he got. "Screw it. Guess there ain't nothing I can do about it. Well, the least you can do is give me one of the beers you've been guzzling."

"No problem, Skinner," Frank said. Reaching into a small ice box that stood in the corner near the bathroom, he opened two bottles of Fitzie's ale with the church key he pulled out of his green, oil-stained coveralls. Handing one to Dad, he looked up and noticed me standing there. Without saying a word he reached in and grabbed a small bottle of Coke, opened it, then handed it to me.

"Thank you," I said.

"No problem, Kid."

Dad said to Frank after he finished his beer, "I hope to be back with another load in a week or so and they better pay more or I'm gonna look elsewhere," knowing full well that he couldn't get a better deal. Frank knew it too and laughed back at Dad.

"Ya gotta do what ya gotta do. By the way, Skinner, why don't you see if your old lady wants to come by with you this weekend. She's never been to our place, ya know."

"I told you a thousand times, Frank, she ain't ever going to come up there. I mentioned your proposition to her and she almost whacked me with a frying pan. Never again. Besides she's always home with the kids and that suits me just fine."

That was the one and only time I met Dad's friend, but I had heard lots of stories about him when Ma was sitting around the kitchen table with Winnie, Helen, and my sister Kathleen, venting about Dad's suspected indiscretions. I usually never understood what they were talking about, especially when they began talking about swapping and bathroom diseases. I heard lots of "stuff" sitting quietly in that dark corner. I guess most times they forgot I was even there, and if they did realize I was there, they thought I was too little to understand anyway. I didn't understand most times, but I always found their conversations intriguing.

CHAPTER SEVENTEEN

Earning Your Keep

Even with Dad finally taking notice of me that year, I was still pretty much a lonely little boy at times. Harry Moore was a neighborhood icon, respected for his helping out needy families in our neighborhood. He was like a surrogate father to kids like me—kids whose fathers often weren't home for long stretches, either by choice because they didn't want the responsibility of fatherhood, or because they found odd jobs which took them out of town.

Harry would give kids chores to do around his store, then reward them with small amounts of money, free candy or a soda. He did this mostly with the older kids like Denny, Frankie, Alan and my brother Cliff. He would have them help fill up his coolers or sweep out the store, take out the garbage or pick up litter on the street near his store. Sometimes he'd have them deliver food to elderly people on the street for him. Harry was trying to instill a work ethic in kids. It was subliminal. They were learning life lessons and didn't know it. Harry's motto was this: Treat people with respect, and if you want things in life, you have to work for them. This became a simple but poignant message which most kids in my neighborhood carried into their adult lives. Of course, it wasn't a linear path to adulthood and we faltered many times along the way, but the basic goodness and ethic he espoused served us well.

I can still remember the time Harry gave me my first chore. I was hanging out in front of his store one hot summer morning, around midday. Most of the older kids had headed up to Prospect Park to go swimming. I was all alone, because none of them wanted me tagging along. So, there I was sitting on the steps that led down to Eighth Street, lonely and daydreaming like five year olds do. Suddenly, I sensed this hulking presence hovering over me. It was Harry.

"Hey, little man. What are you doing? How come you didn't go up to the park with your brother and his buddies?"

"They didn't want me tagging along, even Cliff. So I'm just sitting here counting how many cars go up the street."

"Well, you just can't sit there blocking the steps. I got a job for you to do."

"You do?"

"Yep, so get off your behind and come here," Harry said gruffly.

"Ok." I meandered over to Harry, who was standing by the door holding a small bucket and a trowel.

"See those weeds sticking up between those bricks, dandelions and such?"

"Yes, sir, I do."

"Well, I want you to start digging them all out and put them into this bucket, ok?"

"Yes, sir, Harry."

"When you're done you come in and tell me, and don't be all day about it, and whatever you do, don't block the door! You hear me?"

"Yes, sir, "I replied.

"Good, so get started, and don't dawdle."

So, I got my first experience at earning my keep. I started up by the porch, located about eight feet from the door. It was a real struggle trying to yank out those dandelions. Pulling them out by the roots was impossible, with my scrawny arms and hands. It seemed like the roots were bigger and stronger than my arms. That's when I used that curved trowel Harry had given me. By using it, I was able to pry at the bricks a little, edging my way under the plants, which allowed me to pop them out.

This painstaking task seemed to take forever, especially, when customers would laughingly ask, "What ya doing there, Herbie?"

As he walked past me, Mr. Barrow chuckled, "Looks like Harry's got you working in the salt mines." I didn't understand what he meant. I did hear Harry and him laughing heartily in the store, assuming they were probably laughing at me.

Soon after Mr. Barrow left, I finished my chores and let Harry know. I was covered from head to toe with dirt and had grass stains on my hands and knees. Harry smiled at me and said, "You sure get into your work, Herbie. Let's go out and see what kind of job you did." As he came around the counter, he put his arm around my shoulder and we headed outside. "Hum," Harry pondered. "Looks like all the weeds are gone. Where'd you put them?"

"I put them over there in the bucket you gave me," pointing to the porch.

"Oh, I see them now, Herbie. Well! It looks like you did a pretty fine job, young man, I must say. Now take that bucket and dump it in the barrel by my back yard, then come see me."

"Ok." Weary, I trudged up the hill and emptied the bucket then headed back to the store to get my just rewards. I didn't know for sure what he'd give me, but I hoped it would be an ice cold Coke from his cooler. I was parched by the hot sun and all that strenuous work.

When I entered the store, a beaming Harry said, "I'm really proud of you, Herbie. You did more work than the older kids usually do. So as a reward, grab a soda from the cooler and pick out a bag of candy. Thrilled, I pushed up the sliding metal door on the cooler and reached down into the arctic depths to get the coldest, wettest bottle of Coke I could reach. I then went over to the penny candy counter and started picking out my favorites: Squirrel Nut Zippers, Necco Wafers, Tootsie Pops, Dots and of course *Nigger Babies*. (I never knew the derogatory nature of that name until I was much older. It offends me now. However, at the time, it was just yummy candy.)

After filling my bag to the top, I turned to leave. That's when Harry shouted, "Wait a minute, young man."

"Oh, no." I thought. "He's mad because I took too much candy."

I was just about to hand him my bag, when he moved around the counter and said, "Put down that bag, Herbie, and open you hand." I sensed he was going to take away my goodies because I had been a little greedy. Instead, he surprised me. He handed me two nickels and said, "Since you did such good job, you deserve a bonus. But you have to put one nickel in your piggy bank for emergencies. You can spend the other on anything else you want. You just can't spend it today. Do you understand?"

"Yes, sir."

"Remember! It's important that you always put something away for a rainy day." That was a lesson that I carry to this day. Even though I don't have a lot of money saved, I do have a little something to tide my family over in case of an emergency. It was a few short weeks later that would change our neighborhood forever.

It was 7am when Winnie appeared at our front door, frantic and crying uncontrollably. "What's the matter, Winnie?" Ma pleaded, while at the same time trying to console her.

"He's dead, Mabel! He's dead!"

"Gene?" Ma cried back. Gene was Winnie's husband.

"No, Mabel, Harry Moore. He died of a heart attack during the night. Virginia told me this morning when I was sitting on the porch."

"Oh, my God," Ma shrieked, bursting into tears herself.

By midday the entire neighborhood was in shock and mourning, myself included. Being so young, I'd never experienced this type of emotional trauma before, the death of a beloved friend. Harry was indeed loved by the entire neighborhood, as though he was a member of everyone's family. I remember the sadness in Ma's eyes, as she, Kathleen and Dorothy dressed in their Sunday best to attend Harry's wake.

It took a long time for the neighborhood to recover from that loss. But they did, as Mae continued to run the store with the help of Ronnie, who was forced into adulthood because of this tragic loss.

Although summers always seemed to be the best time in our neighborhood, this summer didn't because of Harry's death. However, life went on. The summer still gave Ma a break because we weren't always under her feet and could burn up some of our energy outdoors.

I didn't play as much with Eddie as I would have liked after the bike incident. He went over to his twin cousins' house to play more often. Even so, I found another kid about my age to play with later that summer. Ironically, he wasn't one of the local kids.

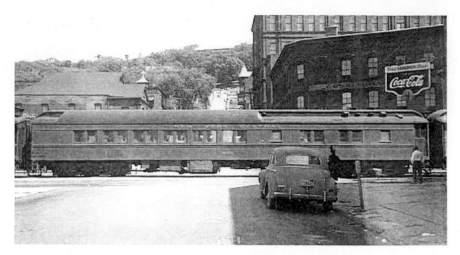

New York Central train headed toward the Sixth Avenue tunnel.

CHAPTER EIGHTEEN

Melvin Snee

Alan Sydner had a cousin named Melvin Snee who lived in Brooklyn but visited Alan's family for a few weeks every summer. He was the family's sunshine kid shipped out of the big city to spend time in the "sticks" of upstate New York. However, Troy was not exactly the "sticks." In fact, it was cosmopolitan in many ways, with its Victorian architecture, striking brownstones, pocket parks and city squares similar to those found in New York City and Boston. However, within a few miles of the city you would be in the "sticks," with rolling hills, dairy farms, and many lakes and ponds. Also within an hour's drive are the Green Mountains of Vermont, the Berkshire Mountains of Massachusetts and the Catskill Mountains of the Mid Hudson Valley, while ninety minutes to the north are the majestic Adirondack Mountains.

Melvin was a character and about the same age as me, as best I remember. What I do remember for sure is that we played together a lot. Although Alan was supposed to keep an eye on his cousin during the day, he would instead dump Melvin off on me. Alan thought it was demeaning to babysit his little cousin; plus, he wanted to do things with the older, mini gangsters in our neighborhood and he couldn't do that if he had to watch Melvin. (Alan was about ten, Melvin eight and I was seven, going on eight.)

Being pushed off on each other as we were, Melvin and I became fast friends each summer and would hang out together all the time. Being from the big city, Melvin was a fearless, prepubescent provocateur and I was his eager follower. Together we'd do things I would never consider doing by myself.

When Alan's Uncle Charlie took his daily walks, me and Melvin would sneak into his basement apartment. A narrow overgrown back street housed the family's wooden storage garage, which could be easily seen from the corner of College and Eighth, if anyone cared to look down there. Melvin and I would rummage through the old codger's beat up refrigerator, looking for goodies and occasionally unearthing some kind of frozen snack. However, more often we'd discover a half-finished bottle of beer or a cheap bottle of wine with a screw cap on it. We, of course, would help ourselves to anything we wanted, inevitably opting for the beer. On several occasions we smuggled a full bottle of beer out of his apartment and down to the old beat up garage which served as our clubhouse.

Yuk! That beer tasted like shit to my seven year old palate during those unofficial taste tests which served as an exciting experiment into the world of adult beverages. My first "official" tasting would come a few years later at which time I would learn to enjoy drinking beer, my beverage of choice, often drinking to excess as my hangovers could attest. Luckily, I didn't become a lush or alcoholic, but like most of my peers, I would overindulge many times during my youth and early adulthood.

Being very skilled little sneaks, we knew we had to cover our tracks after stealing the old fart's beer. So we'd add enough tap water to the bottle to bring it up to level. However, it looked more like a light pilsner now, rather than the hearty Ballantine Ale it was originally. I can just imagine now how shitty that beer must have tasted to the old coot when he went to finish it. However, as I look back now, he must have suspected that someone had been doctoring his beer, but being pretty much shit-faced most of the time, he downed it anyway.

Alan's uncle stored lots of stuff in his dilapidated garage down back. Amid the wooden work bench, tools, ladders, empty paint cans and paint-soaked rags, he stored his old beat up Chevy sedan. Although the car hadn't been driven in years, the smell of gasoline and motor oil still permeated the air. This garage became our hideout during the several weeks Melvin was here each summer. It was a place where we could play and keep ourselves out of everybody's hair. Melvin and I were pretty much unimpeded and able to do anything we wanted. A frequent pastime was checkers, with Melvin always beating me. (To this day I hate checkers and "Slap the Jack.") We'd also practice pitching pennies, a must-have skill to compete with the older guys who were always trying to hustle me out of the few pennies from my meager allowance or what I earned doing neighbors' chores.

Occasionally we would become extremely adventurous and sneak over to the old Day Home, which was located just beyond the fence that bordered our hideaway. This place was mysterious and scary to us little kids, because we never knew what really went on there. It was an old two-story, brick building consisting of a main building and two massive wings that created a U-shaped courtyard on the north side. Some windows held black wire grates and frosted glass. Rumor had it that that these frosted windows prevented anyone from peering inside and seeing the unspeakable and hideous deeds being perpetrated on young kids in the stark chambers within this edifice. Despite all the scary stuff we had been told about this place, it seemed odd that it also had some fun things like sand boxes, a hobby horse, merry-go-rounds and a large swing set.

The older kids spread horror stories about how kids our age were dragged into the home kicking and screaming, never to be seen again. I can still hear some neighborhood moms reprimanding their kids, warning them that if they did not behave the cops would come and haul them away to the "Day Home." Used by both parents and older siblings as a behavioral tool to keep them in line, the Day Home became a frightening urban legend for seven year olds. In reality, the Day Home was a day care center, and kids would scream and cry simply because of separation anxiety.

The vacant Day Home and its environs became both a social and athletic stomping ground for many of the older youths who used it to burn off much of their testosterone-fueled energy. I was told by my Eighth Street buddies that some of the older guys even got laid down there by some girls who lived on lower Ferry Street or the public housing projects on Seventh Avenue. Of course, at the time I couldn't figure out what the hell they were talking about, because I didn't know what the term "getting laid" meant, and I didn't want to be called stupid by asking. I already got picked on enough for just about anything, from my big ears to being called "Scurvy Herbie" by kids who had already taken fifth grade science.

I still remember vividly when several of my buddies had coaxed some older guys to help them build a huge tree house next to the Day Home. It was perched about thirty-five feet up in the crotch of an old oak tree and was fashioned out of old packing crates, 4x8 planks, and tar paper. As the local newspaper noted the day after the fire department dismantled it: "Trees are for the birds: A tree house was built by enterprising would-be young Tarzans. Some of the young 'Tarzans' volunteered the information that 'It was some job getting the stuff up there—now look what happened.'"

The neighborhood kids also used the large area bordered by Eighth Street to the east, the Day Home to the south and School 5 to the west for pickup games like baseball, stickball and touch football. However, most of the time we played the majority of our games either in the roadway on Eighth and Ferry Streets or in Prospect Park. One of the things the older kids were doing caught my attention at a very young age: smoking cigarettes. Most didn't do it in front of their parents, many of whom smoked themselves. Being naive and impressionable, smoking seemed like a cool thing to do. Camels, Lucky Strikes, and Kools were the weed of choice by most guys. How they got them remained a mystery. I assumed they found ways to steal them, either from their parents or from one of the local corner stores—except Harry Moore's store. No one stole from Harry, because he was a good guy. But his second cousin Eddie's store, well that's another story; he was always fair game.

Melvin and I were down at our hideout one Saturday morning discussing the virtues of smoking even though we'd never smoked ourselves. Melvin professed how cool it was watching the older guys compete at blowing smoke rings in order to determine who could make the biggest, or whose would last the longest before it vanished into thin air.

Smoking seemed like such an innocuous habit to Melvin and me. We never gave it a second thought that smoking could some day make us sick or kill us. The warnings about the dangers of smoking would not come until many years later. We were enthralled watching these "Cool Guys" smoking, blowing smoke out of their noses, and then flicking the still smoldering butts onto the sidewalk. They could have just as easily snuffed them out with the heels of their highly polished baby duck shoes. They, of course, chose not to because they were "Kool!"

Out of the blue, Melvin started a heated discussion about how we could easily steal a pack of cigarettes from Eddie Morris's store, just like the big kids. "Hey, you could pretend that you're looking for a can of beans or something for your Ma, along the back shelves. He is definitely going to follow you back there because he doesn't trust you or any of us as far as he can throw us. So that's when I slip in the front door and snag a pack of Camels. What do you think? Great plan, huh!"

Being a wimp, I whined back. "Are you nuts? With my luck, I'll get arrested and thrown into reform school like my brother Cliff."

Agitated, Melvin then came up with a monumental brain fart. "Ok, chicken shit! You know what? I bet we can find some cigarettes in the Old Geezer's apartment. He's still out so let's hustle up." Reluctantly, I rushed back with Melvin as we ransacked his apartment again, but this time coming up empty.

"Ok, smart ass. Now what?" I carped.

Now very perturbed, Melvin pondered. Earlier that morning he had seen some corn in the refrigerator while looking for goodies. "Well, at least, I found a box of matches so now we can snag these two ears of corn and make our own cigee's from the corn silk. They'll be just as good as the real thing, I bet." Then, pushing me out of the door he declared, "Quick, let's get the hell out of here before he gets back!"

So off we raced down to our hideout, reaching it just as the old codger opened the gate at the top of the hill. Luckily he didn't notice us down there as he sidled slowly down the wooden stairs.

Thinking ourselves now safely out of site, Melvin proceeded to make us a couple of cigees. He ordered me to rip off some thin pieces of the corn husk to use as wrappers. He then began pulling the smooth corn silk out of the second ear of corn, making neat little piles. "Ok, Herbie. Hand me a piece of the corn husk so I can start wrapping our cigees."

"Here ya go," I complied, handing Melvin a long, thin strand of shiny corn husk. He took the husk, piled a heaping portion of corn silk onto it, then began to roll it up, sort of like the way Ma used to roll up her jelly roll cakes. Before I knew it, he had made two big fat "cigees." Of course, these handmade gems looked nothing like the ones the guys smoked. But hey! It's the best we could do with what we had.

All this prep work now done, it was time for the real adventure to begin: our first journey into the joys of smoking. This would be our right of passage into the world of the "Big boys," or so we thought. Since Melvin did most of the work creating these little beauties plus the fact that he had the matches, he, of course, insisted on smoking the first one. Being his submissive minion, I gladly acquiesced.

Melvin quickly reached down and grabbed the biggest of the two amateurish cigarettes. Then this cigarette impresario proudly stuck that green stogie into the corner of his mouth, champing down on it to keep it in place, looking a bit like Old Man Manino, but not as mean. His saliva made the end of the stogie a dark green, soggy mess. Not a very appealing sight. He then tried unsuccessfully to light several of the matches he'd stolen. He scratched the tiny, red and yellow knobs against the abrasive lining on the side of the box several times, without success. When he finally was able to get one started, it would burn his fingers before he could get his cigarette lit. He was forced to drop the still red-hot match into dirt and weeds, where it began to smolder, unnoticed by Melvin.

I didn't notice the impending danger either, because I was too busy laughing my ass off at his ineptness. After several more futile attempts, Melvin finally got one match to stay lit. He then proceeded to light his prized stogie. It started off quite innocuously as the corn silk smoothly burned, a trail of light smoke drifting into the air. However, when Melvin tried to inhale those noxious fumes, he started coughing and gagging uncontrollably. Ripping the soggy butt from his mouth he chucked it into the tinder-dry, smoldering weeds next to the garage.

Melvin was still bent over wheezing and gagging as I tried to hand him a half filled bottle of beer we'd snagged earlier that morning, in hopes it would stop his coughing jag. After several more frightful seconds Melvin was finally able to regain his composure and stop coughing.

After helping him to straighten up from his gagging episode, I noticed how ashen his faced looked. "You ok?" I worried.

"Yea, I guess," Melvin sheepishly replied, spitting the remnants of that ghastly stogie into the smoldering weeds, now expansive and reddish and glowing.

Just as Melvin was finally gaining his composure, a sudden breeze swept across the lot, and within seconds those smoldering weeds erupted into a raging brush fire, right before our disbelieving eyes.

"Holy shit!" Melvin screeched, as the fire began racing along the ground at an amazing pace. "We gotta put this damn thing out or it's gonna hit the garage." He then began stomping on the flames as I grabbed an old broom lying against the side of the garage and began slapping at the flames, which by now were dancing around Melvin's feet. My heart almost jumped out of my chest as Melvin screamed, "My pants on fire! My pants on fire!"

That gave new meaning to the old saw: "Liar, liar, pants on fire." However, Melvin wasn't lying. His pants were on fire. "Oh my God!" I cried, as I looked over and saw the bottoms of Melvin's dungarees starting to burn. In a panic, I ran over to Melvin and started whacking him with my broom, forcing him out into the dirt road alongside the building and out of harm's way. I kept whacking and whacking him until he screamed.

"Stop it, you friggin asshole! They're not on fire anymore, and you're killing me with that friggin broom."

"I'm sorry, I'm sorry" I gasped, looking up at Melvin's tormented face. "I was afraid you were going to burn to death." Suddenly, we heard this loud whoosh and felt a strong, hot wind, rush past us—just like the whoosh we'd hear when the trains came out of the railroad tunnel on Sixth Avenue. Now with the hair on both our necks standing on end and fearing the worst, we warily turned toward the garage. Ka-boom! It exploded into a huge fireball.

"Oh shit, oh shit, we're in friggin trouble now," Melvin exclaimed. "We gotta get the hell out of here before anyone sees us or we're sure as hell going to reform school."

With our hearts racing, Melvin and I took off, racing north along the old dirt road that led to Seventh Avenue. At the end of the road was a beat up chain link fence with a gaping hole at the bottom. Without breaking our stride, we dived through the opening, then crawled on our bellies like soldiers until we reached the other side. Racing through the parking lot near School 5, we then headed north along Seventh Avenue, tripping several times on the uneven sidewalks in our haste. Just as we neared the base of the RPI Approach, we heard the first ominous sound of sirens emanating from the central firehouse, located on State Street a few blocks away.

Out of breath and exhausted from the tremendous adrenaline rush, Melvin and I now peered up at the huge Doric style columns rising up to the sky, like two ancient Greek soldiers stoically guarding the acropolis, the RPI Approach. We knew that we couldn't wait any longer to traverse this huge edifice in order to reach Eighth Street and safety. So off we raced, gasping for air again as we reached the top landing, now we could see the billowing smoke and the shooting flames. Within the secrecy of our conscience, each of us rued: We didn't do it on purpose, but nevertheless, we did do it!

A large group of kids came racing up Eighth Street to see what all the commotion was about. So Melvin and I simply blended in with them as they continued their rambunctious jaunt to see the fire. The closer we got, the more frenzied the scene appeared. With a second alarm called in there was now a bright, red, pumper truck hooked up to the hydrant just south of Alan's house. Fire hoses ran all the way down the gangway, spraying copious amounts of water onto the now fully involved garage. The gathering crowd ooh'd and ah'd, as small explosions erupted, apparently from containers of chemicals stored in what had been our hangout, which now had become a raging inferno.

As we neared the Mayes's house, we found the area cordoned off by the cops, who told everyone to either go back up the street or to cross over to the other side. Melvin, still scared shitless, decided he didn't want to go any further and headed back up to the wall by the basketball hoop. However, I was still feeling some of the adrenalin rush and headed down to Moore's store in order to get a better view of the conflagration. As I got closer, I saw a crowd standing by the steps that led to the road on Eighth Street. Walking a little ways up College Avenue just past the entrance to Harry's store, I was able to see the shooting flames and smoke over the heads of the other onlookers. That was when Mae Moore spotted me as she turned away from the crowd.

She slowly walked up the hill towards me with quizzical look. "What do you think of all this commotion, Herbie?" she inquired.

Puzzled by her question, I replied. "Well, I , uh, don't know what to think of it right now, Mrs. Moore."

 "Well, then. How do you think the fire might have started?" she succinctly probed. "You think it was an accident or something else? Like maybe it was set on purpose!"

Her caustic inquisition was beginning to make my stomach churn and give me goose bumps. In total dread now, I blurted out. " I, uh, don't think it was set on purpose. No one would do that on purpose. It must have been an accident or something, Mrs. Moore."

"You're sure, Herbie? Right?"

"I'm sure. I would never do anything like that on purpose," I stammered.

"Herbie, I saw what happened!" hissed Mrs. Moore.

Almost passing out from the shock of those words, I abjectly grieved to myself, "Oh my God. Now I'm friggin screwed. I'm going to reform school like my brother Cliff and Ma is going to kill me."

"I'm sorry, Mrs. Moore." I sobbed. She then quickly walked me into the store without anyone noticing. "It was an accident, I swear, Mrs. Moore." She then had me sit on the chair in her back room, where no one could see or hear us. She began to lecture me and finally console me, even though I didn't deserve consoling.

"Do you understand now, why your Mom always told you not to play with matches?"

"I do now, Mrs. Moore. I really do. But, I, uh, didn't have the matches. Melvin did," I wangled. "We just wanted to smoke like the big kids. So Melvin made a couple cigarettes out of corn silk for us to try."

"Listen, Herbie, don't you try to hoodwink me, because I didn't just fall off the turnip truck. Remember, I told you that I saw what happened."

"I'm sorry, Mrs. Moore, I'm just so scared. I don't want to go to reform school like my brother Cliff."

Uncharacteristically, the usually placid and soft spoken Mrs. Moore continued her relentless grilling regarding the fire. I have to believe she was determined to sear all the horrible details of our dumb stunt into my psyche.

"Ok, ok, Herbie. You can stop your whining now," she declared unsympathetically. "I hope you understand that when you do foolish things, there are usually bad consequences. People's lives were put at risk because of what Melvin and you did!"

Gradually, her demeanor returned to normal as she began talking like the benevolent person she always seemed to be. She then proceeded to explain exactly what she saw.

"I was sweeping the sidewalk a little while ago when I noticed you and Melvin playing down by the garage. At first, I wasn't sure exactly what you were doing until I saw Melvin trying to light that cigarette. I saw him throw it onto the ground after he started coughing. It was then that I realized that there could be a serious problem. Even so, I was shocked when the weeds started on fire and spread so quickly to the garage. I was even more shocked when it exploded into flames. I saw you and Melvin try to put out the flames and it was then that I ran in and called the fire department, because I thought you boys were going to be killed. However, by the time I came back outside, you were gone. I didn't know where you went but prayed you were ok. Thank God you're safe. But, where is Melvin? Please tell me he's ok."

Now feeling a bit relieved, I responded, "Melvin was too scared to come down here. He was sitting on the wall the last time I saw him."

"Thank God for that!" Mae whispered.

I then meekly probed. "Are you going to turn us in to the cops, Mrs. Moore?"

"I could! But I have decided not to. I know it wasn't done on purpose. It was a very foolish accident and I hope you've learned a very serious lesson from this experience."

I ran over to Mrs. Moore and hugged her, sobbing. "Thank you! Thank you! I will never do that again I promise; I will never try to make a cigarette again. I was so afraid I'd be going to reform school, that Ma would disown me, and that I'd be kicked out of the family."

"Don't you worry, Herbie," Mae said soothingly. "I won't turn you in and I won't tell your Ma as long as you keep your promise."

"I will. I will. I promise."

The newspaper headlines would note that an old abandoned garage was burned to the ground from what appeared to be careless smoking, and two young boys had been seen fleeing the scene. However, they were never identified or caught.

Mrs. Moore kept her promise and never turned us in. Apparently other neighbors may have seen what happened too and decided not to turn us in either, at least to the cops. However, Melvin's summer vacation was cut short. He returned to Brooklyn two weeks early. It was also the last year that Melvin came to visit for the summer. I often wonder if his family was told what happened. I also wonder today how Melvin turned out.

Another lesson learned: Although you may do many stupid things in life, people can be forgiving if all the facts are known. Turning us in for this stupid accident may have done more harm than good in our development. Instead of having to face the penal system, I think we learned more about the honor system. We were given a second chance. To this day I don't think Ma ever knew what really happened that day. Additionally, I never became a smoker.

CHAPTER NINETEEN

The Iceman Cometh

During the late 1940s and early 1950s, before the fledgling super market industry evolved into the colossus we know today, neighborhoods were serviced by the local corner store, usually a mom and pop operation. We also had a wide variety of street vendors who would ply their wares, usually from the back of their trucks or wagons.

Some of the more notable vendors came around on a regular basis: The Chicken Man delivered his puny-looking poultry weekly, mostly to some of the older, Italian families living on our street; the Ice Man came to our homes several times a week to replenish small, wooden "ice boxes"; the Milk Man delivered fresh milk and eggs on a daily basis; the Freihofer Bread Man delivered bread, rolls, and their famous chocolate chip cookies from the back of his horse-drawn wagon; and finally the Vegetable Man delivered his locally grown vegetables once each week, usually Saturdays. The local corner stores had their vegetables delivered to them more frequently, usually by commercial vendors from the Little Italy section of South Troy, known as the Market Place. The Rag Man came around less frequently, usually every several weeks because it took several weeks for people to accumulate newspapers and used clothing or rags. (People could also bring their rags and newspapers to the Rag Man's business on Ferry Street if they wanted to.)

Several door-to-door salesmen also came to our homes selling anything from bathroom products to clothing. Weekly or monthly they collected their payments, because people back then bought these products on "time" but without the excessive interest charged by today's financial institutions.

As a means of letting these vendors know when a family needed their products, most families kept a collection of colorful signs to put in their front windows. Each vendor had their own colored sign, and on any given day neighborhood moms might have a veritable rainbow of signs in their front window if they were short of needed staples.

Many families including, of course, my family, still relied on the ubiquitous ice box. It was well into the 1950s before we would have one of those newfangled high tech gadgets, known as a "refrigerator." I think we received our first used refrigerator from one of our neighbors, who had purchased a new one and instead of trading in their old one, generously gave it to us. So up to that time, especially during the summer, we kids would eagerly await the arrival of the ice man. We quenched our thirst on a hot day with the ice chips that covered the cold wooden floor of the ice man's truck. He would separate huge blocks of ice into a manageable size with his ice pick. It was a real treat for us kids and it didn't cost anything. We just had to wait until he went into people's homes to deliver their ice before we'd climb up on his running board to snag our cooling treat, sometimes snagging a sliver in our fingers in the process. We became accustomed to seeing this handsome hulk of a man, with massive arms and bulging chest, easily traverse as many landings as needed in order to deliver his fifty pound block of ice to waiting and often times "lusting" homemakers.

Each day before the ice man made this trek up to our third story flat, Ma would have a couple of us kids help her to empty the overflow tray which contained the last remnants of the previous block of ice. This was a logistical nightmare at times. We struggled to maneuver this heavy, rusted piece of sheet metal, filled to overflowing with rust-colored water and indecipherable goop to the kitchen sink. Sometimes we didn't make it and this slimy mess would flood the floor, causing even more headaches for our stressed Ma.

It seemed odd to me that almost every time this guy made his rounds to our house, Ma's friends, Winnie and Marilyn Zelner managed to mysteriously appear at our door minutes before he arrived, ostensibly to have coffee with Ma. They'd just pop in out of the blue, knowing of course that Ma always had a pot of coffee going and enjoyed their company most of the time. Ma needed to have some adult companionship once in a while to maintain at least a modicum of sanity. She had to deal with our antics twenty-four hours a day without help, and these little respites with her friends allowed her that needed break.

Being so young, of course, I never sensed the sexual undercurrent wafting through our apartment in Winnie and Marilyn's conversation. However, Ma did and would chastise them for their cattiness. For some reason, Winnie always seemed to run to our front window on these days to check on the status of the object of their affection, the Ice Man. Then she quickly returned to the kitchen, throwing herself into a chair, her legs and arms splayed wide and acting as though she had fainted from the "vapors" at the sight of this guy. She then fanned herself with Ma's folded newspaper to cool off. "Phew," Winnie sighed. "He's so gorgeous, I'd let him put his shoes under my bed any time."

Marilyn then chimed back laughing, "So would I. In a heartbeat!"

Sitting in the corner by the stove, I wondered to myself, why would anyone want to have some strange man put his shoes under their bed? It's usually messy enough under the bed already, and putting some strange guy's shoes there would make it even messier. Suddenly, now exasperated by her friends' mid-life delusion and girlish fantasy talk, Ma upbraided them for their snickers and giggling. "Stop the crap, you two. I have kids here, and he'll be here soon. I don't want to be embarrassed by you two."

"Oh, don't get your britches in an uproar, Mabel." Winnie shot back. "We won't attack him in front of the kids."

Ma then reached over and whacked Winnie on the arm and laughingly declared, "You SOB, Winnie! It's a damn good thing you're my friend."

Suddenly, everyone shut up. The ice man was knocking on the door and hollering to Ma, "Ice here." Ma yelled over to me to run and open the door, which I immediately did. Standing there was this giant of a man in coveralls and plaid shirt with a fifty-pound chunk of melting ice on his burlap-covered shoulder. He said, "Thanks, Sonny."

Confused, I blurted out, "Hey! I'm not Sonny, he's my big brother, I'm Herbie!"

Amused, the ice man softly chuckled, "Oh, I'm sorry, you just looked big for your age" at which Ma, Winnie and Marilyn burst into an uncontrollable fit of laughter. Stunned, confused and not seeing the humor in what I said, I slunk back into my chair by the stove and watched the amazing hulk finish his delivery to the glee of his two swooning admirers, Winnie and Marilyn. When he finished and Ma was paying him the fifty cent fee, Winnie brazenly asked if he'd like to stick around and have a cup of coffee with them.

He looked up knowingly, smiled at Winnie and said, "No, thanks, ma'm, I do appreciate your offer though but I'm really behind and have to finish my route before it gets too late." With a twinkle in his dark brown eyes he winked at Winnie and Marilyn, who were just about drooling by this time and said, "Maybe some other time, darlin's, when I have a little extra free time on my hands."

After he left, Marilyn leaned over to Winnie and I heard her softly whisper, "See, Winnie, I told you he is the guy who messes around and I bet if the circumstance were right..."

"Damn it, you two, stop it right now! Can't you see Herbie's all ears over there in corner? He doesn't need to hear this crap from you even though he probably wouldn't understand anyway!" Well, Ma was right about that because I had no clue about what they were yapping about. However, I found out several years later what it was all about from my older buddies.

I guess I was around ten or so when I heard Denny, Billy and Alan talking about how they'd hang out at Belcher's store near Spy Hill and Farm Street with Frankie, Yummie and Bobby. Mrs. Belcher lived over the store in a modest apartment. She ran the store during the day, while her husband worked his full time job at a local paper mill in Watervliet. She closed the store during dinner hour each night, and after dinner he came back down and reopened it until closing, which was usually around 8:30 or 9pm, depending on business. It was a tiny storefront that kept his wife busy during the day while he worked and also made them a little extra money. It definitely kept her busy during the day in a variety of ways.

The store had a small wooden counter, several coolers which held ice used to chill the beer and soda, plus several shelves of canned goods, cereals, cigarettes, various candies and dry goods. In the back of the store was a door which led to a small outdoor storage area and steps leading to the rear of her apartment. On the right side of the front entrance to the store were stairs that also led her apartment.

Billy was laughing his ass off as he detailed to us the time Mrs. Belcher asked Yummie and him to watch the store for her one afternoon a couple months earlier. It seems that she had a lot of vendors who came by while her husband was away at work and collect their unpaid bills. Apparently on this particular day the bill collector was the ice man. Of course, Yummie and Billie were glad to help her out because they could pilfer a few things for themselves while she was away, plus she always gave them a few bucks to keep them quiet afterwards.

"You know what the hell da're doin up dare Billy?" Yummie quipped with his inimitable lisp.

"Nah, no idea Yummie, what?"

"He's futtin her, you dummy! Ha," snickered Yummie, "That's how she pays her bills."

"No shit! Wow! How the hell do you know that?" spouted Billy, dumbfounded.

"Because, I seen her doin it wit my own eyes."

"You did? Geez, how the hell did you see that?"

"Well, me and Bobby Vittner was hiking up Spy Hill one day and stopped to catch our breath in back of the store. We was just sittin there bullshittin behind a bush when dis futtin, fat, bald headed guy heads up the back stairs shortly after we saw Mrs. Belcher go in. Sure as shittin, a couple minutes later who opens up da back door but Mrs. Belcher, in her futtin birthday suit. We almost futtin pissed our pants from da shock."

"Holy shit, Yummie, did she see you?"

"Nah, but she left the shade up in her bedroom the whole time and we saw the whole damn thing. After dat, me and Bobby figured she was bangin half the guys who delivered stuff to her place. Dat's why she lets us watch the store for her when we're around."

"Hey, Yummie, maybe you can bang her someday yourself."

"Nah, wid my luck she'd give me the crabs or somethin, she's screwed just about everyone in sight by now."

When Billy finished his story he was still laughing so hard that he almost choked on the wad of gum he was chomping on. "So," Billy told us, "from now on when you see that 'Closed for Lunch Sign' in her store window and one of them delivery trucks parked in front of her store, she's probably upstairs paying off her bills."

CHAPTER TWENTY

Spy Hill and Prospect Park

As youths, we hung out at a place called Spy Hill like the older kids had done for a generation. It was a rocky precipice overlooking Congress Street and could be accessed either through gangways that ran between several houses near the crest of College Avenue or by craggy trails etched out over time by generations of daring kids, who climbed the escarpment from its base which abutted Congress Street. Spy Hill rose seventy feet above Congress Street and was covered with prickly brush, stones, and small trees. This urban, geological treasure was flanked on either side by two giant advertisement billboards. On the east of the hill were several row houses and businesses, including Yate's Grocery Store, while on the west were more row houses, small shops and businesses including Sam's Barber Shop and Helflick's Meat Market.

Directly across the street from Spy Hill, Ferry Street merged into Congress. We called that "The Point," and we'd meet there for various activities, such as playing stickball on the Ferry Street side or planning various gang escapades. The Point housed an appliance store, and just west on the Congress Street side were more row houses, along with Stickley's Grill on the corner of Rock Alley near Pantera's house and Pantera's store. Further down the street was Eddy Morris's store.

For us kids, climbing Spy Hill was like scaling El Capitan. We, of course, didn't know what the hell El Capitan was. This place was a mountainous hiking trail for poor city kids, so instead of traveling to Yosemite, we just went up Congress Street for our adventures.

As I look back on it now, Spy Hill was a cool, fun place for kids to hang out, but it also provided cover for us to be little delinquents, doing some pretty stupid, dangerous things. Sometimes we'd hike the craggy trails to the top or hide behind the billboards that overlooked Congress Street and chuck little stones or pebbles at the neighborhood kids who were making their daily trek to Prospect Park during the summer months. Other times we'd be good, just playing tag or sitting on the billboard scaffolding watching cars go by.

Winter was our most daring time on Spy Hill. We would take empty cardboard cartons and slide precariously down some of the jagged trails, risking life and limb. However, the most daring and dangerous thing we did on those bleak winter days was chucking snowballs at passing cars going down Congress Street and scaring the wits out of the unsuspecting drivers. It was great fun for us, but not for them. Many of them would slam on their breaks or spin out on the snow-covered road. Some drivers would even get out of their cars and swear at us, but we'd just laugh at them from our hideout in the scraggy brush high above that jagged hill.

One incident stands out above the many I experienced on that treacherous hill. It involved Alan Sydner, Billy Finch, Carl Redmond and me. I remember it vividly. The day was overcast with light flurries and miserably cold, and the ground was covered with six inches of wet snow. However, the miserable conditions didn't stop us from our appointed rounds of peppering as many cars and kids as possible before heading home for supper that ominous winter day.

The wet snow made great packing for our arsenal of snowballs. As per our usual modus operandi, we'd take turns pelting our innocent victims. Tires screeched, cars spun out, people swore and neighborhood kids ran home crying. Just as we were about to quit for the day, Carl decided to hurl one last snowball for good measure. It was the largest one we'd made all day. However, the result of that decision was dire as it hit a beat up sedan with two brutish looking guys inside. Within a split second the car skidded, spun out, and then screeched to an abrupt stop forty feet below us. Suddenly, two goons jumped out with their fists flailing at us and screaming at the top of their lungs, "You fuckers are going to pay for this! We're gonna kick your ass!"

For some reason that threat sent chills down my spine. However, it apparently didn't seem to bother anybody else, because Carl immediately responded in kind by screaming right back at them. "Fuck you, assholes! You can't touch us." To add insult to injury, he then hurled another hard one that splattered at their feet. He laughed cavalierly as they quickly jumped out of the way. From past experience we figured there would be no repercussions, because our targets could never run up the hill fast enough to catch us. Feeling smug, Carl then gave them the finger as we laughingly sauntered back up the hill toward College Avenue, our mission accomplished for this day and oblivious to any dangers that might lay ahead. We figured these two brutes would drive away, just like all the others had done in the past.

Being really pissed, these guys didn't just go away. They had revenge on their minds! Instead, they quickly hopped back in their car, turned right at the corner, and headed up Eighth Street just like so many of our other victims had done in the past. However, instead of just driving away and forgetting about it, they abruptly made another quick right turn and raced straight up College Avenue without us noticing. Unfortunately for us, the street had just been plowed and sanded a couple hours earlier, which made it easy for them to make it up College Avenue and come after us. Soon, all hell would break loose.

Alan and I decided to head home for supper by taking the narrow alleyway next to the McMaster's house on the southwest side of College Avenue. Meanwhile, Billy and Carl headed up to Billy's house to hang out, waiting until Billy's mom got home from her job cleaning houses for the rich people living on Brunswick

Road. So instead of taking the way that Alan and I had, they followed the rocky driveway which separated several row houses on the south side of College Avenue.

The driveway was several houses further east of where Alan and I had exited. The driveway also served as a parking lot and was wide enough for several cars to park. Unbeknown to Carl and Billy, one of the cars now parked there was the one Carl had peppered with snowballs, not five minutes earlier. Those two angry brutes were now lying in wait, ready to impose their revenge.

Minutes after Alan and I headed down College Avenue, we heard a loud commotion coming from up the hill, not far from Billy's house. Although we couldn't see what was going on, we could hear swearing and cursing soon to be followed by Carl's wailing as he was being punched, kicked and knocked to the ground. He had been blindsided and didn't know what hit him. It sounded as though he was being torn limb from limb, pleading for them to stop. "Stop it you bastards, stop it," he screeched. "Don't hit me anymore, I'm sorry, I'm sorry!" He continued to plead, but they didn't stop.

Alan and I knew there was real trouble for Carl, but we decided that it would be too dangerous for us to try to help. Instead, we sped toward Moore's store to tell Ronnie, Harry's son, what was going on. We figured Ronnie could call the cops because things were really getting out of hand. We also knew that Ronnie would probably go up the hill and kick the crap out of those two guys himself. (You see, Ronnie was a big, tough, burly brute himself.)

Ronnie, already having heard the commotion, briefly listened to our frantic pleas, then abruptly ripped off his apron, threw it towards his mom, and yelled at her to call the cops. He then darted off, racing up the hill as fast as his lumbering body could take him. Just as he reached the alleyway, police sirens began wailing in the distance. Without warning, the dilapidated, rust bucket those two goons were driving hurtled out of the driveway, skidding on two wheels and knocking Ronnie to the ground as he grabbed for the door handle. His corpulent torso rolled over several times before coming to rest in a heap by the curb as they screeched away, tires smoking and rocks flying everywhere. As they roared off into the distance, Ronnie pulled himself up and rushed over to tend to Carl, who lay bleeding from the nose and mouth and writhing in pain. Although Carl was pretty beat up, Ronnie, thankfully, suffered no ill effects from his tumble, just a slightly bruised ego for not getting there in time to help poor Carl.

The cops arrived shortly after the muggers had fled and called for an ambulance to haul Carl away. Although his injuries seemed severe at the time, nothing was broken except for his spirit, and he suffered no permanent damage, only a big black eye, busted lip and bruised ribs for several weeks.

Alan and I learned more details of what happened that day when Billy came out of hiding. He recounted to us how he and Carl approached a bunch of innocuous looking cars parked in the driveway near his house but didn't recognize the one Carl had pelted earlier. Suddenly, two bruisers jumped out of their car and accosted Billy and Carl. The biggest guy grabbed Carl by the scruff of his neck and threw him to the ground. Billy was able to tear away from the other guy, racing up the hill like a cheetah past his own house. He didn't want them to know where he lived. He then scurried down the fifty or so concrete steps that led past Farm Street, ending up on Congress Street where he found refuge at his friend Carl Sorreinto's house.

Although Carl got the shit kicked out of him by these two goons, they were never tracked down by the cops or brought to justice for mugging him. (We later learned that they were allegedly RPI football players. A neighbor of ours happened to work as a maintenance man in their dorm where they bragged about how they had kicked the crap out of some Troy urchins who had snowballed their car.)

Regretfully, this was the first of many times that we heard these disparaging remarks by a minority of students who thought they were better than us. They seemed to revel in referring to us as "urchins and Troylets." That contemptuous attitude served to foster resentment in many of us, skewing our perception of all students who attended the school, not just the few. As an adult, I often wondered if poor kids in other college towns were treated in a similar manner. Was it the norm or just an aberration in our town? My sense is that it was not an aberration, it was not unique to Troy, and it probably continues to some degree today. However, from personal experience, I believe that a larger percentage of students are altruistic in nature, have a better understanding of the troubles facing poor inner city youth, and gladly volunteer their free time to help the community. A daunting task given their course loads.

Thankfully, it only took a couple weeks for Carl to regain his renegade spirit, laughing at what happened. Carl, being Carl, went right back to chucking snowballs as though nothing had happened. Luckily, he never got mugged again. I guess the lesson we learned from this experience was: Two wrongs don't make a right, and punishment doled out, in this case Carl's mugging, isn't necessarily commensurate with the crime. So, I guess you can say it was a *wash*. We pelted them with snow balls, they pummeled Carl. Luckily, Alan, Billy and I didn't get hurt. Only poor Carl. He got hung out to dry.

Another of the many places where we played as kids was Prospect Park, one of the first planned community parks in the country. It covers several acres of green space and served the needs of Troy's residents for decades. The west end of the park overlooks the entire city and beyond. On a clear day you can see for miles. To the south you can see the skyline of Albany and the foothills of the Catskill and Helderberg Mountains. To the west you can see the city of Watervliet and the Latham area, while to the north lay the city of Cohoes and the Majestic Cohoes Falls.

Prospect Park housed the city's largest swimming pool, tennis courts and playgrounds. It also had several large picnic areas and ball fields. The above ground pool was located at the upper southeast corner of the park and was huge. It had both high and low diving boards, boys' and girls' locker rooms and a food stand to buy summertime goodies. I can still remember the acrid smell of chlorine permeating the locker rooms. The price of admission back then was a dime but was raised to a quarter in later years.

You got a key at the front counter after paying your admission fee and then in turn gave that key to the locker room attendant. Locker room attendants locked and unlocked lockers and in return gave you a brass tag to pin on your bathing suit. That pin identified which locker held your clothes. The attendants kept control of the keys. In order to get your clothes back when you were done swimming, you had to give them the pin so they could unlock the locker for you.

Kids would lay their colorful beach towels on the concourse and sun bathe when not swimming or hang them over the railings when they were swimming. However, if they didn't keep a watchful eye on them, they might be snatched by little bandits hiding in the bushes below the pool deck. They would reach up and yank towels off the deck then scamper down the nearby hillside. Some headed to the Little Italy section of South Troy, while others headed to the Ida Hill section of Troy east of the pool. As one might expect, scuffles would erupt in the ensuing days when these daring little thieves came back to the pool brazenly flaunting their new found towels.

Adjacent to the swimming pool were several tennis courts which hosted many city and regional tournaments. A large two-sided practice wall (used to hone a player's tennis skills) was located on a small hill that overlooked the courts. I learned to play tennis at that wall and played there often with my school buddies, Bill and Larry. Nearby was a large basketball court where the city recreation department held basketball clinics. They also hosted summer league basketball games in which me and my Eighth Street buddies played. We used to play skins and shirts to delineate teams since the city didn't provide uniforms.

To the west of the basketball court was as a large playground for the younger kids and a wading pool to cool off on those hot summer days. It was at that wading pool that I saw my little sister Brenda almost drown. Some dirt-bag kid from the projects was holding Brenda's head underwater for what seemed an eternity. Luckily, my brother Cliff was nearby that day and pulled my sister free, then kicked that snot-nosed girl in the ass. To this day Brenda can't remember why that kid did what she did. I think Brenda was an easy target because she wasn't the tough, tomboy type like my sister Patty. Brenda was a very pretty little girl who, unlike, Patty projected a quiet demeanor which made her prey to a jealous bully.

The park's ballfields included what was called the main diamond, located near the park's entrance and the largest of the park's ballfields. It was bordered on four sides: St. Francis Church and several buildings on the north, a large hill on the south, a backstop and bleachers on the east and a tree lined roadway to the west. The field was used for baseball during the summer and football during the fall.

The place we affectionately called "Squirrel Diamond" was much smaller and was located a few hundred yards west of the main diamond. It was sequestered on top of a hill among a large cluster of trees. There was just enough open space between those large maple and oak trees for us to set up a miniature baseball field. We fashioned bases out of old cardboard boxes and put rocks on them to hold them in place. Even though it was pretty much hidden in the woods, it felt like a major league stadium to us.

Picking sides worked the same way for baseball and basketball. Usually, the older guys picked the teams—Yummie, Frankie and even my brother Cliff. If they weren't around, the responsibility fell to the next oldest: Denny, Alan and Billy Finch. The method of picking teams was supposed to be impartial. The oldest guy tossed the bat to the next oldest guy across from him. That guy then wrapped his hand around the bat at the point where he caught it. Then the guy who threw it placed his hand on top of the other guy's and they alternated hands until they reached the nub. At that point, unless the other guy had called nub-see's in advance, the guy with his hand closest to the nub got the first pick. We played basketball just about every morning and baseball just about every afternoon during the summer. That was, of course, unless we went swimming at the pool or at Snett's or were getting into some type of trouble.

The city had a pretty good amateur baseball league when I was a kid. Their games were played on the main diamond in the evenings or during the day on Sundays. People often parked their cars alongside the roadway or on the street located behind home plate. Since the park didn't have fences, the roadway that ran along center field served as a fence and St. Francis Church served as the right field fence. Any ball hit in the air over the road or the church was considered a home run. Any ball hit on the ground into the road or into the hill on left field was a ground rule double.

Of course, fans who parked in the roadway risked getting their cars smacked, but that rarely happened. A vendor behind home plate sold popcorn and cotton candy. Two small sets of bleachers flanked the back stop on the first and third base sides. However, most fans enjoyed the games from the grassy knoll in left field or from their cars.

The city league had several teams that played there for decades: The Emerald Club, the Paper Makers, the PAL and the Haymakers. (The Haymakers, by some local accounts, was said to be one of the first professional baseball teams in the country, dating back to the late 1800s; some claim the team was the predecessor of the New York Giants, now the San Francisco Giants.)

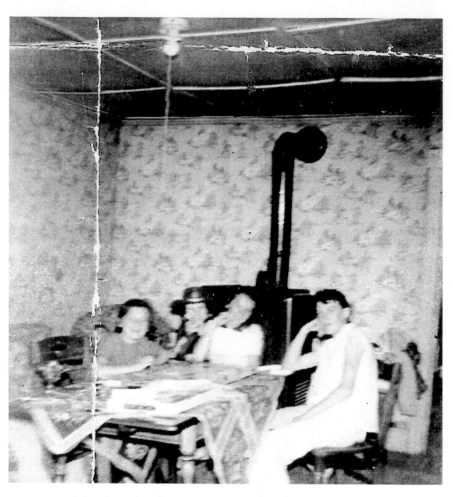

*My sister's playing Monopoly after we moved
into the Koch's house.*

CHAPTER TWENTY-ONE

Hanging out on the Corner

Before I became a "mature" youth, I'd sometimes hang out with my older buddies from the Congress Street gang: Frankie, my brother Cliff (when he wasn't in reform school), Denny, Alan, Billy Finch and a cool kid named Billy Bryce, who looked like the Fonz from TV's "Happy Days" with his slicked-back hair and D.A. He lived next door to Eddie Morris's store where we usually congregated. When I wasn't hanging out there, I spent the majority of my free time at the Boys Club.

Many of the guys bore tattoos on the top of their hands or forearms—part of the gang's initiation ritual. (I was never initiated and always remained kind of an outsider because of my young age.) Unlike Indians—where you became blood brothers by slicing your wrists and exchanging blood, these guys tattooed new members of the gang usually in the shape of a cross. They took a large sewing needle, heated it up with a lit match, dipped it in a bottle of India ink, then injected it into the skin until you bled.

Another gang ritual prohibited wearing a tee shirt with even a small hole in it. If you did and the guys spotted it, they would tear it off your back and then give you a bowzer. (Bowzers were painful welts you got when each gang member took turns hammering the soft muscle near your bent elbow with their bony knuckles.) Since most of the older guys smoked, they found great glee in the ritual of snuffing out their butts in the rolled up cuffs of their unsuspecting buddy's dungarees and giving him a hot foot.

On most days, the older guys stood in a circle bullshitting, spitting on the sidewalk and making a disgusting mess. Other times they tried to raise mucous-filled hawkers then see who could spit the furthest. Cliff always won, once hurtling one over the top of a telephone line. Yuk, it was pretty disgusting.

"Damn it, Cliff, you're the best," Billy Finch yelled after coming in second. "You got more lungers coming out of you than those poor bastards in Marshall's Sanitarium TB ward."

"Fuck you, Billy," Cliff hacked and laughed. (Little did my poor brother know, his disgusting prowess in making hawkers may have been a sad precursor to the lung cancer that would eventually take his life at age sixty-three.)

When not making a mess, the guys usually bullshitted about how to pilfer goodies from store owners they hated like Eddie Morris, who was constantly yelling at them for messing up his store front. Other times they'd bullshit about how to get laid, who had the rag on, or how they could start a gang war. I couldn't figure out what the hell "rag on" meant for the longest time. In my innocent mind, I surmised it was one of those "booby" contraptions Mrs. Pelham always hung on her clothes line. It took me several years to figure out what it really meant. You'd think, living in a house full of women, that I'd have known what that expression meant much earlier.

Aside from selling groceries, kerosene and dry goods in his dingy, store, Eddie Morris also sold vegetables kept on a display outside—potatoes, tomatoes, cucumbers, assorted cabbages and squash neatly laid out on angular wooden shelves. Eddie's second cousin worked the store with him and she was as mean and miserable as he was. The older guys laughed and called her *stinky pants*. They claimed the reason the store always smelled so bad was because that she had a rotten fish in her panties. I could never figure out why she'd do that. However, I did notice that whenever I went to the store, she did reek. The smell was like a cross between my brother Cliff's dirty socks and Limburger cheese.

I do know they did sell Limburger cheese. Tony Fermetti, who was like my fourth brother, always complained about the smell when he'd run errands for Aunt Annie Keller, a spinster who lived in the basement of Virginia Famundi's house. He loved this little old Irish lady. He'd run down to Eddie's for her and return with a pint of Fitzie's ale, along with stinky package of fresh Limburger cheese wrapped in butcher's paper. Tony would share her ale but not her Limburger cheese. Instead, he laughingly complained to Annie about how the old hag at Eddie's store smelled, usually when Annie was making herself a Limburger and onion sandwich.

"She smells like an old douche bag," Tony complained. "Even worse," Tony snickered, "she smells like that God awful sandwich you're making, Annie!"

Those offhand remarks always got a rise out of Annie. That's when she'd whack him on the arm "Stop yur malarky and respect yur elders, ya little twit. Yur gonna be old some day too, ya know."

"I know, I know." Tony said, rubbing his arm and laughing. "But, I'll never smell like her." That's when Annie would slap him again, for good measure.

Aunt Annie was one of several memorable characters who lived quietly on our street and rarely bothered anyone. These characters included Maggie O'Byrne and her brother Jiggs, who lived directly across the street from us in a tiny, asphalt shingled bungalow. They were small in stature and looked like leprechauns.

She had a round face, squinty green eyes and wore wire-rimmed glasses. Her silver hair was pulled back tightly into a neat bun. I think the bun was as big as the rest of her head. The colorful print dress she wore never changed. Neither did her white apron. Her tiny, black leather shoes were topped by white, embroidered sox.

Jiggs had a wrinkly, weathered face, and his bushy eyebrows were so long you could tie them in braids. His head was topped with a greenish felt hat that partially covered his humongous ears. His ears actually stuck out further than mine. Hard of hearing, Jiggs always carried around his trusty ear trumpet wherever he went.

No one knew what they did for a living, but I suspect they baked cookies under the old, oak tree in their back yard. Although we rarely saw them on the street, we often heard them having drunken arguments inside their house on warm summer nights. When Jiggs was working outside the house, painting or cleaning up weeds and debris, he set his ear trumpet down on his front porch. If by chance, he went into the house without it, Alan or Denny would swoop down and snag it before he came back. They then hid it under the Magano's porch, next door, usually right near Annabelle Smither's basement apartment. She was very sexy and rumored to be a tramp. Some guys even claimed they had seen her walking around her apartment naked or in sexy nightgowns.

Sometimes when they knew she was home, guys would huddle in the alcove next to her parlor window, hoping to get a sneak peek. Unfortunately, I never saw her naked, but I did fantasize about her being naked.

The guys were pretty clever when they hid Jiggs's ear trumpet. If they couldn't see Annabelle through the window, they put the trumpet right in front of her door. After ringing her door bell several times, they ran up on the Magano's front porch, directly above the alcove. There they could peer down at her when she came to the door, hoping to see her knockers. Depending on her mood, if she saw the guys gawking at her, she'd either open her bathrobe a little, flashing them, or scream and call them perverts.

Annabelle used to play mind games with the older guys—Tony, Louie Fermetti, my brother Sonny and Babe Famundi. She knew they all wanted to get in her pants. But none of them ever did.

Tony told about the time he and Annabelle were standing by Helflick's, listening to a couple who had just moved into the third floor apartment across the street. The woman was half naked in the window and threatening to call the cops. Within minutes, smoke began to drift out the window along with this woman's screeching.

Tony ran into Helflick's and called the fire department. Shortly after, a fireman escorted out a scraggly looking woman, wrapped in a blanket. Then four other firemen struggled to drag out a huge four hundred pound man, put him in an ambulance, and haul him away. Luckily the building wasn't burned to the ground. Soon after Annabelle went home, but Tony hung around with the guys until the firemen finished cleaning up the mess.

Annabelle had the uncanny ability to whistle so loud, you could hear her a block away. Suddenly, Annabelle got the guys' attention with her whistle, then waved for them to come up to her apartment. Quizzically looking at each other, they thought they were finally going to get lucky and raced up the street to meet her. Seductively waiting in her sexy nightgown, she invited them in. Once inside, she silently locked the door behind them, and then asked in a sultry voice, "Would you guys please help me clean my apartment, I'm very tired today. I'll give you all a real *treat* when you're done."

Exhilarated by her promise, and anticipating a chance to sow their wild oats, they made her apartment spotless.

However, when they finished, instead of giving them a sexual treat, she brought them each a piece of double chocolate cake she'd made earlier. "Thanks for all the help, guys," Annabelle smirked.

"Is that all we're going to get? A stinking piece of cake?" Tony whined.

"You ungrateful snot, Tony. What the hell did you think you were going to get?"

"A hand job, at least!" Tony said.

"A hand job! You pervert." Annabelle screamed at him. "What do you think I am, a whore or something?"

Dumbfounded, Tony Blurted out. "Well, Eddie Morris told us you gave good hand jobs."(There had been rumors swirling for months that she was sleeping with Eddie).

Now she was totally pissed at them and Eddie. That's when she screamed, "Get the hell out of here or I'll scream, 'Rape!' Do you hear me?"

"Jesus, Annabelle! Don't do that again. We'll leave," Tony yelled, as they rushed toward the door. While they struggled to unlock the door, she began throwing cake at them. Tony escaped unscathed. But Sonny and Babe's white tee shirts were splattered with dark chocolate before they could flee.

Tony acutely remembered the night Annabelle *did* scream rape. They were all up at St. Joseph's stealing pears. Tony accidentally brushed against Annabelle's tits while reaching for that one last pear.

Although amused at Tony's innocuous bump, Annabelle took it upon herself to really bust his and the other guys' balls. She immediately began screaming, *Rape! Rape! Rape!* at the top of her lungs. Ignoring Tony's pleas for her to stop, Annabelle raced ahead of them, flailing her arms and screaming as neighbors watched in stunned silence. When she reached the alcove by her apartment she bent over, gasping for air as she laughed her ass off.

Once back on the street, the guys had to walk past the probing eyes of their inquisitive neighbors. Although no one actually questioned them about what went on, they felt like they were unjustly accused of being sex fiends.

Tony and my brother Sonny's generation were our role models. They did a lot of the same things we ended up doing. But they never ended up in part time school or the city lock-up like some of my buddies did. They apparently got close to the line but never quite stepped over like my buddies did.

For some reason my brother's generation seemed more mature at our age. In fact, Tony, Babe and my brother Sonny were allowed to play in weekly (baseball) beer games at School 14. The games were between our fathers' team, (mine not included) and teams from the Armory Grill, Walsh's Grill and the Emerald Club. In fact, Ed Barrow let Sonny play cards and drink beer on his porch during his nightly poker games each summer. Sonny became friends and drinking buddies with Walt and Luke Howard as well as Dick Lempke.

In addition to the weekly beer games, Tony loved it when Terry Small was tending bar at Stickley's Grill. He let Tony hang out and drink even though he was underage. Although Stickley's was not a *real* restaurant, Charlie Dunson, a regular customer made spaghetti and meatballs on Sundays. It was a real treat because Charlie was a good cook. The only distasteful part of the meals was smelling Socksie O'Hare. He'd get plastered, fall asleep at the bar, then shit his pants.

Brenda and me with our first, new Easter outfits, ever!

CHAPTER TWENTY-TWO

Gangs, Fakes, and Fights

Troy was home to lots of local gangs. There was the Congress Street gang; the Ferry Street gang; and the tough Market Street gang from the Little Italy section, as well as a lesser known gang from across the river, the Watervliet gang. With movies like "The Wild Ones," "On the Waterfront," "The Asphalt Jungle" and "Rebel Without a Cause," we found new role models in actors like Marlin Brando and James Dean.

Although none of us had real guns, we did try to make zip guns out of clothes pins, rubber bands and bullets carelessly kept around the house. For some reason, my Dad always kept a clip of bullets on the table next to his bed, which I constantly played with. However, I never found a pistol in the house, and I was never able to successfully make a zip gun although I tried my damnedest. If I had succeeded, I'm sure someone would have been seriously hurt. Me!

However, we did find ways of getting knives, either buying them or stealing them from Cahill's Sporting Goods. Most were stolen. Although they weren't like the switch blades we saw in the movies, we pretended they were, snapping the partially opened blades into place and making them sound like switch blades.

Although we always aspired to be in a gang fight, I can only remember one actual gang fight when I was about six years old. Winnie had dragged me down to the Reese's house on Rock Alley one summer night to visit Mary, Frannie Reese's wife. She had taken me there to get me out of Ma's hair for a while. "Hi, Winnie," Mary said. "I see Mabel's got you babysitting Herbie again."

"I don't mind. She's not feeling well today and she always watches my girls for me. Where's Frannie and Stew?"

"I think they're over at the park near the Little's house. I guess Applehead punched out Willie, Harold's younger brother, during a card game the other day, and now there's talk of a gang fight tonight because of it."

"Oh, no, Mary! I hope not." Winnie said. "Those guys from the Market gang are pretty ruthless fighters. You remember how they broke Felton Griffin's arm with a baseball bat the last time."

"I know, but Stewie says someone's got to stick up for the guys around here or they'll take over Ferry Street, and we can't let that happen."

"Well, I hope nothing bad happens," Winnie said, sipping her coffee.

It was just getting dark when a loud commotion erupted by the park. Quickly, Winnie grabbed me and we all headed down Rock Alley towards Ferry Street. Looking toward Clay Hill at the northwest part of Prospect Park, we saw a dozen guys brandishing rakes, tire chains, baseball bats, and brooms which they had set on fire to act as torches. Young adult men and youths, silhouetted against the setting August sun, ominously poised for battle.

"Oh, my God," Mary screeched, as she heard the horrible thud of a wooden bat against someone's back followed by blood curdling screams and profanity. Within a few minutes, the wail of police sirens arose. Already Stewie's skull had been ripped open by the rake Applehead had allegedly slammed against it. He lay unconscious and bleeding, as the other combatants fled the horrendous carnage and the clutches of the law. Although we weren't close enough to actually see Stewie get whacked, we saw the aftermath as they loaded him into the ambulance, bleeding and moaning as he slowly regained consciousness. Stewie was months recovering from his injuries. Most of the other guys only suffered bruises and cuts. To the best of my knowledge, that fight was the worst and the last fight to occur in the park.

I found out years later that several other guys had seen that fight, including Frankie, Denny, Alan, Billy Finch, Pat McAvoy and Billy Bryce. They would relive that night many times over, embellishing the details with each passing year. They desperately wanted to duplicate that gang fight but were never able to pull it off. The closest they ever came to actual gang fights turned into non-lethal, humorous failures. After several years of being unable to get into a real gang fights, the guys decided to take things into their own hands one warm summer night. "I'm bored as hell tonight," whined Billy Finch.

"Me too," chimed Frankie, spitting into a pile of saliva in front of Eddie's Store.

"Hey, I got a great idea," Billy said to Charlie Coots, a new member recruited to the gang. "Let's start a fake fight. We'll scare the shit out of the neighbors and get a few laughs."

"I'd rather get into a real one," Charlie lamented, "but this could be fun." Charlie was small in stature but pound for pound, the toughest kid any of us had ever met. His reputation preceded him. His fights were legend and no one would dare challenge him. They knew that if they did, they'd have to kill him—in order to beat him.

We were soon joined by Carl Redmond, Carl Sorriento and Stevie Kloyer who just came down from watching the Haymakers up at Prospect Park.

"Hey! You got any old white shirts in your house?" Alan said to Billy Bryce.

"Yea, I do. In fact, I have a bunch of beat up ones my Grandma was going to ship off to the Salvation Army. They're in the front hall, I'll get em."

"Hey, get some ketchup while you're at it." Billy Finch chimed in. "We need fake blood." Frankie told Alan and Denny to get some stickball bats, ropes and tire chains. Alan's Dad always kept his tire chains in his front hallway. I didn't have anything to offer myself so I just stood by as the excitement began to rise.

"Hey, Herbie." Frankie yelled. "See those garbage cans up by Panache's store?"

"Yea, Frankie."

"Go take the lids off and bring them down here." Finally! Now I felt like I was part of the action, quickly returning with three beat-up, garbage can covers. Soon Denny and Alan returned with all their stuff as Billy brought out his bag of shirts. He snapped open his knife and began ripping the shirts to shreds. "Wait! Let me pour this ketchup on them before your rip any more," Frankie demanded.

Billy Finch, Carl Redmond and Alan took off their tee shirts and replaced them with the torn shards of Billy Bryce's ketchup-stained shirts. "Ok, here's the deal," Frankie said. "We go down around the bend near the projects (the Ahearn Apartments) and the Day Home. Cliff, Carl Sorriento and Charlie—you stand by the curb on this side of the street holding one of our short ropes. Stevie, Herbie and me will stand on the other side doing the same thing with our rope. When a car comes by, I'll yell, 'one, two, three' and that's when we yank on our ropes. It'll look like a chain pulled across the road and will scare the shit out of the drivers. They'll slow down as they go around the bend. That's when you guys act like you're fighting. Start banging on the garbage can lids with those bats, throw punches and swing those tire chains in the air."

It worked like a charm for about five cars. You could see the shock in the drivers' eyes as they slowed down and yelled out their windows to stop fighting. "Fuck you," Charlie, Billy Finch and Alan yelled back in unison, laughing. However, within five minutes, neighbors were screaming out the project windows at us too. That's when all hell really broke loose. We heard the sirens and saw the flashing red lights speeding toward us. It wasn't just one car, it was several, speeding from different directions, limiting our escape routes.

I thought to myself, "We're screwed."

"Oh shit!" Frankie screamed. "Get out of here, the cops are coming."

Thank God I was small and quick. I sped through the vacant lot near the bend and then down the alley that dead-ended at a wrought iron, picket fence on Eighth Street. Me and my brother Cliff raced together and he leaped over the fence, almost impaling himself. I couldn't leap the fence, but because I was small and scrawny, I was able to squeeze through the wrought iron bars to safety.

However, Billy Bryce, Frankie, Stevie and some of the others weren't as fast and had to hide under one of the many porches that lined the alley. Luckily, the cops never really pursued them. Instead, they rounded up the guys whom they had trapped with their squads, effectively shutting off their escape routes. Charlie Coots, Alan and Billy Finch got snagged by the cops and hauled off to Central Station on State Street. They got slapped around pretty good by the cops on their way to the station. The next day, after spending the night in the lock-up, they all got off with a slap on the wrist from the judge. He gave them a stern warning for disturbing the peace and being stupid. They were lucky Alan's father was politically connected, otherwise they might have ended up in reform school.

One interesting sidelight to this disaster—Billy Bryce wasn't the tough guy he made himself out to be. Frankie later mocked him, telling us how he had to slap him in the face in order to stop his whimpering while hiding under "Nutsie" Craig's back porch.

The second debacle occurred a year later over a scuffle Charlie Coots had with a Watervliet gang member at the Boys Club. Luckily, Dom Greco and Tony Fermetti broke it up before Charlie put this kid, Angelo Cusio, in the hospital. Charlie was kneeling on his chest, pounding him into oblivion by the time Dom and Tony were finally able to drag him away. News about the beating got back to Angelo's older brother Tony, who was the leader of the Watervliet gang. He vowed revenge, challenging Charlie and our gang to a fight under the Congress Street bridge the next Friday night.

When Friday arrived, I was at the Famous Lunch, devouring a half dozen tiny Greek hot-dogs, slathered in mustard, onions and their famous savory meat sauce, along with a heaping bowl of rice pudding loaded with cream. The best part of eating at the Famous Lunch? The hot dogs only cost a nickel each and the pudding fifteen cents. Luckily, I was able to pilfer enough loose change off my Dad's bedstand that night to have a little spending money. (Of course, Cliff would get blamed for it if Dad noticed any of it missing.)

Also sitting on the vinyl padded, stainless steel stools lining the narrow diner were my brother Cliff, Billy Finch, Alan Sydner and Charlie Coots. Pat McAvoy and Yummie Kiley and Bobby Vittner were sitting on the end stools near the bathroom. They had come because Frankie, Denny and Billy Bryce had begged them earlier in the week to help us out. Of course, neither Frankie, Billy or Denny were here yet. They were still hanging out at Eddie Morris's store, bullshitting. Soon the guys began to get restless and started yelling and swearing about those no good, Watervliet wops and how they were wimps who only picked on old ladies and little kids, how they couldn't stand up and fight like men and wouldn't have the guts to show up tonight.

All the noise prompted some customers to complain to the owner, Nick the Greek, that they couldn't hear the juke box. They had put their nickels into the gaudy, neon Wurlitzer a few minutes earlier and now couldn't hear "The Great Pretender," the latest hit by the Platters. Nick half-heartedly warned us to shut up but we just ignored him. That prompted those customers to leave in a huff, swearing never to return. Nick, with his hairy forearm loaded up to the elbow with hot dogs, gave them the finger as they left. We all burst into a fit of laughter. You see, we were regulars—they weren't.

As agreed to by both gangs, a messenger from the Watervliet gang was to meet us at the diner around eight o'clock to tell us exactly where and when the battle would begin. Shortly after eight, a young kid about my age and height arrived. He looked scared to death and was holding a note in his trembling hands. However, as scared as he looked, he still managed to forcefully yell out, "Charlie Coots? Where's Charlie Coots?"

His mouth stuffed with a hot dog, Charlie looked up and immediately realized this kid was the messenger. Wiping meat sauce off his chin with his arm, Charlie rushed over to the kid and tore the note from his hand. He opened it, pushed the now terrified kid out the door, and screeched, "Tell that wop we'll be there and kick his ass!"

In the blink of an eye, this kid was gone. He looked like a blur, racing west toward the Congress Street Bridge. It was then that Charlie noticed Frankie, Billy Bryce and Denny weren't there. "Where the hell are those clowns?" Now agitated, Charlie yelled over to me. "Herbie! You're fast. Run up to Morris's store and tell those dickheads to meet us under the bridge by quarter of nine and tell em to make sure they bring the 'stuff,' too! You got it?"

"I got it, Charlie."

Boy! Did I feel important now racing up Congress Street. My heart was pounding with excitement as I neared the store and spotted them. Out of breath, I shouted, "Frankie! Charlie told me to tell you dickheads he needs you. There's going to be a fight under the bridge at nine and you gotta be there by quarter of. He said to make sure you bring the stuff."

"Oh shit," Billy whined. "I didn't think they'd go through with it."

"Dickheads?" Frankie lamented. "Well, we did promise to go. Let's get moving. Denny, grab that duffle bag."

"Ok, Frankie."

"Billy, you grab the other one."

"Uh, I got to take a leak, Frankie," said Billy.

"Well make it quick. I'll grab the bag for now. But when you catch up to us, you're gonna lug it."

"No problem, I'll be right behind you." (He never caught up. In fact, he never showed up.)

"Herbie, you stay here. We don't need a little twerp like you tagging along."

"Bullshit!" I yelled back at Frankie. "I just busted my ass running up here to tell you guys about this fight and I ain't gonna miss it."

"Damn it. Cliff's going to be pissed at me if you show up."

"I don't care if he's pissed. I'm still going."

Frustrated with my obstinacy, Frankie griped. "Well, I ain't got time to screw with you now." Soon, the three of us took off with Frankie still grumbling. "You damned well better stay out of the way! You hear me?" I just ignored him.

When we finally arrived under the bridge, the other guys were milling around and bitching. "What da futt took you so long?" Yummie complained.

"We got here as fast as we could, Yummie. We were waiting for Billy but the dickhead never showed."

"That figures," chimed Charlie. "He's a big phony."

"He is," Frankie agreed.

"Hey, what the hell is Herbie doing here, Frankie?" yelled Cliff after spotting me.

"I tried to stop him, but the little shit came anyway."

"Dammit! You better stay out of the way, Herbie, or I'll kick the crap out of you myself!" (Although he acted like he was angry, he wasn't. As my big brother, he was just concerned about my safety.)

"I will, I will." I reluctantly replied. "I just didn't want to miss seeing this fight."

"Ok. But, if things get out of hand, you get out of here quick and run home. You hear me?"

"Yea, yea, I hear you." I replied sarcastically, not wanting to take orders from my brother.

It was really getting muggy out with rain threatening at any minute. That's when Yummie grumbled. "It futtin hot out—and it's after nine. Where da futt are those stupid bathturds? I'm sweatin my ass off and I don't wanna waste anymore of my time."

"Me either," chimed in Bobby.

"Maybe they chickened out, Yummie," laughed Billy Finch.

"Them wops are cowards most of the time," Charlie sniped.

"Well, Applehead sure ain't a coward, said Pat McAvoy. "I still remember when he clobbered Stewie Reese with that rake."

"True. But, at least he's a Troy wop!" said Alan. We all laughed at that.

Suddenly, we heard the muffled roar of the impending rumble approach the bridge. Minutes later, above us the noise built to a crescendo. Then the clanging of metal against metal and the loud cursing began. That's also when we began to feel the sting from the stones they were hurling at us, as we stood just below the north edge of the bridge looking up to see who was there. We couldn't make out who it was but we definitely knew they had suckered us.

"You stupid assholes," they hollered down at us as cars screeched and horns blared. The dozen or so members of the Watervliet gang had blocked the roadway, disrupting traffic. To make things even worse, we could feel warm rain pouring down amid screams of laughter.

"Shit, it's starting to rain," Charlie complained.

"Boy, that's awful warm rain," said Cliff.

"It smells like piss to me," I offered.

The laughter coming from above grew louder the more it poured.

"Hey! Dat ain't rain," Yummie screamed. "Dem futtin guys are pissin on us."

"You no good fucks," Charlie screeched up at them. "I'm gonna kill you bastards. Fight like men, not the wop cowards you are." That's when the wail of sirens rose in the distance. "Uh, oh," Charlie yelled. "The cops are coming."

"Shit, not again," I thought, remembering what happened at the last fight.

"Scram, you guys!" Frankie yelled.

"I ain't getting caught this time," Billy screamed as he raced away.

"Me either," yelled Alan, as we all high-tailed it along the river's edge towards the Green Island Bridge. Luckily, the Watervliet cops were slower than the Troy cops and we were all able to escape.

In retrospect, I think the reason we all escaped this time was because the cops were more interested in snagging guys in the Watervliet gang than us. Apparently, they had been a thorn in the cops' sides for months. Even so, the closer we got to the end of the Green Island Bridge, the more resigned we were to our fate. We fully expected the Troy cops to be waiting for us, but they weren't.

The next morning, I overheard Ma complaining to my sisters about how Cliff's and my clothes smelled like piss. Surprisingly, she never uttered a word to either of us about it. I guess she was used to our clothes being smelly. Since we didn't have many clothes, we'd wear them for days without end. I guess they always stunk by the time she washed them. However, this time they must have smelled really, really bad.

CHAPTER TWENTY-THREE

Part of the Gang, Finally?

Because of my participation in those fights I slowly gained acceptance with the older guys. Charlie even mentioned making me a gang member after the fights but never did. Who knows? Maybe it was my age or size. All I know for sure is that if they had made me a member, I'd now be sporting a nifty tattoo on my arm and I'd be trying to figure out how the hell to get rid of it. Even though they never made me a full-fledged member, they did let me tag along more often and didn't pick on me as much. In essence, I became the gang mascot, their good-luck charm.

We hung by the train tunnel on Sixth Avenue once in a while, playing chicken with the trains heading north toward Union Station. We passed the time in a nearby field arm wrestling, playing stretch or just harassing each other. Once we heard the train whistle, we'd run toward the tunnel. Billy Finch or Stevie Kloyer then put his ear on the track. Once he felt it vibrate, we knew it was getting close, even though we couldn't see it coming around the bend. That's when we raced like hell through the tunnel, as black smoke billowed over the hill behind us.

What a rush that was! We had to get to the other side before the train entered the tunnel or risk getting hit or sucked under the wheels. You had to have perfect timing. On a few occasions some guys didn't make it in time and had to hold on for dear life to the electric cables bolted to the inside wall of the tunnel. Luckily, no one ever got killed or maimed. However, a few years earlier a young kid from South Troy almost did. He was running an errand for some railroad workers when he tripped on the tracks and was knocked unconscious. The train ran over him, amputating a leg and arm that lay draped over the tracks. He survived but was handicapped the rest of his life.

One of the other stupid things we did was steal dynamite caps from storage boxes located strategically along the track. They were used to warn engineers if there was a problem ahead. They were attached to the rails by metal straps and exploded when run over. They were about as powerful as a cherry bomb but could have ripped a finger off if handled improperly. We'd stand behind a tree or car, then throw rocks or red murphys on them.

My older buddies looked for things to keep themselves occupied during those long, hot summers days during the early 1950s. We wandered off to various local swimming holes to cool off both ourselves as well as our emerging hormones. Just outside our town was a swimming hole along the Poestenkill Creek nicknamed White Bridge, which was in the town of Brunswick and was used by local families as a summer diversion for picnics, swimming or to cool off on a hot summer night. It was just a short drive outside the city, away from the oppressive heat that permeated the city proper. It was a quiet, relaxing, family-oriented spot, an oasis of sorts for city dwellers, but without the sand dunes.

However, the restless youths in my neighborhood preferred more daring places during those hot, lazy summers, places along the Poestenkill Creek with colorful names like Snetts, Buttermilk Falls/aka 95 and Jack's Hole. The favorite spot for the guys and young nubile maidens of my neighborhood was Snetts, affectionately known as "Bare Ass Beach." Of course, the swimming holes were totally segregated, not by race, but by sex and distance.

The girls, I was told by the older experienced guys in my group, would swim naked just around the bend in the creek from where the guys swam in the buff. I was never able to verify if that was true. However, I can confirm that I did hear female giggles in the distance the few times I was there, and that several of the older guys went out on scouting expeditions through the thick woods and underbrush. I guess it was a rite of passage for guys to sneak a peek at these naked beauties while the same held true for the girls. They weren't so innocent either. They apparently sent out scouting expeditions too and could be heard giggling in the brush behind where the guys were swimming.

Who knows how many may have actually lost their virginity at these little outdoor encounters, but I would venture a guess that it was only few and far between. Early adolescence in my era was more about curiosity than actually having sex. I was pretty naive about the mechanics of sex for a long time, but once I learned the mechanics, I wanted to *become* a mechanic.

The sex thing would come at later age for most of kids of my era. I realize, of course, that there were exceptions to that notion, but most kids of my generation didn't experience sex until well into their teenage years. For me and my closest buddies, it seemed like an endless stream of clumsy blunders in an unending journey trying to lose our virginity.

One day when I was a little older, my brother Cliff, Frankie, Denny, Alan, Billy Finch, Yummie and Pat reluctantly dragged me with them up at Snetts. I quietly tagged along behind them as they meandered through the old Mount Ida Cemetery on the east side of Pawling Avenue, around Beldon's Pond then through the thick brush that secreted their tarzan swing on the south edge of the Poestenkill.

As we neared the swimming hole, Yummie started pissing and moaning about me being there. "Hey, Hydie, why da futt you gotta drag yur little, snot-nosed brudder wid ya anyway?"

Even though Cliff was pissed that I was there, he didn't like getting his balls busted by Yummie. Cliff and Yummie were about the same age and Cliff wasn't about to be mocked by anybody, including Yummie. "Go fuck yourself, you toothless fuck, Yummie! It was ok when your dumb brother Snowball tagged along with us, wasn't it?" Snowball was Yummie's kid brother, Tommy. (Why they gave Yummie and Tommy those stupid nicknames is beyond me.)

Cliff's remarks stopped Yummie in his tracks. He knew Cliff was right, and he also knew that if he popped Cliff like he wanted to, he'd be in the battle of his life. Cliff was one tough son-of-a-bitch and Yummie knew it. "Hey, Yummie, I ain't too happy about having him hanging around either." So they continued their trek with no bloodshed.

The tarzan swing was made from a thick hemp rope with a huge knot tied at the bottom. The knot was used to sit on while holding the rope as it flew out high over the creek. I was shocked when all the guys started taking off their clothes. Up at the Prospect Park pool you had to wear bathing suits, but I guess out in the wilderness they weren't needed. Cliff didn't let me swim with them that day. He told me to sit on a huge tree stump next to the creek, while the guys took turns plopping their bare asses on that coarse rope. After hopping on, they flew way above the creek, let go, then drop screaming into the creek. The bigger the scream the bigger the splash. Since I barely knew how to swim, Cliff didn't let me ride the swing like the other guys. He was very protective of me even though he hated me tagging along.

I learned later in life that after our little heterosexual excursions along the Poestenkill, Bare Ass Beach became a haven for gay sunbathers and allegedly a gathering place for sexual encounters. Rumors about homosexuality were quietly talked about back then and not part of the social discourse as it is today. Sadly, those hurtful stereotypes persisted for many years and as young boys, not knowing what to believe, we were always on our guard.

Now that I was allowed to hang out more often with the older guys, I also became an accomplice to some of their antics. In fact, I was even allowed to tag along when they snuck into some movie theaters that dotted the city. The first one I remember sneaking into was the Griswald Theater located on Third Street. It was a dumpy old theater with a balcony. The balcony had an exit door that faced the alley. The exit door was about twenty feet off the ground and emptied onto a broken, wrought iron fire escape.

In order to get to the fire escape landing, we had to shimmy up an old oak tree nearby. We then jumped from an overhanging branch onto the rusted landing. That's when Frankie would tap on the door in urban Morris Code. Within a few seconds, the guy who bought the one ticket would open the door for us. Not a bad deal, since it only cost fifteen cents. Once inside, we nestled into whatever seats we could find before the ushers caught us. We made it just in time for the cartoons—usually Tom and Jerry, Bugs Bunny or Wily E Coyote—and the start of the weekly serial that preceded the feature movie. The serial I remember was "Super Man Meets the Mole Men" and it scared the crap out of me.

We also used to sneak into Proctor's in Troy and the Lincoln Theater using similar methods. Proctor's was the largest of the grand old theaters, bigger than Proctor's in Schenectady or the Palace in Albany. It had two balconies and an immense winding walkway. On Friday night lines of people waited to get in. Proctor's proved to be much more difficult to sneak into than the other theaters as they used mostly adults as ushers. However, we were lucky enough to have one adult friend who was an usher there—Artie LeBarge.

We let him know in advance when were coming. He would then station himself next to the exit on the top balcony. It was always pitch black up there. Plus, the street lights behind the theater were always broken, so light never filtered into the theater when the door was opened. However, after several successful sneak entries, we finally got caught en masse on the metal fire-escape. We had brazenly made too much racket outside, upsetting some of the paying customers who complained to the manager.

Poor Artie got fired. We felt bad, of course, but mostly for getting caught. Undaunted, we turned our attention to a new venue.

After befriending the owner's son at the Boys Club, Billy Finch had us set our sights on sneaking into the Lincoln Theater, located directly across from Barker's Park—aka Pigeon Park.

Before sneaking into the movies, we often hung out at Pigeon Park—appropriately nicknamed for its ubiquitous pigeons and its even more ubiquitous pigeon droppings. The park was terraced with several flower and shrub beds and numerous benches dotted the park. The lower level of the park was bordered by St. Anthony's Catholic Church to the east on Fourth Street, and St. Paul's Episcopal Church to the north on State Street. Food vendors, selling peanuts and popcorn, took up residence on the Northwest corner of the park.

The focal point of the park was a large cast iron fountain. On top of the fountain stood a statue of a little boy, holding his pecker and taking a leak into the lower bowl of the fountain. I was shocked the first time I saw it, because nudity, even art-nudity, was a no-no in our house. On most days, little old Italian women and young mothers with their babies sat around this fountain, feeding the throngs of pigeons. Most of the Italian women had just gotten out of morning mass then headed to the park to socialize, gabbing in their native Italian and ogling the babies as though they were their own.

Billy Finch, Alan and I met there one Saturday. That's when Billy took a couple pennies out of his pocket, pennies he'd beaten me out of earlier pitching pennies. He handed one to Alan and they started grinding them against a large rock. "Hey! What are you guys doing?" I asked.

"We're making slugs so we can get candy out of the candy machines when we sneak in." said Billy. "If we grind them down just right, they will be the size of a dime"(the cost of candy in the machines).

"Well, you got a penny I can borrow?" I asked.

"Here's one," said Billy. "But, you have to pay me back two when you get the money."

"Ok," I said to Billy's extortion, hoping he'd forget about it later.

"What time is Seth going to let us in, Billy?" Alan asked.

"I told him we'd be there at quarter after one. The movie starts at one, but he has to take tickets first, so he can't get to the back door until then," said Billy. Just as we had finished our slugs, Billy got a brain fart to beat all brain farts. "Hey, let's snag a couple of them friggin pigeons, stuff em in our jackets, then let them out when we sneak into the movies. Ha, ha. It'll scare the shit out of them kids when they start flying around."

"Great idea!" laughed Alan.

So off we went, pigeons in tow. While we waited at the back door of the theater, the damned pigeon started scratching the shit out of me. "Jesus, Billy! He better open that door soon, or I'm letting this guy go. He's friggin killing me."

"Oh, stop your damned whining. I hear Seth now." Suddenly, the black metal door rattled open and Seth waved us in.

"Hurry! Hurry, before my old man sees I'm missing."

We raced up the stairs following Seth, tiptoeing single file across the hardwood floor in back of the screen, until we reached the stairs on the other side. A small door opened into the theater from there. After opening the door Seth whispered, "Ok, you're on your own now," as he scooted up the aisle to gales of laughter. We thought they were laughing at the cartoons. They weren't. They were laughing at us. They had seen our silhouettes on the screen as we scurried across the stage.

We raced up to the balcony, stopping briefly at the candy machines so we could use our slugs before Seth's Dad made his rounds. He was a miserable old geezer, and if any kids acted up, he wouldn't hesitate to grab them by the scruff of the neck and haul them out. If you knew he was around, you made sure you behaved.

We sat still for awhile, muffling the cooing of the pigeons, as the weekly serial came on right after the cartoons. It was one of my favorites, "Rocket Man." Every week he'd stand on the same gravelly desert road in his atomic-powered rocket suit, with his pointed metal helmet and a power dial on his chest. Once he turned that dial, the adventure began. He took off like a rocket, deftly avoiding the same telephone line he avoided the week before, then quickly traversed the same barren hills in order to save the earth from some dastardly villain. It was science fiction at its best.

Like clockwork, we could smell the putrid stench of the old man's stogie, wending its way through the theater. "Get your damned feet off the seat, you little turd, or you're outta here!" he bellowed.

"Yes, sir," came some kid's timid response. By the time he got to us, we were sitting quietly in our seats, praying the pigeons wouldn't make a racket under our coats. Luckily, they didn't. He just gave us a quick glance then headed downstairs to his office on the first floor.

"All clear," Billy whispered as he came back to his seat having made sure Seth's old man was gone. "Let em go!"

Within seconds, these dirty doves began dive-bombing the kids sitting below us, scaring the crap out of them. Soon they were pecking popcorn spilled on the floor from bags they had wrenched from the hands of those petrified kids. Frightened screams reverberated across the theater and out into the lobby. That's when we heard the office door slam shut. We knew trouble was coming.

"What the hell is going on here?" Seth's old man screamed. Soon the house lights came up, and Seth's old man saw what was happening. "Seth! How the hell did these pigeons get in here? Did you let your damned friends in again? Did you?"

"Uh, no Dad." He lied. Seth could almost see steam spewing out of his old man's ears and knowing he didn't believe a word of it.

"Hurry up, you guys!" Alan laughingly screamed, as we scurried down the stairs on the opposite side of the theater from where the old bastard was haranguing those innocent kids and his son.

Exiting safely onto Third Street, we laughed our asses off as Billy proudly took credit for pulling off this brilliant stunt. The next week at the Boys Club, Seth approached Billy. He was sporting a black eye his old man gave him for letting us sneak in.

"Thanks! I thought you guys were my friends."

"We were. But I guess we're not now, huh?" said Billy. That was the last time we ever snuck into the Lincoln. Instead, we'd wreak havoc at the Boys Club during their Friday night movies.

One Saturday during the fall, we were hanging out by Eddy's Store, making a mess and annoying customers. Angry, Eddie came out and threatened to call the cops if we didn't move. Not wanting another episode with the cops, we moved across the street to Helflick's.

Forcing us to move across the street really pissed Frankie off, so he concocted a scheme to get revenge. He sent Carl Redmond and Stevie Kloyer down to Pipe Alley, where they would circle around to Ferry Street and sneak back through the alleyway between Eddie's Store and Billy Bryce's house. From there they could peek through the store window until Eddie went into the back room. That's when they snagged as many tomatoes off Eddie's wooden vegetable stand as possible. Carl grabbed a whole bushel of tomatoes while Stevie grabbed a shirt full of potatoes. They then hightailed it up to Spy Hill, where we were waiting.

That night around dusk, we splattered Eddie's windows with the stolen tomatoes, swearing and screaming as we raced away. Later that night, we celebrated Frankie's revenge with a rustic potato roast. We dumped all the stolen potatoes into a fiery pile of dried leaves up by our basketball court. Twenty minutes later, when the smoldering embers cooled off, we pulled them out with wooden sticks. Billy Bryce then sliced each one open with his switch blade. Yum, there is nothing like the smoky aroma and taste of roasted potatoes slathered in butter on a cool autumn night.

Only one kid never really accepted me—Denny. He pretty much picked on me until he moved away in 1958. But by then, I was so used his taunting that it hardly bothered me. Besides, I started to fight back when things got out of hand with him. God forbid, if my sister Patty saw him beating me, she'd pull him off and kick the crap out of him.

I could never understand why Denny felt that way. He really seemed to admire my brother Cliff but not me. Maybe it was my age or size or just me. Maybe I just wasn't destined to be a tough guy like all the others thought they were.

Denny even made fun of me for wearing my new Little League uniform with my beat-up black sneakers. I was so proud of making the majors and getting that uniform—I think I used to sleep in it. Since Ma couldn't afford to buy the fancy rubber cleats Denny had, I was forced to wear the used Keds that the Boys Club provided.

Although Denny was a couple years older than me, we both made the major leagues that year. I was on the Emerald's Club and he was on the PAL. That was my first year in the majors, but it was Denny's second and his last playing Little League. The Armory Little League had just moved to their new field on Fifteenth Street and Boght Road, next to the Troy Armory. It was named the O'Brien-Baker Field—in honor of William J. O'Brien and Thomas Baker, men who were awarded the Medal of Honor for heroism in 1944 during the Battle of Saipan in World War II. Before then, the league played at Catholic High School's Notre Dame Field in Lansingburgh.

Early one evening I was proudly showing off my new duds to anyone who'd notice. I felt so proud, tossing that ball up in the air under the streetlight. That's when Denny spotted me and decided to bust my balls. "Hey, scurvy Herbie! What ya doing? Showing off?" he sarcastically yelled.

"No! I'm just practicing," I lied.

"Bullshit!" he screamed back at me. "You're just showing off because you finally got a uniform. You shouldn't have made the majors in the first place because you stink." That remark really hurt my feelings. I knew I deserved to make the majors, no matter what he said. Not letting up on the insults he continued, "Boy, do you look stupid in those ugly sneaks. Why don't you get a pair of spikes like mine?"

Hurt and insulted, plus knowing Ma could never afford to buy me a pair, I yelled back at him, "I don't need those stupid spikes. Besides, I can run faster than you ever could—even in your stupid spikes and you know it." (In my heart I really wished that I did have a pair of those spikes, because they looked like the ones the Dodgers always wore.)

I guess that really pissed Denny off because he immediately raced over, grabbed me by my new jersey, and started shaking me. He then punched me in the arm and yelled, "Don't you ever say you're better or faster than me, you little dickhead." He then put me in a vice-like, head lock, knocking my cap and glove to the ground.

"Let go, Denny! You're hurting me," I screamed, trying to pull away before he could punch me in the nose. The harder I tried to pull away, the harder he squeezed. Realizing I wasn't going to be able to get free and not wanting another bloody nose, I did something drastic. I hauled off and whacked him in the nuts, as hard as I could, causing him to gasp for air as he released me from his painful headlock. He tumbled to the ground, doubled up in pain, screeching. "Ouch! Ouch! Ouch! You little prick. I'm going to kill you."

I realized I'd better skedaddle, quick, before he recovered. Gathering my stuff, I raced for home. However, within seconds, I could hear Denny's thunderous hoofs behind me, swearing louder the closer he got. I threw open the bottom door to our house, then raced up to the first landing with Denny in hot pursuit. Just as I started up the second set of stairs, he grabbed my leg and started punching me in the back as I tried kicking him away, all the while screaming for Ma.

"Ma, help me, help me." I briefly managed to free my leg from his grasp and headed further up the stairs. Just as I was about to reach the top landing, he grabbed me again and started punching as hard as he could. "I'm going to kill you, you little fucker!" Suddenly, the door burst open and out ran Patty and Ma, screaming at Denny to let me go. Ma then began kicking at his hands as Patty pounced on his back and started pummeling him, harder than he was pummeling me.

"Stop it, stop it!" Denny pleaded as he pulled away and tumbled down the stairs, landing in a heap. "He punched me in the nuts, he punched me in the nuts!" Denny whined.

"I don't care what he did," Ma screamed. "Leave him alone and don't ever come here again." That's when Patty took his cap, rolled it into a ball and threw it at him.

That was the last time Denny ever picked on me. But that episode also made me acutely aware of the fact that we were poor. Being insulted because of those beat up old sneakers really hit home to me. Although I had been sensing for several years that our family was different because we didn't have the things other kids had, I tried to ignore it. However, after this last incident with Denny, I realized that I didn't want to be poor. I wanted the same things he and other kids had and that Ma couldn't provide. I developed a growing awareness and sensitivity to our plight as a family and felt the stigma poverty imposed on us. It hurt. I also began to realize that times and attitudes were rapidly changing, even in our neighborhood.

CHAPTER TWENTY-FOUR

I Guess We Are Poor

A few years earlier my sister Dorothy dragged me and my younger sisters down to the Salvation Army for their annual Christmas party. I think Cliff was away at Vanderhyden Hall that year and Patty refused to go. This was the first and only time I remember us going to that party. Apparently, this was one of the bleakest Christmases we ever had, because Dad had not gotten much work, and when he did, he drank away most of the money. Plus, Grandma and Grandpa Davenport were in a financial crisis. Sales had slowed and they didn't have much extra money that year. (I learned later that my grandparents were the ones who always made sure we had Christmas gifts under the tree. They were our "Santa and Mrs. Claus.")

Ma was silently crying at the kitchen table that day because things had gotten so bad. She knew we wouldn't have any gifts under the tree. "What's the matter, Ma?" I asked innocently.

Looking up at me with tears running down her cheeks, she smiled, then hugged me and said, "Oh it's nothing, honey, I'm just feeling the blues. I'm ok now." With that she wiped her eyes with her dish towel and went back to drying the dishes.

An hour later, Dorothy came into the parlor where we were playing and told us all to make sure we were dressed. "Why?" Patty complained.

"Because Ma said we all just got invited to a Christmas party down at the Salvation Army, and Santa is going to be there." Ma had been getting invitations for several years now but never sent us, because that would be an admission that we were poor and that she couldn't provide us a proper Christmas. However, this year was different. She was desperate and truly believed that going to this year's party would be our Christmas, providing us the only presents we'd get.

"Really," Brenda said gleefully. She loved parties and loved to dress up, while the thought of seeing Santa Claus sent chills of excitement up my spine. "Can we get dressed up special?" Brenda asked Dorothy.

"Nope. Just wear what you have on. It's going to start in about a half hour, so we got to get moving, get your coats on, now!" Of course, we didn't have many special clothes. Come to find out, most of our "new" clothes were actually used clothes from the Salvation Army. As kids, we could have cared less where we got them, because they were always new to us.

"Well, I'm not going!" Patty sniped. "I don't want to be with all them kids. I don't want to be like them." Dorothy didn't want to argue with her because she knew time was running close. Patty stayed home in her room that day.

We soon began the long trek down the RPI Approach to Broadway, making sure we stayed on the opposite side of the street from Gaynor's Gay spot. At Fourth Street and the Post Office, we turned north into the freezing cold winds and snow flurries that were buffeting the city that brutal December day. Just north of Fulton Street, Dorothy ordered us to stand behind a group of grungy looking kids, dressed in tattered clothes like ours. They had been waiting patiently for the door to open.

We shivered in the freezing cold for about fifteen minutes, when a volunteer finally opened the door. She counted each laughing kid as they raced gleefully past her and up the creaky wooden stairs. As Dorothy reached the front of the line, the volunteer said regretfully, "I'm sorry, I think we're full up."

I know this poor girl must have felt terrible seeing the sadness in Dorothy's eyes and us little kids shivering behind her. With tears welling in her eyes, Dorothy pleaded, "Can you please see if you can find room for us? My little brother and sisters have been standing in the cold for a long time, and they haven't had real meal in days."

That was true. We had been eating watered-down pea soup and stale bread for the past week. Ma made the soup from a leftover ham-bone and a bag of dried green peas Winnie had given her the week before. She knew Ma had nothing left to eat in the house. Being the proud woman she was, Ma refused to add to the tab at Harry's. She was embarrassed because she couldn't pay him what she promised. She had been hoping that Dad would soon be home with some money. But he never came. He'd already been away for a week, supposedly cutting Christmas trees with Frank Lanquid. In past years, he'd sell them from an old ice fishing shanty he kept illegally on a vacant corner lot behind Helflick's.

Sensing our disappointment, the girl said to Dorothy, "Let me check and see if we can fit you in." She disappeared for what seemed an eternity as we continued to shiver in the cold. Just as we were about to leave, she returned to the door smiling. "We do have room. Quick, come in out of the cold and warm up."

With tears of joy, Dorothy replied, "Thank you so much. You don't know how much this means to us." As it turns out, we were the last kids allowed into the party.

As we reached the second floor, we heard the raucous laughter of dozens of kids and saw the festive lights shining out into the darkened hall where we were standing. As we warily entered the room, smiling volunteers dressed in the soldier-like garb of the Salvation Army and Santa hats handed each of us a colorful candy cane and a small cardboard box, decorated with snowflakes, a wreath, or pictures of Frosty the Snowman with hard candy inside

On the table were bowls filled with snacks—popcorn, pretzels and leftover candy corn from Halloween. Christmas carols were playing and a huge Christmas tree stood in the corner with piles of presents underneath.

We had made it just in time because, as soon as we took our seats, the leader asked us all to stand and bow our heads as he led grace. The volunteers then began serving dinner. Of course, this turkey dinner wasn't as delicious as Ma's but it sure did fill the void in our empty stomachs. Just as we were finishing our meal, out came small dishes filled with colorful red and green Jell-O, topped with whipped cream and a cherry for dessert. That was yummy!

After all the plates were cleared away, the sound of sleigh bells were heard and in came a jolly old man about six feet tall with a fake white beard, a pillow stuffed into his bright red costume, black leather belt and shiny black boots. He was accompanied by several colorfully dressed volunteers that looked like the Keebler Cookie elves.

Each of us made our way forward to the front of the room to sit on the lap of this oversized Santa. "I'm scared," I said to Dorothy as we got closer.

"Oh, don't be afraid, Herbie. He's got a nice toy for you, I bet. You've been good, right?" Dorothy questioned with a smile on her face.

"Oh, yes, I've been good," I fibbed. Knowing that I had done a few things that might get me disqualified, I hoped Santa would overlook them. Luckily, he did. When I was forced to sit on his lap and near tears, he immediately asked me that very question. Scared to death he wouldn't give me a toy, I was unable to speak or look him in the eye. I was frozen in place.

Sensing I was petrified, he gratefully said, "I've heard from a good source that you've been pretty good this year."

That's when he handed me a wooden train with a big smoke stack, huge wooden wheels and a coal car attached to the back of the engine by a tiny metal hook. I was thrilled to death as I jumped off his lap, running back to Dorothy, my train clutched securely in my arms. That Santa was so smart. He knew exactly what I wanted for Christmas. In turn, each of my sisters received little girl dolls with colorful dresses. They were so happy to have their wishes granted, just like me. It was amazing how Santa knew exactly what each of us wanted, even this gangly Santa.

Strangely, it didn't feel quite as cold as we raced back home that afternoon, eager to show Ma what Santa had given us. We rushed into the kitchen, pushing and laughing to be the first to show Ma our goodies. She just stood there with a big smile on her face. Grateful to see us so happy, Ma hid a sense of melancholy that hung over her spirit. This was the first time I think she really doubted her worth as a mom, heartsick that we might not have food in our bellies or toys under our tree. Having to send us to that party broke her heart.

Ironically, as bad as Christmas was destined to be that year, our Grandparents did manage to help out again and brought toys and clothes for under the tree. Later that night they'd make the long trek back to Bennington, secure that Santa and Mrs. Claus didn't forget us. Dad was able to sell some Christmas trees that year, and even gave Ma money to buy a ham for Christmas dinner before he managed to piss the rest away getting plastered down at Stickley's Grill on Christmas Eve. But, at least Grandma and Grandpa were there, with Grandpa laughing and telling us jokes.

A few hours later, we all awoke to a horrible crashing sound coming from the parlor. We rushed in to find Dad laughing on the floor, the tree tipped against the parlor window. He had staggered into the parlor and fallen on the tree, knocking it partially over and breaking some of the ornaments and lights. Tinsel was strewn everywhere.

Of course, he lied to a horrified Ma about what happened, blaming our poor cat Mittens. He said he was trying to pull Mittens off the tree when he and the tree fell. Of course, Ma didn't buy his story and quietly seethed with anger, wondering how he could he do such a thing on Christmas Eve.

"Oh, I brought a case of bananas for you," he slurred, pointing to the broken cardboard box, bananas scattered across the floor.

She knew he was plastered, but with all us kids awake at one o'clock in the morning, she he didn't want a fight that would ruin our Christmas. Instead, she had us all help her straighten up the tree and put back the ornaments on our "Charlie Brown" tree.

Once we had picked up the mess of tree and bruised bananas, we spotted all the presents that had been hiding under the tree. Now realizing Santa had come, Brenda and I screamed in unison, "Santa came, Santa came!" We then rushed to find our presents. That was the earliest we ever opened our presents. Even with all the mini-disasters we encountered, that Christmas stands out as one the best I can ever remember.

As I started getting older, I began noticing things that set our family apart from others. Ma would send my sisters Dorothy and Patty and my brother Cliff up to the Troy Armory on Fifteenth Street to pick up surplus food because welfare had cut back on our monthly food allowance. They came back carrying cartons filled with surplus: powdered milk, flour, butter, oily peanut butter, orange-colored cheese, chipped beef and lard.

Patty would cynically complain, "Why do we have to get this stuff, Ma? All those people in front of us looked like dirt bags." I think Patty already realized we were poor and hated it. However, she didn't see us in the same light as them. We weren't dirt bags, even though an outsider looking at us might think so. Our clothes looked pretty ratty looking, too.

I think the difference between us and many of the other poor kids was that Ma always tried to make sure we were clean and neat, even if our clothes were a bit ragged. The exception was me and Cliff. We were a bit slovenly and lazy at times, especially when it came to bathing and changing our clothes. It seems ironic because for most of my early years, I relished the weekly bath Ma gave me in the kitchen sink.

When we were a little older, it became our responsibility to take our own baths, usually in cold water, because the hot water tank always seemed to be broken. We had to sit, often shivering, in a rust-stained, cast iron tub with claw-foot legs. Those cold water baths were always brief. When we were lucky enough to have hot water, I couldn't stay in the tub long enough. Usually my sisters would be banging on the door for me to get out so they could take their baths or whining to Ma because I had used up all the hot water. (My wife complains about that today when I take a shower.)

Me in cap and Patty standing next to my left...The other kids are all neighborhood kids dressed for Easter...we had the ratty clothes on.

CHAPTER TWENTY-FIVE

Strike up the Band

Troy played host to at least a couple of parades downtown each year. One of them was a Halloween parade, sponsored, I believe, by the City of Troy and several local merchants. It was usually held in the late afternoon or early evening the Friday before Halloween.

The other parade was sponsored by the RPI student government and several fraternities as the culmination of their Grand Marshall Week when student leaders were elected. After the results were announced at the RPI approach, the newly elected Grand Marshall would don the traditional top hat and soon after, the parade would commence downtown.

As the parade snaked its way through city streets, a huge cadre of RPI freshman in night shirts ran the gauntlet of upper classmen. This ritual signified their transition to sophomore status. Various campus fraternities joined in, decked out in various garb from togas to tuxedos. Even city kids jumped in line and marched along the parade route. Some might be lucky enough to ride in the back of a fire truck or one of the many festive or sometimes irreverent floats.

The floats were cobbled together with materials like papermâché and colorful crepe paper. Police cars led off with their lights flashing, followed by the school's marching band, with a fire truck bringing up the rear. After traversing the many archaic cobblestone streets and city squares downtown, the Grand Marshal Parade eventually wended its way up Federal Street, terminating at North Field with a huge beer party and bonfire at '86 Field.

I remember several of those beer parties quite well. I was about eight or nine years old and about five feet tall when I first tagged along with Frankie, Denny, Alan, and Billy to one of these parties. It was a grueling chore for me to plod up the tortuous granite steps from Eighth Street to the field. I usually ended up gasping for air and wheezing for several minutes because of my asthma. Thankfully, I recovered in a short period of time and joined in the festivities.

I had never experienced the exhilaration of being among a horde of young, hedonistic revelers. Although this event was sponsored by fraternities with Greek-sounding names, the aura that hovered over the celebration was more like that of Saturnalia, the week long Roman celebration of revelry and licentiousness. I heard the band blaring out "Hail, Dear Old Rensselaer" and smelled the aroma of burgers and hot dogs sizzling on the grill. It was so exciting.

Frankie, who had snuck his way up to the front of the line, grabbed a bunch of hot dogs and passed them back to us. Meanwhile, Billy had worked his way to the keg and snagged a glass of beer as a huge kid in a toga chugged two glasses of beer nearby. Frankie and Denny also snagged a beer.

However, when I reached for one, a big goon in a toga snorted "Well looky here, who wants a beer—a little urchin. You really want one, kid?"

"Yes, sir."

That's when he took a plastic cup filled with beer and said, "Here ya go, little Troylet." He threw it in my face, burning my eyes and forcing me to wince in pain. My tee shirt was now soaked in Fitzie's brew. The worst part for me? He kept laughing and joking with his friends about me. "Hey, Joe, ya think that little Troylet enjoyed his beer? Ha, ha, ha!"

I quickly regained my composure but hearing their raucous laughter pushed me over the edge. I glared up at that laughing dickhead, then kicked him in the shins as hard as I could. "Fuck you!" I yelled, as I sped off. His beer was now splattered on his face and he was doubled over in pain like I had been. He should have known better than mess with us *Troylets*. We have feelings too, ya know.

Aside from the beer parties, I had lots of good times playing up there with Butchie Grillo after school or on Saturdays during RPI's football games. On the southwest side of the quadrangle encased in concrete was a WWII era tank and a set of deactivated ack-ack guns. We pretended we were shooting down enemy planes or soldiers coming up over the hill. We also played games underneath the huge concrete and brick grandstand or raced endlessly around the cinder track surrounding the football field. Back then they would hold track and field events and cross country meets at 86 field. That field was a wonderful, magic place for us kids and served as the heart of most campus activities. It was recently closed, as RPI built a beautiful new $100,000,000 East Campus Athletic Village behind the Houston Field House, including a brand new 5,000 seat football stadium. However, 86 Field will never be forgotten.

The Halloween parade was more kid and family oriented. The reviewing stand was located in Barker Park, directly opposite the Lincoln Theater. Usually my older sister Dorothy took me and my younger sisters to see the parade. It usually started around 4pm and lasted about ninety minutes, just in time to go home for supper. This year I asked Dorothy if I could walk around by myself to see what was going on. She reluctantly said ok, but I had to meet her by St. Paul's Church after the parade.

This was one of the first times I was ever alone downtown and it was kind of a scary but exciting adventure. I meandered down to Fourth and State Street where a large, cream-colored brick building housed the telephone company. Just north of there was the majestic Proctor's Theater.

I struck up a conversation with a legless WWII veteran who was selling pencils near the telephone company. He said he felt like a beggar at times but he was forced to do it because of his handicap. I said to him, "Do you make a lot of money begging? Is it hard?" He looked up at me and said, "It ain't what I want to do, but I need the money bad."

I felt kind of bad for him with no legs and all. But when I saw kids buying balloons and kazoos from the vendors near Barker Park with money their parents had given them, I felt left out and decided I would ask people for money and see what happened. I begged for money to buy a kazoo. It was hard because most people looked at me with disdain and didn't give me a cent. But a few felt sorry for me and I got enough to buy my kazoo. Of course, Dorothy asked me how I got the kazoo and I told her some nice people gave me the money. However, I didn't tell her I begged for it.

CHAPTER TWENTY-SIX

Fourth Grade

At first, fourth grade seemed more boring than third. However, Billy Finch and I became pretty good friends that year and he helped alleviate some of that boredom. Having flunked third grade like I flunked second, he and I were able to stay together through most of grade school. He always found ways to make things interesting, in and out of class.

We had Mrs. Grantham that year, an older, matronly teacher who was nearing retirement. She was a really sweet woman who pushed our writing and math skills, but not in an aggressive manner. She reminded me of "Old Ma Perkins" whose show Ma listened to on the radio.

Having several poor kids in her class like Billy Brazier, Billy Finch and me, she was acutely aware of our plight and offered homespun advice. If she sensed one of us was having a crisis at home, she would take us aside, console us and make sure we were ok. (Those were the years before schools had child psychologists.)

I don't know if it was because of her advancing years or a health problem, but she had an uncanny ability to nod off for about ten or fifteen minutes every day, right after lunch. It was our study period, and of course with her dozing, we did little studying. Instead we'd have spit ball fights or Billy and I would sneak off to the boys' room.

Billy, who had already started smoking, knew some older boys would be hiding there smoking and hoped he could mooch a cigarette. I tagged along for the fun of it but never smoked. With my

breathing problems and the fact that I had already had some bad smoking experiences with Melvin Snee, smoking wasn't my thing. As you would expect, sucking in all that secondhand smoke wasn't a very bright thing for me to do, because I usually ended up going back to class wheezing slightly and smelling like a smoke stack.

Billy and I often walked home from school together and along the way, he'd show off his boxing prowess. Billy had a natural talent for boxing, while I didn't. He'd throw a jab and I would be forced to put up my hands to defend myself. He'd then throw another, then another, then another.

Eventually, defending myself from Billy's everyday pounding began to try my patience. I felt like I was becoming his personal punching bag. Although he never intentionally hurt me, I quickly tired of my daily whooping and soon found ways to avoid going home with him. Billy eventually became one of the best amateur boxers in the area, winning the golden gloves as a welterweight.

Billy's interest in boxing started in back of Alan Sydner's house. I vividly remember when Clyde Koch, who was a bit crazy, held boxing matches and even handed out prizes to the winners like a coke or candy bar. He set up a small ring in the dirt lot near the Day Home—pounding two-by-four stakes into the ground, then fastening clotheslines around them to simulate a boxing ring.

The unique part of these boxing matches was Clyde only had one set of boxing gloves. But being crazy and ingenious, Clyde found a way for it to work. With left over clothesline, he would tie one hand behind each boxer's back, fastening the remaining rope around their waist. In essence, they were one-handed boxers.

At first, it was hilarious watching the guys try to fight with one hand. However, standing in back of the crowd watching while the older kids took their licking, I became scared to death at the thought of having to fight. Seeing one kid after another get knocked down or their noses bloodied didn't seem like fun to me. Before I was able to slither away from danger, Clyde abruptly grabbed me by the arm.

Tying my right hand tightly behind my back, he forcefully stuffed my left hand into a smelly, sweaty glove, then pushed me under the rope and into the ring. Swearing and screaming at the top of my lungs, I used every expletive known to man.

"Let me go, Clyde, you M@&%$#, F@&#@*&, C@#&S%#+@& asshole," I screamed. My tirade didn't help as I was forced to fight Alan, one of my regular tormentors. He was two years older, several inches taller, and about thirty pounds heavier than me. I was petrified to say the least, especially since I didn't know the first thing about boxing. So, when Alan came at me, I started running around the ring with my gloved hand in front of my face trying to protect myself, as all the older kids cheered. I felt like a sacrificial lamb being thrown to the lion. When I woke up on the ground, I saw crazy Clyde holding Alan's victorious hand in the air, waving to the crowd. To this day I still don't remember that punch.

Bobby Mathers was a quirky kid whom I'd visit after school or during the summer from time to time. He was so laid back and slow moving that we nicknamed him "Speedy." He wasn't very athletic, so when I came over to visit, we usually just hung out and played checkers or cards with his sister Lilly. Bobby went through the rest of grade school with me and Billy. However, while Billy and I managed to flunk earlier grades, Bobby managed to flunk eighth grade. He ended up in my sister Brenda's class right through high school. (Sadly, I recently learned that Bobby passed away. His obituary stated that he was a good family man, volunteer and a decorated Vietnam veteran.)

I also had a very smart kid in my class that year, Tommy Howgan, whose father was an RPI professor. Tommy led to my budding interest in the RPI hockey team, which won the National Collegiate Hockey Championship in 1954 and again in 1985. Coach Ned Harkness became legendary in national hockey and lacrosse circles. His team won the national championship in lacrosse in 1952 at RPI, and three in hockey: One at RPI in 1954 and two at Cornell in 1967 and 1970.

I remember vividly all the commotion the night the team triumphantly returned to Troy with the 1954 hockey championship. The players were all loaded onto the back of fire trucks and proceeded through the city. The thunderous sounds of the truck's air horns pieced the chilly air along with the high pitch whining of their sirens. In the muted background was the school band triumphantly playing their victory song. The city, fans and local residents all reveled in that amazing feat. (My wife and I, along with about 5,000 local residents, were lucky enough to attend the 1985 Championship victory in Detroit. I was hoarse for three weeks.)

Fourth grade was also the first time I ever saw a dentist. As was the case with most poor kids, oral hygiene wasn't a priority in our house. Twice a year, the school brought in a dental hygienist to check our teeth. I dreaded the thought of having someone playing with my mouth, especially after hearing horror stories about how painful it was from other kids. Sitting in the waiting room, I heard the whirring sound of a mechanical toothbrush, along with the muffled groans of unwilling patients. Shortly after the whirring stopped, a kid emerged looking like a chipmunk, cheeks stuffed with cotton gauze. Shortly after the last kid came out, I was called in and seated in a dingy, gray dentist chair. The masked hygienist turned over a tiny hour glass and put it on the window sill, tied a bib around my neck and ordered me to open wide.

The suction hose inside my cheek felt like it was going to suck the tongue right out of my mouth. Afraid, I grabbed her hand and that's when she told me to stop acting like a baby. Forcefully prying my hand away, she soon began to prod my teeth and gums with her wretched hooks and snares. I tightly squeezed the side of my chair, praying the agony would soon end. All during this torture session, she complained about the greenish goop and tartar that coated my teeth, claiming it was because I didn't brush. She was right, I rarely brushed. The session only lasted a half hour, but it seemed like an eternity. After rinsing my bloody mouth into a round porcelain sink, the hygienist finished the session by brushing my teeth with that same whirring machine I'd heard earlier. After rinsing again, she then stuffed cotton gauze in my cheeks to stop my gums from bleeding further. Like most of the other poor kids, I was sent home with a note to see a dentist.

Eventually, the Welfare Department approved minimal dental care for our family. Prior to that, our dental care consisted of Ma pulling out our baby teeth, which we then put under our pillows for the tooth fairy and usually got a nickel for each tooth. However, if we had a bad toothache Ma would put a whole clove into the cavity to numb the pain. When I finally went to Dr. Sutter, the Welfare dentist, he told me that several of my permanent teeth were so decayed that they couldn't be filled or saved. So he pulled them, leaving empty pockets in the back of my mouth where molars used to be. Luckily, he didn't have to yank any front teeth.

Because of that horrible experience, I made sure that I brushed my teeth regularly. However, Ma wasn't so lucky and eventually had all her remaining teeth yanked out. Dr. Sutter referred her to an oral surgeon, affectionately nicknamed Dr. Ripper, who was apparently a very nice guy but freaked me out the day Ma dragged me along for her first checkup. We waited so long to see the doctor that morning that Ma admonished me for fidgeting. Apparently I was beginning to annoy people who were waiting patiently. Finally it was Ma's turn. We met a short, cross-eyed man in a gray dentist smock, wearing horn-rimmed glasses and a miner's light on his forehead. He looked like a goofy cartoon character to me. Not a comforting sight when you're awaiting surgery—a cross-eyed doctor!

He yanked out her remaining teeth and cleaned out the infected gums and bones in her mouth. Eventually he made her a set of pearly white choppers which ended up in a large, water-filled glass on her nightstand. She didn't wear them because they didn't fit and were painful. After several painful trials, she was given a new set that did fit. From that point on, Ma never went without her shiny new teeth. The only time she didn't wear them was at night, when she put them in a fizzy, Polident solution. (Ma looked so much younger and prettier with her shiny new teeth.)

That year was also filled with all kinds of adventures with my neighborhood buddies: stickball on Ferry Street, baseball in Prospect Park, hoops up the street and at the Boys Club, sleigh rides down College Avenue in the winter and sneaking into as many movie theaters as we could. Ironically, my sisters and I used cardboard box covers as sleighs because we didn't have a real one. Sometimes kids let us use their sleighs or they let us piggyback down the hill with them.

Sleigh-riding was a treacherous treat in our neighborhood. We always had a kid stationed at the bottom of the College Avenue to warn us of approaching cars. Timing, of course, was crucial in order to avoid tragedy. I can't remember the number of times kids aborted their rides by quickly turning into the vacant lot near the bottom of the hill in order to avoid a passing car or truck.

Two extreme incidents still stick in my mind. One involved me, the other involved the Kloyer brothers who lived on lower Congress Street. Stevie was keeping lookout as his older brother Leon came careening down College Avenue at breakneck speed. Just as he was approaching the intersection, a Fitzie's beer truck suddenly appeared out the blue. Spotting the truck at the last second, Stevie waved frantically, but it was too late. Disaster seemed inevitable. Leon and the truck entered the intersection at exactly the same moment. Stevie turned his head and screamed along with the rest of us at the inevitable tragedy. We fully expected to see our friend crushed to death, lying in a bloody heap under tires of that huge truck.

However, as the truck continued on, we opened our eyes to see Leon lying in a pile of deep snow against the Day Home fence, totally unscathed. Miraculously, he went directly underneath the body of the truck without being touched. As I said before, timing is crucial and this wasn't Leon's time.

That same winter, the first full winter after I got my Radio Flyer from the RPI Christmas party, I ventured down the hill just like Leon Kloyer had done a couple of weeks before. Since my sled was still very new and the handle bar grips still pretty tight, I had a difficult time steering it. My sister Patty was at the bottom watching out for cars. But just like what happened to Leon, a truck came barreling down Eighth Street as I neared the bottom. Seeing the truck at the last second, Patty screamed and waved frantically, "Turn, Herbie, turn!"

Seeing the truck out of the corner of my eye, I tried desperately to turn into the lot adjacent to the street, but the handlebars were too tight. At that point it was do or die. Out of desperation I made my fateful decision and rolled off my sled into a heap in the vacant lot. My sled wasn't so lucky. It got crushed under the wheels of a King Fuels coal truck. My brand new Radio Flyer was now a crumpled mess of wood and bent metal. The handlebars turned easily now, but everything else was wrecked. After that near disaster it was back to the cardboard box covers we'd become accustomed to.

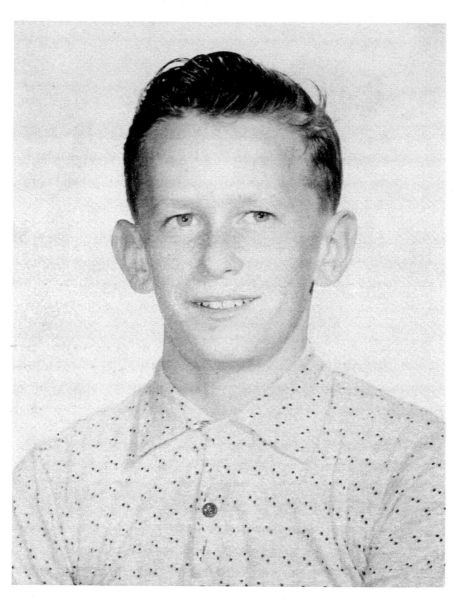

Me (Herbie) with freckles and all cleaned up.

CHAPTER TWENTY-SEVEN

Fifth Grade

I started my year in Mrs. Megan's fifth grade just fine, sitting in the first seat of the first aisle. But because I wasn't good at flash cards, I ended the year sitting in the last seat of the aisle. It seemed that Mrs. Megan punished those who were struggling by moving them back in the row if they continued making mistakes. I couldn't take the pressure of giving quick answers. My mind didn't work that fast, plus, I was easily distracted. Instead of helping struggling students like myself and Billy Finch (who ended up sitting next to me in the last seat of the second row), she devoted most of her time to the smarter kids. By the end of the year math scared me to death. Because of that fear of embarrassment, I chose not to participate much in class.

Somehow I managed to squeak by and pass math that year. However, I really didn't understand the concepts needed to progress to signed numbers, which started in the sixth grade with Ms. Mahew. Because of that fear, I never pursued advanced math courses in high school and instead opted for art, music and business courses where the math wasn't as complicated.

Billy couldn't stand fifth grade and whenever he got the chance, he skipped school, much to the dismay of his Ma and the truant officer. On a few occasions when he did make it to school, he mysteriously disappeared during the day right under Mrs. Megan's watchful eyes. She often visited with other teachers in their classrooms during quiet time in our room.

"Hey, Herbie!" Billy leaned over and whispered. "I'm outa here when she goes next door."

"Ok," I replied, unfazed by Billy's statement.

Billy was like a spider and had the uncanny ability to climb anything: trees, telephone poles, rock cliffs and, in this case, the outside of School 14. Our school had concrete ledges that wound around the entire school which was made of brick. Along with their architectural flair, they also served to separate each floor of the building. Because of the school's unique design, these ledges could actually be walked because they were fairly wide. In addition, several perpendicular wings were built out from the main part of the building. Bricks that jutted out from the main facade provided just enough space between them to allow a person to climb them like a ladder. That is, if you had the guts or were nuts enough to do it. Billy was!

Billy knew there was a vacant classroom just above ours and during lunch he snuck up to that room and unlocked the window. That way, whenever he decided to pull one of his Houdini disappearing acts, all he had to do was to climb out on the ledge, up the brick facade, push up the window and make his escape. He pulled this stunt three times, much to the dismay and amazement of Mrs. Megan. She knew he was missing but could never figure out how he disappeared or where he went.

He finally got caught when a passing motorist saw him clinging to the side of the building. Fearing Billy might get killed, the motorist stopped, ran into the school and told a flabbergasted Mr. Damnesian who raced outside and saw firsthand what Billy was doing. He didn't say a word, for fear he might startle Billy. Instead, he went back into the school, raced up to the third floor and collared Billy as soon as he stepped outside the classroom. Mr. Damnesian read Billy the riot act and then suspended him for three days as punishment. Punishment? Go figure. I guess the end justified the means. In this case Billy got what he wanted, three more days out of school.

By seventh grade, Billy would eventually be sent to a place we affectionately referred to as PTU (Part-Time-University) where he would join my brother Cliff and other school haters. It was located on the first floor of School 5. Cliff described his initiation by the older truant boys when they hung him by his shirt collar on coat hooks. He floundered around for a good ten minutes until a teacher came to his rescue. Cliff continued to flounder his way through PTU and never graduated, having served stints in Vanderheyden Hall and reform school along the way for what would be relatively modest indiscretions.

Sadly Cliff was charged for starting a fire at Prospect Park that he didn't start. The fire had gotten out of hand and almost caught several homes on fire. Although Cliff didn't start the fire, he was with Stevie Kloyer who did. Cliff was the one who got caught while the real arsonist slipped away. Cliff wouldn't rat on the other kid and ended up in reform school. Cliff was too damned loyal!

In addition to my math struggles, Mrs. Megan humiliated me one day in front of the entire class because of a fight I had outside of school with a black kid named Billy Smith, Tommy Smith's cousin. Billy lived on lower Ferry Street and was one of Mrs. Megan's favorites. Ironically, the fight started because of a girl. Go figure. It would be the only fight I'd ever have over a girl.(However, I actually did have a fight once with a neighborhood girl. That's another story.)

At the beginning of fifth grade I made friends with a pretty, blond girl named Lois Volker. I used to walk down College Avenue with her twice a week, carrying her books while she carried her clarinet case. She was taking music lessons at Miller's Music store near Proctor's Theater on Fourth Street. As it turned out, we had a few things in common. We both liked music and singing (I sang and played the harmonica with the Troy Boys Club harmonica band), we both knew Linda Bissell, her neighbor and close friend, and we were both very close to our families. We had a lot to talk about. We really hit it off but were too young to understand what a crush was.

We had been walking together for several weeks without a problem, although some kids teased us occasionally. Even my sister Patty made remarks like: "Herbie's got a girl friend, Herbie's got a girlfriend, I'm gonna tell Ma!" I picked up a stone and hurled it at her as she ran away laughing and sticking out her tongue at me. Patty knew how to bust my chops.

Lois was a special friend I could confide in. However, I didn't realize at the time that Billy Smith had a real crush on her. I found out later that he had told friends in class that he liked her, and he didn't like me carrying her books. He sat next to Lois in the front of the class and apparently was smitten. However, Lois didn't know this. Neither did I. As the weeks passed, I began to notice Billy and some of his friends walking behind us making barely audible remarks. I couldn't tell what he was saying so I ignored them.

Apparently carrying a girl's books was sort of an unspoken code that you were her boy friend. I didn't know the codes at the time but apparently, Billy did. On the day of our fight, Billy and his friends approached us. Billy said to me out of the blue, "Give me the books!"

I looked at him, confused, and said, "Why? I've been carrying them for weeks and I don't mind carrying them."

"I don't care if you mind, I want to carry her books."

That's when Andy Joules, another black kid who lived near Billy, chimed in. "Let him carry her books. He's going to be her boyfriend."

Soon, Mary McCaffrey who sat next to both Lois and Billy butted in saying, "Yea, Billy likes her. He wants to be her boyfriend so let him carry her books."

I looked at Lois, who was now totally scared and confused and said, "Do you want him to carry your books?"

She was starting to shake and meekly said to me. "I, um, don't want any trouble, I just want to go to my music lessons. Please stop arguing," she pleaded. It was then that Billy slapped my hand as he tried to pull the books away. He scratched me in the process, making my hand bleed and causing the books to tumble to the ground.

I was baffled and incensed at Billy's actions. I angrily struck back in an act of self defense, smacking Billy in the face and knocking his glasses to the ground, bending the frames. He started whimpering and whining that I hit him and broke his glasses so I yelled back. "You started it, you friggin' asshole. You cut my hand. Now, leave us alone."

That's when Mary and Andy both started badgering me that they were going to turn me in to Mrs. Megan as they helped a still whining Billy retrieve his glasses. They quickly headed toward Congress Street, screaming at me and calling me a trouble maker, insisting that I would pay for what happened.

I turned my attention back to Lois who had gathered up her books and clarinet and was heading down the hill without me. I yelled for her to wait but she walked even faster. I pleaded to her. "I'm sorry, Lois, don't be upset. It wasn't your fault." By the time I finally caught up to her front of Moore's store, she was in tears.

"I'm so upset" she said. "Now I'm afraid to walk with you anymore."

"It wasn't my fault. Billy cut my hand and I just reacted."

"I know. But I'm still afraid. I don't want to be the cause of you guys fighting."

"It's not your fault. You're my best friend, Lois. Please don't be mad at me."

With tears trickling down her cheeks she headed towards the approach and said, "Please don't follow me. I'll see you in school tomorrow." I watched her rush away as my heart sank.

I got to school early the next morning hoping to see Lois before class but she wasn't there. Apparently she was so upset about what happened that she didn't come to school that Friday. Instead of straightening things out with Lois that morning, I ended up facing an inquisition. Mrs. Megan called me to the front of the class and told me to stand there and not say a word. She lectured me about picking on kids. She related how she was told by several reliable witnesses—Billy, Mary and Andy—that I had picked a fight with Billy for no reason. (That, of course, was a lie.) She said that I had hit him and bent his glasses. (That, of course, was true.) I tried to speak in my defense but Mrs. Megan would have none of it.

Instead, she said, "You're a mean boy for doing that to poor Billy" (her pride and joy). "I'm going to send a note home to your mother about this incident and I hope she punishes you severely. I would punish you myself if I could but I can't. It didn't happen on school grounds. Otherwise I'd have you suspended for what you did." All I could do was stand there trembling in anger and shame, tears welling up in my eyes. I felt like all my classmates hated me now for something I didn't start. I was some kind of beast. I felt ashamed and humiliated more than anytime in my life with no way to defend myself. She continued to scold me, saying that I was mean and a trouble maker. I knew in my heart I wasn't. She then told me to stand out in the hall and not say a word. Everyone in school would now see me and know I was a trouble maker. I had to stand there for the entire first period, and when the sixth graders changed classes, they all pointed at me and laughed which made me feel even worse.

The next week Mrs. Megan was out sick and we had a substitute teacher for the entire week. As I slunk back into my chair that Monday morning, Lois walked over and said to me, "Linda told me what happened. I'm so sorry. Why didn't you speak up for yourself? You know Billy started it."

I looked up at her with soulful eyes and said, "I tried, Lois, but Mrs. Megan wouldn't let me say a word."

"Well, when she comes in tomorrow, I'll tell her what happened."

"Don't." I said. "The damage is already done. They got their way and she won't believe you anyway. Billy's her pet."

"Well, I'm going to tell her anyway, before I move away."

"Move away?" I was suddenly heartsick. "What do you mean, move away?"

"My dad just got a new job in Connecticut and we have to leave by this weekend. But I will be sure to tell Mrs. Megan tomorrow what happened."

"Forget about telling Mrs. Megan, she hates me and nothing will change that. I'm just so sad you're moving away. You're my best friend, ever!"

"You're mine too, and I will miss you and our little talks. I'm sure Linda will keep me up to date with how things are going." Before I could pour out my heart further, my dismay was further deepened by the annoying cackle of what sounded like an old hen.

"Ok everyone in your seats," shouted Mrs. Hector, a frumpy old lady with silver-blue hair, flowery pink dress and embroidered white collar. Her wire-rimmed glasses hung at the end of her nose, and her cheeks and double chin hung down to her collar. She looked like she had just escaped from a chicken coop or the local nursing home. Lois knew she'd better get back to her seat right away or Mrs. Hector would make her day miserable. Mrs. Hector was a retired teacher but did a lot of substituting the past several years. Glancing back as she was leaving, Lois must have sensed the depth of my sadness, knowing we might never see each other again once she moved away.

Because of her family's imminent move, she was needed to help her parents pack. Sadly, she never returned to school and I never got a chance to say good-bye. I was heartsick, overcome by a feeling of emptiness I'd never felt before. It was as though someone had died and in my young life I had yet to experience the loss of a loved one. The closest I came to feeling like this was when Harry Moore died.

It took me a long time to get over losing Lois. She was the only person who really seemed to listen to me and understood and accepted me for who I was. Although she was an only child in a loving family who lived in a middle class neighborhood, she didn't have airs about her. She had an inherent sense of the challenges that poor families faced. Although we never talked about my being poor, she knew I was and didn't ostracize me because of it. Instead, we'd talk about things we had in common. She was a great listener and empathized about how the kids on the street picked on me because I was younger and smaller than them, and because I didn't have the same "creature comforts" like new clothes, bikes, shoes, etc.

Although she didn't have any sisters or brothers, she seemed to understand how much my family suffered because of the lack of a strong father figure and how much I wanted and needed that male interaction. She had that close bond with her Dad that I lacked; I think she was keenly aware of the importance of a strong father figure in all families.

Too often, women in impoverished homes face the challenge of being both mother and father to their kids and there are usually few outside resources available to help them. From my personal experience, I saw how difficult it was for my mother raising us, basically on her own. I'm amazed how she was able to give us the love and attention we needed with her limited resources. She imbued in us a positive attitude that allowed all of us to build a better life for ourselves when we became adults.

CHAPTER TWENTY-EIGHT

Knifing and More Hard Times

Ironically, Andy Joules, the snot-nosed kid (his nose was always running) who had lied to Ms. Megan about me, turned out to be a *true* juvenile delinquent and was always causing trouble with kids both in and out of school. A couple of months after Lois moved away, I saw Andy taunting Johnny Waltham during lunch recess near Myer's corner store, located directly across the street from school.

Johnny lived a few doors up the street from Billy Finch. The day before, Johnny and Billy had been playing catch in front of Johnny's house. They stopped briefly to go into Johnny's house for a snack. That's when Billy, who kept his baseball mitt with him, thought he saw Andy scurrying away. He didn't say anything to Johnny because he wasn't sure what he had seen. However, when they came back out to play, they realized Johnny's mitt was missing.

"Where the hell's my glove?" Johnny yelped.

That's when Billy remembered what he saw. "Oh, shit, Johnny. I think I saw Andy Joules on your porch but didn't say anything because I wasn't sure it was him."

Instead of running down to his house and confronting him that night, Johnny waited to ask him about it the next day. Since Johnny didn't know Andy very well, he figured Andy would give it back once confronted. Johnny could prove the glove was his because he had secretly carved his name on the inside of the leather strap.

Johnny soon found out what a jerk and criminal Andy really was. Apparently, he had recently been on a petty larceny spree in the neighborhood, ending up in Juvenile Court several times, but each time they let him off the hook with probation. By then, I guess he thought he could get away with anything.

The next day, there was Andy, flaunting Johnny's mitt in front of his face, trying to provoke a confrontation. However, Johnny tried to avoid a fight and kept asking Andy nicely to give it back. But Andy was intent on stirring up trouble and just laughed, "Try and get it!"

Still not wanting a fight, Johnny continued pleading, "Come on Andy, give it to me, you know it's mine."

"Prove it, shit-head. If you think it's yours, try and take it from me," said Andy, arrogantly.

Now totally pissed and frustrated, Johnny angrily yelled back, "Give me the friggin' mitt, you little bastard."

Andy continued laughing as he put his other hand behind his back. Exasperated, Johnny lunged at him to retrieve his mitt and that's when I saw the swift, metallic flash of Andy's switch blade slash Johnny's face. Johnny screeched in pain, grabbing at the gash on his cheek just below his left eye. Hearing the commotion, Jimmy Myer's, the store owner, raced outside to see what happened as scores of kids scurried away screaming, mortified by the bloody assault they'd just witnessed.

In his haste to escape, Andy stupidly tossed his bloodied knife into the garbage can sitting by the storefront window, in plain view of Jimmy. Within a few minutes, the cops arrived, along with an ambulance to bring Johnny to Samaritan Hospital to get stitched up. Andy was soon apprehended and dragged down to Juvenile Court again. But this time, he didn't get off lightly. He was kicked out of school and sent to reform school for six months. From what I have been told, Andy ended up in jail several times as an adult for similar crimes. I guess he was one of those kids that could never be reformed.

The rest of the year would not be the same without Lois. However, Billy Finch made school interesting with his antics inside and outside of class, and that helped to lift the funk that had overwhelmed me with the loss of my first love. He came from a poor family too and we used to kid each other about who was poorer. I remember the day we were joking down by Harry's store with Billy's brother Dickie, trying to one-up each other. Alan and Denny, who weren't poor, were there too, taking it all in. They stood by smirking in their clean, new, pin striped shirts, corduroy pants and leather shoes. Shoes, of course, with no holes in them.

I laughingly said to Billy, "We're so poor we have to put cardboard in our shoes and sleep by the pot belly stove every night during the winter because it's freezing in our bedrooms. It's so cold that we sleep in our dirty clothes and holey socks. Plus, we have to use our coats to cover up with because Ma doesn't have enough blankets."

"Hey, Alan! That's why Dumbo stinks so much," Denny bellowed.

"Frig you, Denny!" I said, giving him the finger.

Then Billy retorted, "Big deal, Hydie! We have to do the same thing in our house."

"Don't call me Hydie! You know I hate that," I shot back in feigned anger. "Some days my Ma doesn't have anything in the house to eat but bread and butter. Since we don't have a toaster, we slap the bread on the side of our sooty stove to make toast. If we're lucky, Ma might give us some butter and sugar to put on it."

"Well," Billy chimed back, "we're so poor we can't even afford coal for our stove. Our Ma makes us toast using a lit match. Now, beat that."

"Well, I bet you at least have hot water to take a bath," I shot back. "My Ma has to heat up pots of water on our kitchen stove, when it's working, for our weekly baths. When it's not working we have to take them in icy cold water."

"You only take baths once a week, Dumbo? No wonder you smell like an elephant in the zoo," Denny guffawed, smacking Alan's arm.

Now flummoxed by Denny's snide remarks, I gave him a double finger and told him to go fuck himself which made him laugh ever harder. Alan just stood by smiling passively, taking it all in.

"Well, we're so poor we don't even have toilet paper to wipe our asses," bragged Billy as he made a subtle glance at his brother Dickie. He and Dickie shared a bed every night when not sleeping next to their stove.

With a look of bewilderment on his face Dickie asked Billy, "Well, hum—then how did you wipe your ass when you took a shit?

"I wiped it on you!" Billy shot back as we all burst out in laughter.

Poor Dickie took the brunt of Billy's joke that day. But worse still, he had also taken the brunt of an awful bike accident a couple years earlier. It happened about a year after he and I crashed turning up Eighth Street. Billy and his older brother Sonny were hassling each other over the fact that their poor Mom, whose husband had abandoned them years earlier, was always working. Sonny was pissed at her because he wanted lunch and she wasn't home. He argued that he was going to call her and demand she come home and feed him. If she didn't, he'd jump off the roof of their dilapidated house which hovered above College Avenue. Sadistically, this prank worked the first time he tried it. Now he thought he could do it again but Billy insisted she wouldn't fall for it.

When Sonny pulled this stunt the first time he made a lifelike dummy out of a shirt and pants stuffed with dirty underwear. He then made a head from a small stuffed pillow case which he attached to the body. On the head he taped his favorite Dodger's cap. When it was done, it looked like a real person from a distance.

When his Ma finally got home later that day, Sonny was hiding on the roof with his dummy. Exhausted from work, she wearily trekked up the steep stairs leading to her front porch. Just as she neared the porch, Sonny hurled his lifelike dummy over the roof, screaming to his Ma as it fell. "I told you I'd jump!"

Horrified, she screamed. "Oh, my God! Why, Sonny, why?" as the dummy thumped against the porch roof and tumbled into the thick hedge below. Desperately sobbing, she ran to what she thought was her mangled son.

"You damn fool, Ma! You actually thought I'd kill myself?" Her wretched son laughed from his roof top perch.

Now on her knees, his poor Ma sobbed. "How could you do this to me, Sonny? How could you be so cruel?"

"Well, you didn't come home and make me lunch," he blurted without remorse. "So you got what you deserved. Besides, it was only a joke." (Some joke.)

I guess he took after his father.

Billy and Sonny continued their tirade over Sonny's mean antics toward their Mom. In the meantime, Dickie was wheeling his beat-up bike nearby. Suddenly, Dickie started screaming as he sped down the hill past them. "My brakes don't work, my brakes don't work. I can't stop. Help me!"

Engrossed in their heated argument, Billy and Sonny barely managed a glance at their brother. Their debate ended, with a horrific thud in the distance and people screaming. Quickly realizing that thud may have been their little brother, they quickly raced down College Avenue, their hearts in their throats. They could now see a shattered bike and a shattered little boy lying in a pool of crimson. A crush of people hovered over poor Dickie as he lay helpless in the road, unconscious, his head ripped open.

"Oh, my God! Oh, my God," Mrs. Sydner cried out. "Call the police, call an ambulance!"

"No time, no time," Jack Schlegal, Mae Moore's son-in-law screamed back. "Call Samaritan Hospital's emergency room and tell them I'm on my way." Just as Billy and Sonny neared the scene, Jack ran by with Dickie bleeding profusely in his blood-splattered arms. He screamed to Billy, "Open the door, Billy, quick." Petrified, Billy opened the door as Jack lowered Dickie into the back seat.

Billy then jumped in beside him. Sonny quickly hopped into the passenger's seat of that old Nash Rambler. "Billy, hold this towel as tight as you can on his head and don't move it, no matter what!" Jack shouted.

"Ok," Billy replied, numb with fear. Billy, Sonny and their Mom spent five horrifying hours waiting in the hospital, praying, as doctors tried desperately to save Dickie's life. Late that evening the doctor came out and told a beleaguered Mrs. Finch that Dickie would make it.

If not for the quick reaction of Jack Schlegal, Dickie might not have survived. He had severed a major vein in his head and was almost scalped. His forehead had been torn back from the impact of his collision with the hood of a black Chrysler sedan parked on the Street. The immediate loss of consciousness and temporary amnesia allowed Dickie to heal while not suffering any permanent psychological harm.

Luckily, two years later, the only remaining testament to his near fatal accident was an ugly scar running along the length of his hairline. To this day, Billy still laughingly claims that Sonny and Dickie were both a bit wacky.

CHAPTER TWENTY-NINE

Sixth Grade

The summer before sixth grade, I took a walk to see where a new shopping center was to be built on Hoosick Street, in the same spot where the old Central Market was located. It was sunny and hot that Sunday. I surveyed all the bulldozers and back-hoes and was just about to turn back when I was whacked in the arm by a stupid looking plastic disc I had never seen before. It reminded me of a flying saucer I had seen in a movie. As I reached down to grab this silly looking contraption, two guys appeared on the top of a huge pile of top soil and yelled at me to shoot it back to them.

"What the hell is this thing?" I yelled back.

"It's a frisbee," the fat kid with a brush cut yelled back.

"Frisbee? That's a stupid name."

"Stupid name, but lots of fun," shouted a tall, skinny kid wearing horn-rimmed glasses and also sporting a brush cut. Little did I know at the time that these two guys would be lifelong friends.

"What's your name?" asked Billy, the fat kid.

"Herb. What's yours, and who is your friend?"

"I'm Billy, and this clown is Larry." Billy then whacked Larry on the arm playfully. "Where you from, Herb?"

"I live down on Eighth Street near College Avenue."

"That's quite a walk." Billy shot back. "How come you're up this way?"

"I was bored and decided to see what they were building up here. I heard they were building a shopping center and I've never seen one before."

"Yea, they are and they tore down lots of our neighbors' houses to put this stupid thing in here." Larry offered. "My Dad says that's progress."

"I don't think so if they tore down all your friends' houses for it," I said.

"But my Dad also said they paid them lots of money for their houses, so I guess it's ok."

"Hey, you want to try frisbee with us?" Billy ventured.

"Sure, but it still looks stupid to me." Boy, this frisbee game turned out to be challenging as Bill and Larry tossed and caught the disc with ease, while I could rarely touch it. There was a certain level of skill needed to play well and Bill and Larry had attained that skill. History would show that the frisbee would prosper for decades to come, especially among college and high school kids. I never fully understood its fascination and it always seemed like a sissy sport to me.

I spent a lot of time with Billy and Larry and also met another of their friends, Ronnie, who lived on Fifteenth Street. When not hanging out at Billy or Larry's house we ventured off to Beman Park where Ronnie lived to play basketball or tennis on the courts next to Samaritan Hospital. Although I didn't have a racquet, Billy and Larry let me share theirs.

It was a fun summer, and the best part was I got away from my tormentors on Eighth Street for a while, although I still hung out with them too. Just not as much. As it turned out Billy, Larry and Ronnie attended School 17 but would transfer to School 14 for sixth grade. They would become my classmates right through high school. Eventually, they replaced my "Eighth Street buddies" whose families began moving out one after the other. Our close-knit neighborhood was slowly beginning to slip away.

Sixth grade was interesting because it was the first time we were required to change classrooms for each subject. We were exposed to different teachers and teaching styles. Some were nice, others not so nice, like Ms. Mahew, our math teacher who looked like Mr.

Bluster on the Howdy Doody show. She was highly respected by her peers and the smart kids in class. However, I wasn't one of those smart kids and was terrified by her style of teaching. I didn't want to be singled out as being stupid or lazy. To her credit she did try to help me but to no avail. After the first few weeks of equations and brackets around letters, I pretty much gave up. Of course, bringing up my sister Patty the first day of class didn't help either.

"Boy, I hope you're not like your sister Patty," she carped. "She was one tough cookie to teach."

"Great," I thought to myself. "Now I'm totally screwed if I need any help." However, by the time she was done complaining, she grudgingly admitted she liked Patty's feistiness. Although she didn't suffer any fools, she did try to help me at times. But I just couldn't grasp math. Even as bad as I was, I managed to forge a D for the year.

Sixth grade would also begin the long, slow, coming-of-age process. It was a seminal time in my life and the lives of most of my new buddies who transferred in from other grade schools that year. Seminal in the sense that our minds, bodies and masculine traits were rapidly beginning to evolve as our testosterone levels increased. During this time most guys had to contend with strange new physical anomalies that seemed beyond their conscious control: their voices were beginning to change and even more uncontrollably, they began to get daily boners. Oh yes, most guys knew that the penis wasn't just for peeing anymore. They had probably innocuously played with these little gifts from God since they were toddlers. However, they never had the sense of urgency that now made their dungarees stand up like miniature tents. They'd just pop up out of the blue and without warning or provocation, usually around ten o'clock during Mrs. Doyle's social studies class. Also our homeroom teacher Mrs. Doyle was a buxom beauty who always dressed in form-fitting dresses that accented her voluptuous figure. She had black silky hair that framed her oval face, dark brown eyes and ruby red lips. Her cleavage was a magnet for our admiring eyes as well as her long supple legs ensconced in silk stockings. She was a beauty to our mesmerized eyes, especially after she'd been out drinking the night before at Callahan's Bar and Grill.

It was hilarious to see a group of guys standing in the hall after social studies class holding their books in front of their laps praying that these little anomalies would go away before they were found out. We soon learned the quickest way to get rid of an unwanted boner was a swift swat in the nuts. It became a morning ritual with Bill, Larry, me and sometimes Ronnie taking turns whacking each other lightly in the nuts or goosing each other after class, while girls like Linda Bissell were warily watching us, trying to figure out what the hell we were up to. Linda was a cute, ditzy blond in junior high, who would become a sought after hottie in high school. Eventually most of us were finally able to control the problem with will power. However, the nut whacking turned into a goosing ritual that continued through grade school.

The one guy whose anomaly seemed most out of control and who usually had the biggest tent was a black kid named Tommy Smith. He was a character, always showing up late for class, and when he did show up he'd rush through the door breathless with the flourish of an actor. We nicknamed him "Hollywood." He played his role to the hilt and got away with it because Mrs. Doyle usually got a kick out of his antics. He came up with all kinds of lame excuses for being late or not having his homework: my chauffeur got stuck in traffic, darling; I had to fix the toilet because the plumber got hit by a bus; I left my homework on the floor and our pooch crapped on it. However, if the excuse was too lame or he used it too often, she made him stand in the hall for a half hour as punishment. Part of his punishment was to keep on his ratty raincoat, scarf and ever present sun glasses. It really was punishment because it could get quite uncomfortable standing there with the temperature hovering around eighty degrees.

Our homeroom had two-piece wooden desk sets, consisting of a chair and a free standing desk with a cubbyhole to store books. There was also a pen holder on top. These desks were unlike the old fashioned one-piece metal and wood desks of earlier grades. The tops of the desks were pretty beat up from earlier students who had carved their initials or cartoon characters or stick figures into them.

A large cloakroom spanned the length of the room and had sliding wooden doors that closed to conceal our coats and boots. Some days before class started, guys would take turns hiding in the cloakroom and scaring the shit out of unsuspecting girls who went in to hang up their coats. They would jump out from behind a coat or sneak up on them when their backs were turned and grab them. They would then run off laughing. Of course, the teacher was never around when this happened. She was usually a few minutes late or came into class shortly before it began. She may have gotten up late or she may have been hung over. You could usually tell when she was hung over, because on those mornings her lipstick didn't quite match her lips, but her knockers always look perfect.

Mrs. Doyle was called out of the room one morning for a ten-minute conference. That's when Tommy leaned over to ditzy Linda and asked her if she and Cindy wanted see a magic trick.

"You know magic, Tommy?" gullible Linda asked.

"Not really, but I do have one trick I've been practicing that I think you'll like."

"You do?" Linda squealed. "What is it, what can you do?"

"Well, I can make my desk lift off the floor without using my hands.

"Really? That's impossible."

"You think that's impossible? Just watch me" Tommy bragged, as he clasped his hands behind his head and started humming the snake charmer's song, "Da,da,da,da,da...da,da...da, da, da,da,da!"

"Wow!" Linda gasped as the desk slowly started bouncing up and down as Tommy hummed.

"Oh, my God," Cindy shrieked, then whispered to Linda, "How does he do that?"

Overhearing Cindy, Tommy laughed, "It's not really magic, I just have a big pet snake in my pants."

"Agh, I hate snakes! Let me out of here" gasped Cindy, running from the room.

"Gee, Tommy," Linda said. "I'd love to see your snake some time. It's harmless, right?"

"Oh, yea, it's harmless," Tommy laughed. "Let's go into the closet and I'll show it to you. But you have to promise me you won't tell Mrs. Doyle, because we're not supposed to bring pets to school and I don't need to get into any more trouble."

"I won't. I promise."

As Tommy and Linda entered the cloakroom, Ronnie frantically waved to Billy, Larry and me to come over and watch from his ringside seat. We dashed over and peered into the darkened closet through a small section that was still open. We strained to see what was going on. That's when we heard Linda gasp.

"Oh, my God. It's huge and black. I never thought a snake would look like that."

"You want to pet it?"

"I, uh, nah, don't think so."

"You sure?"

"No, I don't think so. It's scary looking."

"Ok, then. But if you change your mind just let me know," Tommy laughed.

"Ok," Linda blurted as she quickly pried opened the partially closed door and we tripped over each other racing back to our seats before she caught us.

We were all laughing our asses off as Tommy quickly headed to the boys' room to get himself together before Mrs. Doyle got back. Minutes later, Cindy meekly returned, asking Linda if it was safe. Linda assured her it was, then told her not to say anything about it to Mrs. Doyle.

"Tommy just showed me his snake in the cloakroom."

"Was it scary?"

"Boy, was it. He wanted me to pet it, but I was too scared. But you never know, I might some other time."

Tommy came back just before Mrs. Doyle returned from her meeting and whispered to Linda, "Remember, don't say a word to Mrs. Doyle about my snake."

"I won't."

"Promise?"

"Promise."

Tommy was our hero after that episode. He knew so much more about sex and girls than all of us put together, plus he had the guts to pull off stupid stunts like the snake saga. (We learned later in high school that Linda had petted lots of snakes.)

On the first floor of our school was a huge auditorium where we held our biweekly assemblies, plays, concerts and graduation ceremonies. Several wood-framed French doors with inlaid glass panels served as the main entrance to the auditorium. The large wooden stage was flanked by two six panel wood doors and in the back of the auditorium stairs led to a large balcony. The auditorium was a separate wing of the building and had large windows on the north and south sides of the room.

Each time there was an assembly we all had to stand in line outside and wait until signaled to enter. The girls lined up in front of the boys and entered the auditorium first. Attempts to segregate boys and girls as much as possible weren't too successful. The boys constantly teased and agitated the girls whenever the hall monitor wasn't looking, evoking squeals and complaints.

One day Tommy got into line late and whispered in Ronnie's ear, "Hey, Ronnie you want to play cards?"

"How can we play cards standing here in the hall, Tommy?"

"This is a special deck, Ronnie, want to see it?"

Overhearing Tommy's remarks made all the guys ears perk up. "Hey, Tommy can we see too?" chirped Larry.

"Sure, you can all see them but keep quiet, ok?"

We all rushed to look over Tommy's shoulder as he broke out the cards. They weren't your regular cards. These cards showed naked men and women doing all kinds of interesting things—things most of us had never seen before but had heard plenty about.

"Wow! Where the hell did you get them, Tommy?" Billy shouted.

"Geez, Billy, keep it down, will ya? You're gonna get me in trouble."

"Can I get a deck too?" Billy squawked back.

"No! I stole this deck from Charlie Markan's barbershop the other day. He'd kill me if he found out I snagged them." (Charlie was a black barber who ran illegal poker games in his shop after hours. Apparently a customer had left this pornographic deck on a table and Tommy copped it before Charlie saw him.) Of course, Tommy wanted to brag about his find and share it with us guys, risking suspension if he got caught.

Hearing all the commotion Mr. Latito immediately headed over to see what was going on. Sensing imminent danger, Tommy quickly put the cards back in their box and slipped them into a nearby waste basket.

"Ok, wise guys, what's all the racket about?"

"Ah, nothing, Mr. Latito," Tommy said. "Billy was just trying to give me a bowzer."

"Stop this stupid crap, you guys. If you don't, you're going to the principal's office. You hear me?"

"Yes, sir!" We all smirked back.

"Phew, that was close" Tommy sighed, knowing he'd have been in deep shit if he got caught. "Thanks, Billy, you dickhead. You almost got me thrown out of school."

"Sorry, Tommy, I just got carried away when I saw them."

Seeing these images certainly opened our naive eyes about what goes on between men and women and served to make us even more anxious about our emerging sexuality. Prior to that, the only titillating pictures I saw were in *National Geographic* or the Montgomery Ward's catalogue with pictures of women modeling bras. When juniors in high school, Billy's brother Art showed Billy, Larry and me an old, black and white X-rated movie he found.

CHAPTER THIRTY

Harmonic Band

Playing the harmonica and singing became two of my greatest joys as a kid. I wasn't very good at first, but over time I became a pretty decent harmonica player. Because I was a boy soprano and the band's regular singers' voices had changed, I became the band's new singer. I guess all the civic and church groups got a kick out of hearing boy sopranos singing the favorite tunes like "How Much Is that Doggie in the Window," "On Top of Old Smoky," and "When Irish Eyes Are Smiling." I continued to be the band's lead singer right up when my voice changed to baritone. That's when I was unceremoniously dumped for the next boy soprano, Donny Parcimo. I continued to play right up to high school and Donny and I became pretty good friends.

One of the great things about being in the band? I'd get out of school on the days that we played for groups like Rotary Club, Kiwanis Club, Chamber of Commerce or the Masonic Temple. The Boys Club had made arrangements with the school for me to be excused during these events. It was also an opportunity to have a really good lunch or, in some cases, dinner when we played at classy places like the Hendrick Hudson Hotel, the Troy Club, Germania Hall or the Tavern, which was located directly across the street from the Hendrick Hudson Hotel on Broadway in Troy.

In fact, it was at the Tavern where I saw my first live lobster. Dozens of them were crammed into some type of aquarium case in the lobby. These prehistoric monsters had beady little eyes and huge antennas sticking out of their tiny heads. The mammoth claws they shuffled along on were tied together with rubber bands. Their long, bony bodies had dozens of furry, little legs sticking out of them, sort of like the centipedes I'd seen scurrying around our garbage can on occasion. To us kids, they looked like weird pets, put there for our amusement.

Little did we know that people actually ate these humongous creatures until we sat down for dinner that first time. When the waiters began bringing out dinner, there they were, plopped in the middle of huge white plates. They weren't moving and were now bright red and dead looking. They looked like they had a horrible sunburn.

With my eyes bugging out of my head, I looked over at Johnny Bancino, my best friend in the band, who was bug-eyed too. I whispered, "Yuk, I ain't going to eat them ugly things, are you?"

"No way! I'll puke my guts up if they force me to eat one."

Luckily, we didn't have to worry, because they soon brought us out turkey dinners, with mashed potatoes, dressing, green beans and cranberry sauce. Thank God for that. However, it was a struggle for us not to get caught staring at all those hoity-toity folks. There they were, elegantly dressed in tuxedos and evening gowns, with paper bibs wrapped around their necks, laughing out loud as they scarfed down those prehistoric aquatic arthropods.

It was hilarious watching those same folks, looking as though they might barf up their primal delicacies, when our instructor Ray Milkens began playing; he always did this routine where he'd play the harmonica with his nose. Then he would take the same harmonica, put it into his mouth and continue to play with his hands behind his back.

Having seen this routine many times ourselves and having recovered from the initial shock, Johnny and I developed our own little routine while he was playing. Behind his back, we'd pretend we were gagging. We grabbed our throats, then bent over and stuck out tongues out as if we were ready to puke. Instead we turned our backs to the audience and quietly laughed our asses off. Ray never figured out why people were laughing, and we weren't about to tell him.

Our band was actually quite good and the only of its kind in our area. We performed on the Forest Willis radio show and also on local television shows. I remember singing on the Gary Stevens show, a daily music show on WRGB in Schenectady. We also played on Home Fair, a local morning show featuring TV icon Ernie Tetrault and weatherman Howard Tupper. We also played on a Friday night television show that aired on WROW-Channel 10, now known as WTEN. The show that followed our performance featured teenagers led by crazy man Windy Knight, aka Ted Knight, who eventually landed the role of Ted Baxter on the Mary Tyler Moore Show.

I was scared out of my wits as he raced by me that night, wearing thick pancake makeup and red lipstick. All of the performers wore the same make up that enhanced their faces for black and white TV.

Ray Milken was a good-hearted man who dedicated much of his time to the band and the Boys Club for many years. Our band was invited to audition for the Ted Mack Amateur Hour. Sadly, the Club was unable to provide the funding for our trip. I believe Ray left the club because of this, especially after all the donations our band brought in over the years. Sadly the harmonica band ended because they couldn't find a replacement for Ray. Who knows what paths our lives might have taken, had we made it on that show.

In addition to singing for the Boys Club, I sang in the School 14 chorus at the urging of our new music teacher, Miss Miller. She soon became a major influence in developing my interest in music, theater and art. In fact, she even picked me to play the "Littlest Angel" while in sixth grade. Go figure, me! "The Littlest Angel." She also was instrumental in my being named to the All City Chorus. That was a real honor because only the best singers were selected to compete in regional competitions and performances at iconic concert halls. Our performance at the Troy Music Hall was the highlight of my singing career.

It was also in sixth grade that athletics began to have a serious impact on my life. It started with gym class and swimming, along with house league basketball at the Boys Club, and Little League baseball that spring.

Interest in girls also came to the forefront at that time. In fact, a new girl who transferred into my class during the middle of sixth grade piqued my interest. She was a cute, dark haired Jewish girl named Helen Overstein. I didn't really notice her until Christmas day that year. It was almost sixty degrees out and I was dying to try out my new tennis racket. Since there was little snow on the ground, and global warming had apparently just begun, I decided to trek up to Prospect Park. Now I could try out my new racquet against the green practice wall, instead of waiting until spring. I wasn't very good but I really wanted to learn how to play. Coincidentally, Helen was practicing on the opposite side of the wall. She graciously retrieved all my mis-hits and we soon struck up a conversation about tennis.

She had been playing for several years and offered to give me a few pointers. Shocked that she seemed interested in me, I foolishly took it the wrong way and thought she might be my replacement for Lois. I quickly realized she wasn't Lois, and although we talked quite awhile, it wasn't the same. We soon returned to practicing, and when she missed a shot she got flummoxed and shouted Oi-Vey! Not being Jewish, I'd never heard that expression before and thought it sounded cool. Of course, I couldn't resist using it, thinking it would impress her. Instead, it annoyed her and she yelled at me to stop. That's when I realized she was totally different from Lois.

However, she was really pretty and I was a bit smitten with her. We continued to be casual friends, even becoming dance partners during the semi-monthly square dances. But she always seemed distant when we danced. I began to feel that I was just a dupe, an interchangeable partner, someone to dance with but not socialize with. During breaks, she always walked away and talked with other kids, making me feel small and unimportant.

I remember when I told my new friend Tony Yates about her. We played basketball several days a week at the Boys Club and walked home together each night. Since we were in the nascent stage of puberty, girls were the focus of many conversations. Neither of us had ever had a real girl friend or sex, but we definitely aspired to those goals. Neither of us had ever kissed a girl yet, so we fantasized about how great it would be kissing girls we knew: Jeannie Calhoun, who lived up on Fourteenth Street, Patty Jonas who lived on lower Congress Street, and Helen who lived up on Ninth Street.

Tony loved to give people nicknames and thought up a cool one for Helen, at least we thought it was cool at the time. He knew the guys on the street often called me Scurvy Herbie or Dumbo, so once in a while he affectionately called me those names. In turn, I called him Banana Nose, because of his bulbous nose. Neither of us was offended by the other's remarks because we were friends, and we were just busting on each other. Calling each other by those names became a running joke between us.

Since Helen's last name was Overstein, Tony gave her a nickname that rhymed with her last name. The name? *Smellen, Helen, Oderstink.* We both thought it was hilarious and couldn't stop laughing. However, I made the big mistake of telling Helen about Tony's nicknaming skills. She seemed intrigued and laughed at the names we called each other. But then I stupidly mentioned that he had made up a funny name for her.

Curious about her nickname, Helen asked. "Oh, what kind of name did you pick out for me?"

"Are you sure you want to know?"

"Sure do, I bet it's a fun name."

"Well, ok. If you're sure?"

"I am, I am."

"Well, we nicknamed you *Smellen Helen Oderstink*." I laughed.

I immediately realized my major blunder, when she abruptly stormed away, yelling back at me, "Don't you ever talk to me again. You jerk!"

"It's only a joke," I pleaded. But she was having none of it and never talked to me again. I guess you can make jokes about your buddies, but you have to be very careful about other people's sensitivities, especially girls.

When I told Ma and my sisters what happened, they all looked at me like I had two heads. Ma just shook her head and scolded me. "Herbie, Herbie, Herbie! That was not a nice thing to say. You insulted her."

"But, it was only a joke, Ma. Tony always makes up joke names for people and I tried to explain to her it was just a joke."

"Well, apparently it wasn't a joke to her, was it? You better be careful how you treat other people from now on, even if you're just joking. You know how it feels when the guys call you names. Maybe they think it's just a joke too when they pick on you."

Suddenly the light went on in my head and I understood what Ma was saying. I remember how hurt I felt when guys made fun of me. Helen must have felt the same way.

During seventh grade Helen's family moved to Schenectady when her father got a new job at General Electric. Unlike Lois's move, this one didn't hurt.

As the 1950s moved along, things quickly began to change along Eighth Street, College Avenue and Congress Street. It started on Congress Street when Helflick's Market moved away. Shortly after, Sam's Barber Shop moved down to Seventh Avenue for a few years, then moved again to River Street next to Nelick's Furniture store. Sam moved because the city was stepping up its supposed building code enforcement, forcing families to move away. The domino effect was set in motion, with no safeguards to slow it down. Quickly, one after another, the small mom and pop stores and restaurants were forced to close or move away because they were losing their customer base. This ignoble period in Troy's history was like the onset of a horrible illness. This was the ugly first stage of what was heralded as *Urban Renewal*. In reality, it wasn't urban renewal, because nothing was renewed. It was the beginning of our neighborhood's decimation, bit by bit.

Troy's urban renewal would hit its low point during the 1960s, when the heart of downtown was pretty much demolished. Not receiving the promised funds and resources to redevelop properly, Troy began withering on the vine. Tearing down all those businesses created an ugly, open sore in the heart of our beautiful, historic city. That sore festered for years. To compound matters, the city found a willing developer who, like the message of a Joni Mitchell song, "paved paradise and put up a parking garage." An equally ugly Atrium never fulfilled its promise of renewal.

If the city leaders had real vision, they would have saved those buildings and restored them, using the same state and federal funds to retain the historical heart and soul of our once vibrant downtown. Troy could have remained a thriving community with a robust retail, arts and waterfront district. Instead, what we've seen for the past several decades in Troy is a tediously slow effort to do what should have been done thirty-five years ago.

Denny soon began attending LaSalle Institute and didn't hang out much in the neighborhood. However, he did stop picking on me and accepted me as a friend. Frankie Brighten and his family were the first family to move out. A new Italian family moved into their house, the Centaninis. Their son Tony was about my age and because of the ethnic connection, Tony Fermetti befriended them, taking young Tony under his wing.

A couple years later, Denny Barrow's family also moved out of the neighborhood, along with the Delechances and the Koches. The Delechances moved to the suburbs and the Koches moved to somewhere out in the boondocks, while Denny's family moved up to Lansingburgh.

Our close knit neighborhood was slowly disintegrating before my eyes. That social safety net of communal altruism began to fray. New neighbors replaced old. Although most were nice, others were not so nice. The Huberts and Klimers replaced the Barrows and the Delachances and both were nice. In fact, my future brother-in-law Andy moved down from Canada and lived with the Huberts until his marriage to my sister Patty several years later. However, others like the Crissmans were awful. They had no respect for anyone and caused nothing but trouble. One time Linda, the oldest sister, started swearing at my sister Patty and tried to block the sidewalk as Patty was running an errand for Ma. Trying to avoid an unnecessary fight, Patty decided to go down the stairs to the roadway to avoid the confrontation. That's when Linda sneaked up behind Patty and kicked her in the back when she wasn't looking and was most vulnerable. Patty collapsed onto the pavement in severe pain, her arms and legs scraped by the rough blacktop. Linda then pounced on her as she lay helpless. She tried to continue her attack, but Pete Fermetti raced over and pulled her off. He had seen the whole episode.

Ma had no choice but to file charges in Police Court against this dirt bag. However, an out-of-touch police court judge wouldn't put her in juvenile detention for her despicable attack. Instead, he gave her a strong reprimand and a suspended sentence because it was her first offense. Patty's back continued to bother her for years because of that cowardly attack.

That year I learned my Father had another side to his personality I'd never seen before. This was several years after he had taken me fishing and introduced me to his friend Frank Lanquid. Dad came home sobbing. He never cried before, so it really surprised all of us. Ma quickly went over to him and put her arm around him, comforting him. "What's the matter, Frank, what's the matter?"

"Frank's dead!" Dad sobbed.

"Oh, my God! What happened?"

"They found him in the saw mill last night, Mabel. He must have been drunk again. He tripped and fell on the conveyor belt while loading logs. He got cut in half, Mabel!" Dad screeched. "He got cut in half."

"Get in the other room, kids," Ma yelled as we gathered to see why Dad was so tormented. That was the only time, other than his mother's death, that any of us kids would feel sympathy towards Dad. It took several weeks for him to return to his normal, mean self. However, suspicion about Dad's indiscretions increased, especially since Dad spent so much time consoling Frank's widow.

Aside from the passing of my sister Bonnie's twin shortly after birth and Harry Moore's death, Frank's was the first time that death had impacted my life directly. Although I didn't like or trust Frank the one time I met him, I know my Dad did. He had a close personal as well as working relationship with him. Seeing him cry for the first time showed another side of him that I never thought existed. He almost seemed to have a caring side that was rarely, if ever, shown to us kids. The mystery of why remains, but I'll never stop trying to understand who he really was.

After Frank's horrible death, Dad soon developed new friendships with guys who hung out at Pat Cleary's place. Dad had rented a small store front that year right next door to Cleary's. He was going to make a killing selling flower arrangements. In order to accomplish this feat, he hired, I mean dragged, Patty and me downtown to help him on weekends and after school. We helped make arrangements then watched the store when things were slow so he could carouse with his new buddies. Needless to say, this venture into the flower business lasted only a few weeks. But, hanging out at Cleary's didn't.

One of his buddies became an important political figure in the city a few years later. John Buckley became head of the Department of Public Works and later city manager. He apparently took a liking to my Dad and that friendship played an important role for Dad several years later.

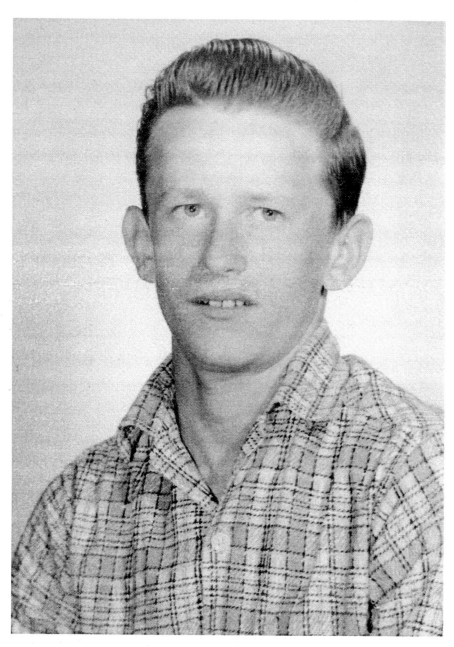

Me during my Georgia Peach Pomade phase.

CHAPTER THIRTY-ONE

Seventh Grade

When I moved on to seventh grade, by the skin of my teeth, I began to take a serious interest in science and astronomy. I became friends with Carl Redmond's brother John who was older than Carl and me, very smart, and really into astronomy. One night, he let me look at the moon through his small refractor telescope. He explained how the moon got all those craters and described how beautiful Jupiter and Saturn's rings were. Unfortunately, you couldn't see them very well through his tiny telescope, so we went to the RPI observatory where we could easily observe the planets through their large reflector telescope. Coincidentally, we ran into my new science teacher Mr. Kirby that same night. He too was an avid fan of astronomy. In fact, that night he and a professor friend of his who worked at the observatory showed us around. At dusk the huge curved doors opened that housed the large and extremely sensitive telescope. Within minutes we were looking at Mars. Shortly after, the full moon appeared over horizon, followed by Jupiter and Saturn. It was a spectacular, colorful show—almost as vivid and colorful as the one I experienced as a toddler, dangling out our front window.

From that point on Mr. Kirby took me under his wing in science class, encouraging me to excel. In fact, the "A" I got in his class was one of the few I had during grade school, except for an occasional "A" in music, art and gym.

It was also in seventh grade that I started showing an innate talent for art. I quickly gained the attention of our new art teacher

Ms. Svanzki, who had just relocated from South Carolina. She was young and had a unique southern drawl. She quickly drew the attention of all the guys in class because of her sexy accent, along with the fact that she was quite developed in the knockers department, reminiscent of Mrs. Doyle.

As would be expected, the guys all jockeyed for position in the front of the class. She often wore low cut tops and short skirts, unheard of in those days, which showed off her cleavage and long legs. It seemed like every day one of the guys managed to accidentally drop his pencil on the floor while she was sitting on the front of her desk. This necessitated her bending down to retrieve it. Guys talked about it for the rest of the day.

It took her a few days to catch on. But once she did, she started moving the guys to the back of the room. The only guy she didn't move was me. Maybe it was because I was already in the second row or I looked innocent or she liked my work. I never quite figured that out. However, she seemed to take special interest in me. Encouraging my pencil sketches, she also taught me the fundamentals of water colors, often giving me special assignments to make for class. I know it pissed off most of the guys in class, because I had such a great view and they didn't, especially when she'd lean over my desk to show me something.

I also enjoyed getting involved in school sports that year. I joined a touch football team along with Cookie Lombardo, Frankie Vumbaco, Dave Rowe, Kenny Mandelbaum and Tommy Fitch. Kenny was one of my first Jewish friends and lived on Tibbetts Avenue, a couple blocks from school. We also played on the school's basketball and baseball teams competing against other area public schools.

During seventh grade we also continued swimming classes that had begun the previous year. Swimming lessons would continue right through high school. Even though I had been to Bare Ass Beach with my brother Cliff and his buddies, I still felt uncomfortable in sixth grade having to swim naked in front of my school buddies. I wasn't the only one to feel awkward about it though, because Larry, Billy, Ronnie and Bobby Mathers felt the same way.

Of course, Mr. Latito didn't make things any easier for us. After we had undressed and showered, he yelled at us to put our towels down, stand up straight and wait in line. We then took turns dunking our feet into some antiseptic gunk before showing him the bottoms of our feet. He had to make sure we didn't have athlete's foot.

Ironically, it wasn't until seventh grade that I got used to swimming nude. It was also when I suddenly began to sprout an occasional, semi-visible, pubic hair. With no brother available to advise me about puberty, I was mystified. So each time we had swimming, I tried to inconspicuously cover my private parts, in hopes that no one would notice my emerging equipment.

Being so insecure about my changing body, I never dared to look below another naked guy's shoulders especially in the locker room, shower, or at the urinal. To this day, I still abide by that unspoken rule that most guys abide by when using a public restroom. "Never let your eyes stray, or they might think you're gay."

We had this farm kid in our class, Cal Oberton, who came from a rural district on the school bus. He was about three years older than us and had failed three grades. He stood about six-two and had thick, bushy red hair on his head and an equally thick, bushy, red pubic forest emblazoned on his private parts.

"Hey, you guys!" Billy whispered to Larry and me. "Take a look at Cal. He's hung like a mule."

"How do you know, Billy?" Larry quipped, refusing to look up. "I guess you've been out to Fairdale Farms too much, Billy, huh?" Larry laughed. That's when Billy whacked his arm, calling him an asshole and a wimp (a wimp, because Larry was frightened to death of water and swimming).

Billy, Ronnie and I stood at the other end of the pool and laughed each time Larry was forced to jump into the shallow end of the pool. He always popped up, wiping his eyes, then began waving his hands like a little girl. "Hey, what's the matter, sissy girl?" Bill yelled. "Afraid to get your hair wet?" Mr. Latito had his work cut out with us. I'm not sure if Larry ever got over his fear of water or learned how to swim.

Fashions and music began to change drastically during seventh grade. All the guys on the street began wearing pegged pants and Cordovan, baby duck shoes with horseshoe taps. They also began slicking back their hair with Georgia Peach pomade or Brill Cream, to emulate their idols like James Dean, Elvis or Buddy Holly.

Rock and Roll had emerged as the new music genre for us kids. Now sock hops replaced square dancing at the school dances. Soon, my sisters Patty and Brenda dragged me down to the YWCA to jitterbug every Monday night. I was no different than most of my buddies, except for the fact that Ma couldn't afford to buy me Cordovans or pegged pants. However, I did start turning up my collar and my lip to emulate Elvis. Before each school dance, I slathered about two pounds of pomade on my head in order to train my hair into a D/A (Duck's Ass). I wanted to look cool for the girls. It didn't seem to work though, and after each dance, Ma forced me to wash the oil slick out my hair.

I got so frustrated not having peg pants like the other guys that I tried to tailor my own. One night, unbeknown to Ma, I snuck scissors, needles and thread into my room in a vain attempt to make my own peg pants. I butchered two pairs of chinos. When I was finished, my pants looked more like pantaloons than the finely tailored pants my friends were wearing. I didn't care. They looked close enough to me. The important thing was I could barely fit my feet through the cuffs, which made my feet looked humongous—exactly the look I wanted. Ironically, my first pair of baby ducks were used ones. Alan gave me his old ones when his parents bought him a new pair. Even though they were too big for me I wore them with pride.

School flew by quickly that year. Before you knew it, it was graduation time. A major accomplishment for our family—my sister Patty would graduate from grade school. Until then, the only other siblings who made it to high school were my sister Dorothy and my brother Sonny. However, both quit for various reasons. After her sophomore year, Dorothy went to work at Montgomery Wards in Menands (*Monkey Wards*, as it was affectionately known). She wanted to be able to buy her own things and help out Ma financially as well. She wanted out of poverty.

A short time later, she met and married a guy named Art who also had a good job in New York State government. They had a son Art but soon divorced. Dorothy found out that instead of working late nights at the office, he was having an affair. That was a troubled time for her and us, since they had been living with Ma when they first got married.

Soon after her divorce, Dorothy went to work at Tiny Town Togs, where she met the real love of her life, Jim Iacketta. Jim was a rough looking guy who drove a big, Buick convertible with a suicide knob on the steering wheel. When Ma first met him, she thought he was a South Troy gangster. Nothing could be further from the truth. Jimmy turned out to be one of the nicest guys you'd ever want to meet and Ma soon learned to accept him as one of the family. Jimmy would do anything for Ma. He loved her like his own Mom. However, he was one tough cookie and very protective of Dorothy and our family. Jimmy was also divorced and his wonderful, young daughter Patty Ann became very close to Dorothy. Dorothy and Jimmy were quietly married in a civil ceremony. They had three children of their own, Jimmy, Danny and Madeline (Maddie). For over forty years, they had a close, loving relationship.

Like Dorothy, Sonny also quit in his sophomore year and enlisted in the army. I think he quit because he wanted to get away from Dad as well as poverty. In order to enlist, he forged his birth certificate and entered the military at age fifteen. In the Army he earned his high school diploma and was selected to be in the Honor Guard. Part of his duty was to guard the Tomb of the Unknown

Soldier. He also served on the security detail for Vice President Richard Nixon. Both were tremendous honors for Sonny. Ma was so proud of him.

An avid baseball fan, Nixon often attended games when the Washington Senators were at home. Sonny, being on security detail, sat next to the Vice President during those games. In fact, Sonny caught two foul balls Mickey Mantle hit; after the game, Mantle autographed them.

When Sonny returned from the service, he gave me one as a souvenir. I, of course, managed to ruin it, playing baseball against the steps. Sonny wasn't a happy camper when he found out. Hey, what did I know! Autographs weren't a big deal when I was a kid. Plus, I hated the Yankees and Mickey Mantle—I was a Brooklyn Dodger Fan.

Soon after his return, Sonny began working at Dauche's Paint Store. But, his real goal was to become a fireman, which he did a couple years later. In the meantime he started dating. A lot!

Sonny was given a room off the hallway in the Koch's house where we had moved a few years earlier. For a tall handsome guy with movie actor looks, finding women was not a problem. Ma wondered why he had so many ladies' earrings on a dish he kept on his dresser but never a matching pair.

One day, Ma began kibitzing with Kathleen and Helen Howard about the earrings. "Damn, I can't figure out why he has so many single earrings on his dresser, Helen."

"Mabel, he's a nibbler," Helen laughed. "I think when he's out on a date and things get hot and heavy, he nibbles the earring off as a souvenir. It's like a notch on his belt."

"You think so, Helen?"

"I know so, Mabel, because he went out with my daughter Diane's best friend Connie Mertins who told Diane what he did. He is a real lady's man, Mabel." Ma blushed and quickly changed the subject.

"You know what else is strange? Sometimes when he's been out on a date, the next morning he complains that his tee shirts are wet and smelly. But I know they were clean when I put them in his dresser."

"Boy, that is a strange one, Mabel," Helen coughed, puffing on her Chesterfield.

Come to find out, Sonny sleepwalked when he was drunk, and thinking he was in the bathroom, he'd open his dresser drawer and pee in it. I remember Ma laughingly recall those episodes at his wedding reception. He married a pretty Irish girl from Watervliet, Marge Halpin and they had four children Mike, Karen, Maryellen and Billy, as well as several grandkids, including a set of triplets.

Because I was in the school chorus, I had to attend my sister Patty's eighth grade graduation ceremony. I would have much rather stayed home and played stickball, if I had the chance. Ma wasn't feeling very well that day. She had been struggling with a headache most of the afternoon and Dad, of course, was among the missing. Dorothy and Kathleen had already promised to go so someone would be there to cheer her on.

"I feel bad I can't go, Patty," Ma said, with a tear in her eye. "I just don't think I can make it up the hill with this headache."

"That's ok, Ma. I know you're not up to it." So, with a sad look in her eyes and dressed in the new white dress Ma bought with the money she made selling pies, Patty headed out the door.

"Stop, Patty, wait a minute, I'll go" said Ma. "Just let me take a couple more aspirins." I guess when Ma saw Patty's forlorn look she knew she had to go, headache or not. Patty was thrilled as they all walked slowly up College Avenue for Patty's big night.

The heat was oppressive that night, which seems the norm for most June graduations. The program started with the Pledge of Allegiance, and *God Bless America*. The graduates then proceeded into the auditorium to the squeaky strains of *Pomp and Circumstance* played by the school band. After all the graduates were seated in he first two rows facing the stage, I returned from the chorus to sit next to my sisters and Ma. It didn't take me long to get bored, as speaker after speaker droned on about how great the graduates were. I couldn't wait for the ordeal to be over, so I could go home and feast on Patty's graduation cake and ice cream.

Within a few short minutes I almost dozed off. However, I was shocked back to reality when the award announcements began. Ms. Mayhew cackled, "The winner of the seventh grade mathematics award goes to Tommy Howgan."

Go figure! Tommy was the smartest kid in my class. Plus, his father was an RPI professor. But then came the *real* shocker. Ms. Svanskie bounced up on stage and immediately, all the males in the auditorium perked up, for obvious reasons.

"The winner of the seventh grade art award goes to...Herbie Hyde."

"What?" I thought, as Dorothy, Kathleen and Ma patted me on the back. I was totally dumbfounded as they pushed me toward the stage to get my award, along with a full-chested hug from Ms. Svanski. I was still so short I barely reached her chest, but I didn't mind. I don't remember which I liked best, the award or the hug.

I hoped I didn't overshadow Patty getting her diploma, because it was her night, not mine. Luckily, Patty wasn't upset. She was just glad to get it over with. She couldn't wait to get home, get out of her dress and eat her cake and ice cream. All in all, seventh grade was a memorable year.

CHAPTER THIRTY-TWO

My Family's Tumultuous Summer

Although school was fun that year, the summer? That's another story. In addition to hanging around with my neighborhood buddies that summer, I also hung out with my grade school buddies Bill, Larry and Ronnie up at Beman Park. I was finally beginning to feel like I belonged.

Everything seemed to be going along swimmingly. I played a lot of baseball and even made it to the Armory Little League all-star team. Several players became well known figures locally. Members of the team included: Tony Eates, one of my best friends at the time, (with his uncanny ability to strike a batter out with the slowest curve ball known to man), Steve Dworsky, Dick Walsh and Angelo Renna, to name a few. Dick Walsh became a well known lawyer, while Steve Dworski became a Troy political fixture for many years. I'm not sure what Angelo ended up doing.

However, from a purely sports perspective, Bobby Weaver became the most prominent and went on to play pro baseball with the Cincinnati Reds as a catcher. He made the all-star team for several years while playing for Cincinnati's minor league club, but unfortunate injuries shortened his career. He returned to the Capital District and became a well known high school basketball coach, as well as Troy's Parks and Recreation Commissioner for several years.

A left hander, Bobby was an incredible hitter for a young kid. Being a bit stout, he reminded me of Babe Ruth. During the all star games alone, Bobby averaged at least one homer per game. They weren't just dinky home runs, barely making it over the fence.

These were bombs, flying over the scoreboard in center field, in some cases almost reaching Fifteenth Street. Quite a feat for a twelve year old!

When not playing ball at night, I sometimes went skinny dipping with Charlie Coots, Frankie, Alan, Billy Finch and my brother Cliff up at the Prospect Park pool. That is, until neighbors complained to the police about the ruckus we made. Usually we loved being chased by the cops, except this one night. Usually, we had a lookout stationed on the hill to watch for cops. He'd signal us with several flashes of his flashlight, sorta like Morris code. This night, for whatever reason, we didn't have a lookout.

I squinted at the blinding searchlight of an approaching car in the distance, yelling to the guys in the pool, "Hey, there's somebody coming!"

"Oh, shit." Charlie yelled. "It's the cops, scram!" Everyone scurried to pick up their clothes, making a beeline over the side of the pool, then racing at breakneck speed down the side of the brush and poison ivy covered hill. Some desperately tried to put their clothes back on as they ran. Most, however, tumbled and stumbled all the way down the hill before the cops could catch them.

How we all escaped that night is beyond me. But we did. However, it turned out to be a tough few weeks for some guys whose asses became covered with nasty blisters from the poison ivy they slid along trying to escape. Those blisters served as a lasting reminder of their folly. Luckily, me and my brother Cliff only ended up with a few scratches and bruises, avoiding the summer long agony of the others. On the other hand, Cliff and I would soon experience an even worse agony.

It was turning dusk that early August evening, as wispy, pastel clouds of pink, yellow, and purple drifted on the horizon. Sitting peacefully on the crest of the hill near RPI's Pittsburgh building with Billy Finch, I suddenly spotted my sister Brenda racing up the hill, breathless, crying and screaming for me to come home, quick. Ma had passed out on the parlor floor.

I raced to our apartment, where Ma was now sitting in the parlor, head in her hands, crying uncontrollably. Winnie and Helen were there, desperately trying to console her. Grandpa Davenport had died earlier that evening of a massive heart attack. When Ma answered the phone, she passed out from the shock. He had died in front of my brother Jack and my sister Patty, who had been visiting Jack and his family for a few days that summer. Soon, the rest of my family arrived to comfort Ma as well as each other.

Things would definitely be different without Grandpa. No more laughter over his well worn jokes; no happy smile to greet us on our trips to visit him and Grandma Davenport. In fact, our trips became infrequent. For many summers after Grandpa's death, Grandma Davenport came to visit us for a few weeks. She was a sweet, dear woman, whom we all loved dearly. She lived into her eighties before succumbing to diabetes. Ma was not the same for a long, long time after the passing of Grandpa. She no longer seemed to have the strength and guidance he had imbued in her. But she was a tough, resilient woman who eventually regained her strength through faith and love from her children and close friends. She was our rock, even after Dad left home for good early the next year and moved into a sleazy apartment with another woman in South Troy.

Ma's heart must have been shattered that fateful day. She didn't see me watching, but I knew she was hurting. She remained strong during that torturous time, but I believe the pain she buried deep inside never went away. Amazingly, from the time he left, Ma seemed more mellow. I guess she accepted what life had given her and tried to make the best of it.

I know they still had some romance in their lives together. My bedroom was next to theirs, separated by a transom window, which they often left open for air circulation. However, along with the air circulating, the subtle, muted sounds of their love making also drifted through that open window. So why would he leave her for another woman if he was still making love to Ma? I'm not sure if the other woman was Frank Lanquid's widow or someone else. But my gut told me it was her, especially after remembering how Dad acted after Frank's death. A few years later I would meet this woman face to face, when Dad's Mother passed away from Alzheimer's at the age of eighty-six.

It was another hot summer day when we got the sad word from Uncle Paul, who was heartbroken at his Mom's passing. He was the good son, the one who cared for her all those years, even as he himself struggled with emphysema and died not many years after his Mother. Although we hadn't seen Dad in a long time, Ma knew exactly where he was living. Since Cliff was out gallivanting somewhere that night and my older sisters refused to go (they were still upset over his treatment of Ma), I was elected to give Dad the sad news. I wasn't thrilled being the messenger, but because Ma asked me, I went. Timidly, I knocked on the door in the darkened hallway. His first floor apartment was located two doors down from the Palm Tavern on Second Street. A thin woman with stringy, gray hair and sad brown eys opened the door and quietly asked what I wanted.

"I need to talk to my Dad. It's very important," I said bravely. She turned and went into the drab looking apartment. A few minutes later, a sullen Dad appeared, wearing a dingy knit undershirt and green khaki pants.

"What do you want?" he groused.

Hurt, I took a deep breath and said, "Your Ma passed away today and Uncle Paul wants you to call him." I fully expected Dad to break down like Ma had when her father died or when his friend Frank was killed. Instead, he just stood there, took a deep breath, said thanks, then closed the door in my face. I was shocked at his reaction. I silently returned home, deep in thought over what kind of man my father truly was.

When I got back home, Ma thanked me, then asked how he took the news. I told her it seemed like he didn't even care. "How can he be so cold, Ma?" I said.

"He is who he is, Herbie. He just didn't want you to see him cry. But I'm sure he did."

To this day I still can't understand his reaction to his mother's death. But, like Ma said, he is who he is. He was still my Dad and as his son I still loved him, even though he rarely acted like a father to me.

The rest of that summer consisted of hanging out at the Prospect Park pool and sneaking into Monday night wrestling at Hawkin's Stadium in Menands with Alan. He and I also snuck into what was probably one of the first Rock and Roll concerts ever held in our area. Called The Tower of Talent, it featured performers likes Connie Francis, Fabian, the Kallen Twins and the Everly Brothers.

Even with everything that happened that year, I still was earning points with my other neighborhood buddies, not just Alan. I played pickup baseball games against kids from South Troy at a place affectionately called "Pig Town." It was a tiny field located near the Poestenkill, right off Spring Avenue. Those South Troy kids were tough cookies, competitive and very proud of their neighborhood, just like us. In fact, they had their own motto that still resonates today: "*South Troy against the world.*"

In early fall, several neighborhood delinquents and I completed our final gang ritual by torching the dried brush on the northwest side of Prospect Park. Completing this last task meant that we were accepted as equal members of the Congress and Ferry Street gangs, which had melded into one gang by that time.

Ironically, my brother Sonny was one of the firefighters on duty that day. He didn't know I had a part in the fire until he saw me standing in back of the Stanton Brewery. The back of my dungarees, stained red from sliding down clay hill to avoid getting caught, was a dead give away. I watched as he and three other firemen put out the fire.

Sonny looked at me with a weary smile. "Hey, Herbie, what are you doing here?" He knew full well why I was there, having gone through the same ritual when he was my age. Sonny became a very good fireman and a union activist after he joined the Department. He was instrumental in making the Troy Uniformed Firefighters Association an effective organization. He learned quickly that being a firefighter was not the glamorous job it was cracked up to be. Shortly after becoming a firefighter, he carried several unconscious children from a burning house on Hutton Street. Someone had placed a washing machine against the back door of the apartment, making entry nearly impossible and costing precious time. Several of the children carried out of that inferno died. He now had to live a firefighter's worst nightmare for the rest of his life. I'm not sure if he ever recovered emotionally from that incident. He never once talked about that fire.

In another twist of fate, he was called to an accident scene early one fall morning, near St. Mary's Hospital. A flatbed truck had tipped over on its side with the driver trapped inside as gasoline flooded the street. The truck could have burst into flames at any moment. The picture in the *Troy Record* the next day showed an heroic fireman, my brother, reaching down through the broken cab window and pulling the driver to safety. The driver of that truck was my father.

Patty attended Troy High for three years. However, she quit in her senior year when her future husband, Andy O'Bomsawin, got her a job at Troy District Shirt Company in Cohoes. Ironically, Patty was only a few credits away from earning her diploma. But, like my sister Dorothy, she fell in love and pursued her quest of getting out of the poverty she detested as quickly as possible.

When Patty and Andy married, Ma decided she'd have a small reception for family and a few close friends at our apartment. Surprisingly, Dad was invited, and came. Patty's wedding was the only one I remember seeing him attend, officially. However, I know he attended my brother Jack's wedding because I saw him in several of the wedding pictures. I also saw him peering into St. Patrick's

Church in Watervliet when Sonny got married, even though he wasn't invited to the wedding or the reception.

Patty's wedding turned out to be a happy day for our family and one of the few times I remember my father laughing, especially when Kathleen's husband Steve got drunk, staggered, then clumsily fell through the curtain guarding Patty's old bedroom. He landed unceremoniously on the bed and snoozed for a good hour. Once awake, he started all over again.

Patty and Andy eventually had two sons, Johnny and Andy, and now have several grandchildren. Patty still laments the time when I was in high school and coerced her son Johnny into saying *shit* on the telephone to my friend Billy. Hey! He had to learn it somewhere. To this day Patty and I laugh about that incident, then she whacks me on the arm for corrupting him.

Kathleen and Steve also had several children—Steve, David, Sue and Wendy as well as several grandkids. Kathleen was so much fun to be around. When she got a bit older, she reminded me so much of Ma. I remember playing "Moon River" on the harmonica for her and Steve's twenty fifth wedding anniversary at Tironi's Restaurant. She was down to earth, honest and never resisted telling you what she thought about things. She became a cook at the Cloverleaf Tavern in Mechanicville while raising her family. (Her golumpkis were to die for.) She later found work in Waterford at the General Electric silicone plant. There she worked alongside my sister Dorothy and Jim Robinson, Brenda's husband.

Like Ma, most of my sisters became great cooks. Both Kathleen and Dorothy were loved by their coworkers for their generosity. They often brought in family specialties to share with their coworkers at the plant. Dorothy's Italian dishes were impressive and tasty, especially since she was a non-Italian, living much of her married life in the tradition laden, Little Italy section of South Troy. My sister Brenda also became a respected and skillful cook, working for both the Troy and Berlin school districts. She also cooked for parties at the Camp Woodstock. To this day she makes a great Jambalaya. Yum! My sister Patty carried on the tradition she learned at Ma's knee with her baked macaroni and cheese casserole. Mmm. I can still smell that pungent garlic. Uh, hum! I, of course, am an excellent cook too, or at least I to pretend to be. My specialty as it relates to cooking is: *EATING*.

CHAPTER THIRTY-THREE

Eighth Grade

When I finally started eighth grade after that tumultuous summer, I was determined to do better and bring my grade average above "C." I was also determined to win the art award again in eighth grade. Art had now become one of my passions and I hoped to continue it in high school. I still struggled with math, English and history, maybe because I hadn't been able to see the blackboard very well for the past couple years.

I did have a vision problem as uncovered by Ms. Mayhew, my math and homeroom teacher. Along with her teaching duties, she also had to check our vision that year. Each kid had to stand in the back of the class by the window, holding an index card over one eye. Ms. Mayhew placed a wooden pointer on various sized letters on a large eye chart. She then asked what each letter was.

When my turn came, I easily read every single letter—right down to the smallest. Thinking I passed with flying colors, I was shocked when she accused me of cheating on the eye exam and insisted I needed glasses. As it turns out, she was right. I was near-sighted and did need glasses. I apparently did cheat but never realized it. I had subconsciously memorized the chart while waiting my turn in line. However, the letters I spouted out were on different lines than the ones she was pointing to.

I made my first visit to an eye doctor as soon as I got approval from the Welfare Department. It took weeks to get an appointment, and once I got my prescription, it took most of the school year to be fitted. The glasses were ugly, clear and pink. They were girlie glasses and all poor kids, male or female, had to wear those effeminate looking spectacles.

In early March, before I got my glasses, I went to the monthly sock hop at school. Ma gave me the twenty-five cent admission, plus another quarter for a soda and cookies. I rarely danced after I lost my regular partner, Smellen Helen. In fact, I had become quite shy around girls and just sat on the sidelines looking through a haze at other kids having fun. Soon after the dance started, I thought I spotted Linda Bissel, big Jim Polechek and a blond haired girl. Big Jim was in my art class and sat next to me that year. Try as I might, I couldn't recognize the blond girl as she waved to me across the gym. But I did wave back not knowing who the heck I was waving to.

The three of them hung out on the other side of the room, laughing and joking as I squinted to make out who this person was. I think I saw her glance over a few times. Most times big Jim had her out on the dance floor, but never close enough for me to see her face. When the final waltz was announced, this beautiful, blond haired girl walked over and stood in front of me with her hands on her hips and a big smile on her pretty face. It was Lois! My heart almost leapt out of my chest. "Lois, I can't believe it's you."

"Hi, Herbie! Didn't you see me waving? I wanted to dance with you so much. Come, dance this final dance with me."

Ecstatic, I took her hand and we danced the final slow dance with her head on my shoulder. It felt so good. "I'm so sorry I didn't recognize you. My eyes are really bad, and I haven't gotten my glasses yet. I saw you come in with Linda and Jimmy and thought you were his date."

"Oh, no, Herbie, I'm not his date. Linda lives next door to him now, and because my family was in town visiting, she thought it would be fun if we all came together. I'm so glad to see you, it's been a such a long time. I miss you and I think of you often."

"I think of you too, Lois. Geez, I wish I knew it was you earlier. I would have danced with you all night."

"Well, since we didn't get a chance to dance much, why don't you come to the Knotty Pine with us. We're getting a pizza and we can talk about the fun times we used to have. Please come, please, Herbie." She pleaded, with a twinkle in her blue eyes and a warming smile on her pretty face.

My heart immediately sank! I was heartsick and began feeling that awful pang I felt when she first moved away. But there was no way I could go. I didn't have any money left and I'd feel embarrassed. Although totally heartsick, I knew I had to make up an excuse. I didn't want her to know that we were still poor, even though I knew she'd understand. So I feigned being upbeat and told her, "I want to go really, really bad Lois. But my Ma's not feeling well and I promised her I'd be home early."

Disappointed, the twinkle in Lois's eyes quickly faded, replaced by a look of sadness. However, being who she was, she sweetly said, "I understand, Herbie, I understand." I think she sensed the real reason I couldn't go. "Stay in touch, Herbie, stay in touch!" Lois said, as Linda rushed her out the door before I could get her address. That was the last time I ever saw Lois.

As the year progressed, I improved my skills in basketball and baseball. I also developed an ego I never realized I had regarding my athletic abilities. That ego would not serve me well when I got to high school.

As graduation approached, so did my anticipation of winning the eighth grade art award and all its ancillary perks. Along with concentrating on my art skills, I even put in extra effort in English and history in order to help raise my average. I was actually able to achieve that goal by getting a B+ in science and -A in art.

Finally, the big day arrived. The weather was like the previous year's ceremony: hot and humid. However, this year Ma couldn't make it up the hill, but my sisters Dorothy, Patty and Brenda did. As usual, the band bleated *Pomp and Circumstance* and the chorus sang *God Bless America*. After my obligatory stint singing in the chorus, I returned to my seat in the first row, anticipating my just rewards for another job well done in art. I would soon be engulfed by the euphoria of winning again and by Ms. Svanski's bosom.

Unlike the previous year when I almost dozed off during the awards, this year I was wide awake and bemoaned how slow the process seemed. Some unknown boy won the seventh grade math award and another unknown girl won the seventh grade art award, receiving an enthusiastic pat on the back from Ms Svanski. "Hum?" I thought to myself. "Why no hug?"

Finally, the eighth grade awards began. As expected, Tommy Howgan won for math again as well as for science. Soon the big moment was at hand as Ms. Svanski meandered back across the stage to announce the next award. Hovering over the mike, she had a smile as big as her boobs. "It is my great pleasure to announce the winner of the eighth grade art award..." My heart was now thumping with anticipation. "The winner is...Jimmy Polachek."

"What!" I thought to myself, as my heart sank and my ego shriveled. "How can this be?" I worked so hard for that award. I was near tears as my sisters came over and hugged me. They knew how much that award meant to me.

Through teary eyes I watched as lanky Jim bounded across the stage to claim his award. He towered over Ms. Svanski as she shook his hand and gave him his plaque. He quickly lumbered off the stage without the heartfelt hug I received the year before. Noting this discrepancy made me feel a bit better, but not much. Thankfully, I was able to recover in time to receive my diploma from Mrs. Nugent, who had replaced Mr. Damnesian as principal that year.

I quietly walked down College Avenue with my sisters, depressed over not receiving the art award. When I got home, there was the graduation cake and a pair of new dungarees Dorothy had bought for me as a graduation gift, but I really didn't care. What a year this turned out to be. First, I see Jimmy Polochek come to the dance with the love of my life, Lois. Then he steals *my* art award.

By the end of that school year, our neighborhood transformation was nearly complete. Families we knew for years had moved away, replaced by those who didn't have the same sense of respect and community. It was sad to watch them leave one-by-one: the Delachances, the Panaches, the Brightons and the Barrows.

On our side of the street, we suffered the painful, tragic loss of Ma's friend, Marylyn Zelner who had died during childbirth a few years earlier. Helen Howard, Winnie Koch and the Gibsons all moved within a few years of each other to better homes in other neighborhoods or the suburbs. Ma had lost most of her female support group and her life became even more difficult. Now she needed to rely on us more than ever in order to sustain our family.

Although it was sad that Dorothy hadn't finished school, she was now able to help Ma financially. In fact, after the Gibsons moved away, she and Jimmy tried to buy that house. However, they couldn't come up with the money quickly enough, and it was going to be sold to another family, the McKeevers. We were all disappointed that we couldn't move into the Gibsons well-kept house. But sometimes fate dictates how things turn out.

Early that summer, I saw Bobby McKeever standing in the alley between our house and the Gibsons. He was looking up at his Dad who was on a ladder fixing some siding that needed repair before they could move in. Even though I was sad it wouldn't be our new house, I wished Bobby and his family luck that day. Bobby was a very smart kid and would be at the top of his class in high school.

In the meantime I moved up to the Babe Ruth League with my baseball friends. I continued to play in that league for several years, making the all star team when I was fifteen. In addition, I started hanging out with my school buddies Larry, Billy and Ronnie as well as Alan. However, hanging out on Eighth Street was not the same, with most of the other kids now gone. One of the fun things I did with Alan that summer was learning how to drive. Alan's Dad had the bad habit of leaving his car keys on a table inside their front door. One Saturday morning his Dad was sleeping in, so Alan decided it was the perfect time to take me on a joy ride up to Prospect Park. He had driven his father's car before and was pretty confident, so I wasn't concerned for my safety. He did a pretty good job as we pulled away from the curb, headed down Eighth Street, then quickly made a left turn up Congress Street, barely avoiding a car speeding in the opposite direction.

He slowly weaved his way up Congress, through the intersection of Ferry Street, then cut off an oncoming driver who had to slam on his brakes to avoid hitting us. Unfazed, we continued our journey, meandering along the winding road that rings the park's perimeter and barely missing the bluff that overlooked the city below. Thankfully, we made it back safely as Alan adroitly maneuvered the car back into its assigned parking spot near the front of the house. However, in doing so he inadvertently backed into Pete Fermetti's car. Luckily, he barely touched it and there was no apparent damage.

Alan forgot that his father was a perfectionist and always parked his car in exactly the same spot: directly opposite his front door. So when Alan's Dad came out later that day, he knew something was wrong. Alan and I were pitching pennies against the front of his house when his Dad slapped him on the back of the head. "How the hell did my car end up here, Alan? Did you drive it again?"

Alan knew he was screwed, realizing he forgot to put it back exactly in its proper spot. "Yea, Dad, I did, I'm sorry." His Dad then whacked him again, admonishing him that if he ever did it again, he would turn him into the cops. A.J, as he was called by the older men on the street who didn't like him, meant what he said.

Tony Fermetti had seen what happened and came up to us after Alan's Dad left. "Hey, if you guys want to learn how to drive, I'll teach you." Tony didn't like Alan's father very much, so he decided he'd teach us just to spite him. Tony kept his word, and the next weekend he took us to St. Mary's Cemetery to let us drive. I guess he figured we couldn't kill anybody up there, since everybody there was already dead. It was fun and challenging, especially for me, since I had never been behind the wheel before. Alan did just fine— but me? Well that's another story.

Tony had a standard shift car and when it came to my turn, I bucked and stuttered my way along the winding dirt road, with Tony and Alan holding on for dear life. I narrowly missed several tombstones and large trees, before finally running off the road and into a ditch. Flummoxed, Tony threw up his hands and snapped at me, "That's enough, Herbie! Get in the back seat." That would be my first and last lesson with Tony. It wouldn't be until I was twenty-two that I'd finally get my driver's license.

I also tried my hand at caddying with Alan at the Troy Country Club that summer. Joe Birchy was the head of the caddies and he picked who would get the good caddying jobs. I know I didn't get a good one, because he assigned me to my church pastor Reverend Hellman, apparently a notorious tight wad. The cheap bastard, *forgive me Lord*, paid me a measly quarter for shagging a whole bag of balls and carrying his clubs for eighteen holes. I decided that caddying was not for me. So did Joe, because he never gave me another assignment. I guess he realized immediately that I sucked as a caddy.

By the end of the summer I was spending more time with Billy, Larry and Ronnie than with Alan. We usually hung out in Beman Park or at the corner of Fifteenth and Hoosick, playing a game we invented called slumball. It was played like a game of handball, but instead of a wall we used the markings on the concrete sidewalk as our court. Our court was directly across from Ned Abbott's corner store, a local hangout for RPI students and neighborhood residents. Of course, we were constantly annoying passersby who were forced to walk in the road to get around us while we were playing.

My life was now moving in a different direction, away from my once comfortable neighborhood. I developed relationships that became much more complex than the ones I had with my Eighth

Street buddies. I guess as you begin to get older, even as teenagers, life starts getting more complicated.

During that summer we still chased after our hormones, with our discussions often turning to girls, women, sex, and the best masturbation techniques. We all agreed, Billy's was probably the best, involving cored out apples and shaving cream. However, *I* never personally tried that particular one. Larry was also creative in trying to engage us in what he concluded were innocuous sexual escapades. He told us how he climbed his neighbor's garage one night and peered into their bedroom window. His lame excuse was that he kept hearing these awful grunts and moans, night after night, and feared for their safety. So there were his neighbors, the Carlsons, naked as jaybirds and humping away to beat the band. Several nights that summer, when Larry saw their light pop on or heard their primal grunting, he studiously observed their adventures and techniques. Larry also turned us all on to the Seton Hall Nursing School dorms, located near St. Mary's Hospital at the suggestion of his trusted mentor, a local fireman named Donny Flavin. On Donny's advice, Larry swore that we'd see the world's greatest strip show up there.

Donny, who was stationed at the Oakwood Avenue firehouse, was like a folk hero to many of the neighborhood youths. He would hold court with Larry, Billy Bennett and others, describing in vivid detail all his worldly exploits and conquests with women. Everything Donny said was accepted as gospel by Larry. When I bragged to Larry about my brother Sonny's exploits, he just shrugged them off as minor in comparison to what Donny had done.

One night Larry persuaded me, Billy and Tommy Berezny, a new kid he had recently befriended, to check out the nurses' dorms. I was nervous yet exhilarated. Luckily, there was a small row of hedges to hide behind so the neighbors couldn't see us in the dark. But if they heard us and turned on their lights, we'd be exposed as peeping toms. So we talked in low whispers, when not panting so loud you could hear us a block away. It was nerve wracking waiting for the erotic show to start. After waiting for what seemed an eternity, the show finally began. However, the only titillating thing I was able to see under the partially drawn shade was a nurse, sensually pulling on a pair of white, silk stockings. Once she finished, she quickly pulled her slip back down and abruptly left the room, shutting off the lights. What a disappointment. We only got to see her knees. However, within seconds of her leaving the room, one of the neighbor's lights popped on. Now exposed, we took off liked a bunch of scared weasels. That was my first and last adventure at Seton Hall.

I also discovered that summer how ultra competitive Billy had suddenly become. He loved to play tennis but hated losing, especially to me. He tried for several years to beat me but never succeeded. He got so pissed off that he slammed his racquet as hard as he could against the chain link fence surrounding the tennis courts.

I don't know why he hated losing to me so much, but he did. I really wasn't that good, but I did have a big serve for a little guy. Plus, I was pretty quick on my feet, which allowed me to return most of his shots.

It finally happened one sunny Saturday morning. Billy and I were playing a very competitive match. The score was tied at one set apiece so we had to play a third and deciding set. For some unknown reason, Billy jumped on top of me early in that last set, and I just didn't have an answer to his aggressive play. He was leading five games to four and had two break points on me in the sixth game. I struggled and tied the score a couple times until Billy got the advantage again. Billy then served deep to my backhand. I barely got my racquet on the ball and it floated softly over the net. Smelling blood, Billy pounced on it, hammering a winner so hard it bounced over the fence. He finally beat me after all those years.

Feigning exhaustion, Billy dropped to his knees like he'd just won Wimbledon. With his arms outstretched to the heavens, he exalted in his victory. From that day on, I never beat Billy again. In fact, Billy would eventually go on to play varsity tennis in college, while Larry and I continued to play recreational tennis, mediocre to the end but still enjoying the game.

In mid-August, Ma, with the help of Dorothy, bought me some brand new chino slacks plus several Ivy League shirts. They wanted me to fit in with all the other freshmen. Having new clothes as I entered high school would give me a huge psychological boost. I knew if I wore my old hand-me-downs, I would have been labeled as being poor.

Dorothy brought me down to Stanley's to try them on. Stanley's was a large department store, similar to Grant's. Most working class people bought their clothes at these two stores. After we finished shopping Dorothy treated me to a huge piece of lemon meringue pie at the Puritan Restaurant. That was one of Dorothy's favorite spots and a favorite of many Trojans for decades.

School was starting in a couple weeks when tragedy struck our neighborhood. I had been playing basketball with Tony Yates at Prospect Park when I heard the ambulance sirens. It was not un-usual hearing them at the park, so I disregarded them. However, when I returned home later that afternoon, I saw a cop car near my house. When I got closer, I saw several neighbors standing around talking to Pete Fermetti and shaking their heads.

Now I was nervous, because all this activity was right by my house. Bad thoughts popped into my mind. Did something happen to Ma or someone in our house? My mind raced back in time to when the Cat Lady, a blind woman who lived on the first floor of our building, almost burned our house down. Because her tiny space heater didn't work very well, she often turned on her gas oven to keep warm, often forgetting to close the door. One of her many cats was taking a nap inside when she closed the door, trap-ping the sleeping cat inside and then turned on the oven to heat up the apartment.

Luckily, my sister Patty heard the old woman coughing and crying a short time later. Patty raced into her smoke-filled apartment. The woman pleaded with Patty to help find her cat, whom she had heard screeching in pain. Noticing a horrible smell and flames licking the oven door, Patty immediately turned off the gas and opened the door. To her horror, there was this poor animal, burnt to a crisp. The Cat Lady had accidentally cooked her cat. Thank God, Patty's quick action prevented a fire that could have spread and burned our house to the ground.

I anxiously raced upstairs to find out what was going on. Ma was sitting at the table with Dorothy and Jimmy having a cup of coffee and speaking in hushed tones. "What happened? Why are the cops outside?" I asked.

"There was a terrible accident," Ma said.

"What kind of accident?" I asked.

"Poor Mr. McKeever fell off a roof on Ferry Street today."

"Oh, no!" I said. "Is he ok?"

"We're not sure, Herbie. Pete told us they took him away in the ambulance a while ago. But it doesn't look good."

Later that night we learned that he died from the fall. It was such a sad time for the poor McKeever family. They lost their hard working father, and now would be unable or unwilling to move into the Gibson's house.

The tragic irony of this fateful event? Dorothy and Jimmy were eventually able to purchase the Gibson's house a year or so later. It wasn't the way they wanted things to turn out, but like I stated earlier, often fate steps in and dictates your future. Now Ma and the rest of us kids still living at home would have a better house to live in, while Patty and Andy were able to rent the downstairs apartment several years later. Dorothy and Jimmy continued to live in their Adams Street apartment in South Troy, close to his family and friends.

You know what? At this point in my meandering journey, I'm still poor! I wonder what fate and high school have in store for me?

All my children (Ma's 70TH birthday).
Back row—Cliff, Herbie, Jack, Sonny;
Middle row—Kathleen, Jan, Ma, Dorothy;
Bottom row—Bonnie, Patty, Brenda.

Afterword

My Father died in 1969 at the age of sixty-three. Although I hardly knew him as a child, his death was very emotional and traumatic for me. I cried like a baby as we drove to the cemetery that day. Although he didn't live at home when he died, Ma insisted he have a proper wake and burial. I know in her heart she loved this man and was heartsick when he died.

After Dad's passing Ma battled cancer, survived and lived quietly for several years. She died peacefully in 1981, surrounded by her loving family at the age of seventy. I cried like a baby when Ma died too. However, unlike with my Dad, I always felt loved by Ma. Her loving spirit remains the heart and soul of our family.

Engraved on their tombstone is a picture of a man and a woman walking hand in hand down a long road through the garden of life. The verse from the Book of Ruth 1:16 reads: "WHITHER THOU GOEST, I WILL GO."

My fervent hope had been to complete this memoir sooner. I wanted to present the first copy to my dear sister Patty, my childhood protector. Sadly, Patty lost her valiant battle with cancer just five days before I received my author copy. However, I know she is laughing her ass-off while reading it to Ma.

The End